MINORITY GROUP INFLUENCE

Recent Titles in
Contributions in Political Science

Principled Diplomacy: Security and Rights in U.S. Foreign Policy
Cathal J. Nolan

Presidential Influence and Environmental Policy
Robert A. Shanley

Professional Developments in Policy Studies
Stuart Nagel

County Governments in an Era of Change
David R. Berman, editor

First World Interest Groups: A Comparative Perspective
Clive S. Thomas

Cold War Patriot and Statesman: Richard M. Nixon
Leon Friedman and William F. Levantrosser, editors

Legislators, Law and Public Policy: Political Change in Mississippi and the South
Mary DeLorse Coleman

Provisional Irish Republicans: An Oral and Interpretive History
Robert W. White

The Political World of a Small Town: A Mirror Image of American Politics
Nelson Wikstrom

Ownership, Control, and the Future of Housing Policy
R. Allen Hays, editor

The Presidency in an Age of Limits
Michael A. Genovese

Leftward Ho! V. F. Calverton and American Radicalism
Philip Abbott

Public Administration in China
Miriam K. Mills and Stuart S. Nagel, editors

Public Policy in China
Stuart S. Nagel and Miriam K. Mills, editors

Minority Group Influence

AGENDA SETTING, FORMULATION, AND PUBLIC POLICY

EDITED BY

Paula D. McClain

Prepared under the auspices of the
Policy Studies Organization
STUART S. NAGEL, *Publications Coordinator*

CONTRIBUTIONS IN POLITICAL SCIENCE, NUMBER 333

Greenwood Press
WESTPORT, CONNECTICUT • LONDON

Library of Congress Cataloging-in-Publication Data

Minority group influence : agenda setting, formulation, and public
   policy / edited by Paula D. McClain.
            p.   cm. — (Contributions in political science, ISSN 0147–1066
   ; no. 333)
      "Prepared under the auspices of the Policy Studies Organization."
      Includes bibliographical references and index.
      ISBN 0–313–29036–9 (alk. paper)
      1. United States—Economic policy—Citizen participation.
   2. United States—Economic policy—Decision making. 3. United
   States—Social policy—Citizen participation. 4. United States—
   Social policy—Decision making. 5. Minorities—United States.
   I. McClain, Paula Denice. II. Series.
   HC103.M56   1993
   338.973—dc20   93–7707

British Library Cataloguing in Publication Data is available.

Library of Congress Catalog Card Number: 93–7707
ISBN: 0–313–29036–9
ISSN: 0147–1066

First published in 1993

Greenwood Press, 88 Post Road West, Westport, CT 06881
An imprint of Greenwood Publishing Group, Inc.

Printed in the United States of America

The paper used in this book complies with the
Permanent Paper Standard issued by the National
Information Standards Organization (Z39.48–1984).

10 9 8 7 6 5 4 3 2 1

To
Jewel L. Prestage,
a pioneer in the study of African-Americans and public policy,
whose intellectual footprints are throughout this volume.
We owe you a debt, both intellectually and personally.

Contents

Preface

Since the early 1930s, political scientists have developed a keen interest in the politics of African-Americans. Beginning with the works of Ralph Johnson Bunche, the modern foundations of black politics have examined a variety of issues and areas, for example, voting behavior, political attitudes, electoral structures. While the New Deal sparked some interest in African-Americans and public policy, the majority of the scholarly interest in racial minorities and public policy issues stems from the passage of various civil rights and social program statutes during and since the 1960s.

Although there has been an intense interest in racial minorities and public policy in the political science literature, most of the research has focused on the implementation of policies after legislative passage, or on the effects of the policies several years after passage. Little work has focused on the predecision stage of the policy process, agenda setting, and the way in which issues of concern to racial minority populations are raised to the agenda. Agenda setting, with its roots in interest group politics, is critical to the framing of the issue, for how an issue is defined, in many instances, determines the direction it will take in the subsequent policy process. Given the importance of agenda setting for public policy issues one would have expected much more attention to have been paid to that aspect of the policy process. Yet, little has been done.

This volume is an attempt to continue to fill the void in the public policy literature concerned with racial minority group access to the agenda-setting process. The editor's interest in this process stemmed from early work on nuclear decommissioning and the influence of the utility industry in defining the issue of decommissioning and narrowing the scope of debate about the question. That research, combined with her interest in racial minority group politics, led her to the question of minority group influence on the agenda-setting process. Most of the authors in this volume contributed to an earlier *Policy Studies Review* symposium on the same topic, yet each has written a new contribution for this effort. Each author recognizes the importance of the agenda-setting process to the policies of concern to racial minorities, and each addresses the influence of racial minorities on that process for his or her particular topic area. We do not intend this volume to be a definitive work on the topic, but a bid to begin a dialogue on the importance of this particular step in the policy process to the formulation of public policies of concern to racial minority groups, and to open up avenues for future research.

As with any endeavor, there are numerous individuals who contributed, knowingly and unknowingly, to the success of the project. I must thank Theodore J. Lowi for his continual pushing to intellectually address serious questions of nondecision making in my urban homicide work, and Harold M. Rose, who has taught me more about research and probing for answers than he will ever know. Each of the contributors is owed a debt of thanks for participating in this project and putting up with my editing of his or her work. They have been real troopers throughout this protracted process. I am very grateful to Steven C. Tauber, my research assistant at the University of Virginia, for his role as *factotum* in all aspects of this book. I also must thank the Policy Studies Organization, particularly Stuart Nagel, for its support of our efforts in this volume and for making this book a part of its ongoing publishing series. Finally, when one thinks about racial minorities and public policy, one thinks about the scholarship and activities of Jewel Limar Prestage. Throughout her career she has been actively involved in the intellectual study of policy issues of concern to African-Americans, and was the founding dean of the School of Public Affairs and Public Policy at Southern University in Baton Rouge, LA. So many of us in the discipline of political science owe her intellectual as well as personal debts, that it is to her that we dedicate this volume.

MINORITY GROUP INFLUENCE

1

Introduction: Racial Minority Group Access and Policy Agenda Setting

Paula D. McClain

Agenda setting is the most creative part of the policy process, for it is the stage at which ideas become policy issues. An issue is a conflict between groups over substantive and procedural elements relating to the distribution of positions or resources (Cobb and Elder 1972:82). Thus, as Roger Cobb and Charles Elder define, agenda setting is the process by which conflicts and concerns gain prominence and exposure so that they come to the public arena for debate and governmental action. Questions concerning the origins of policy ideas and input into the policy process by various segments of the U.S. public are continually debated, in public discourse as well as in the academic literature. The distinctive question of racial minority group—black, Latino, Asian, and American Indian—access to the agenda-setting process has received much less attention, however. Yet, in the wake of the verdict in the Rodney King case and the resultant riots in Los Angeles, the issue of racial minority group access to and representation in the political system is salient once again.

The institutions of most governmental systems, including the United States, are designed to maintain the status quo, which in many instances translates into maintaining the exclusion of certain groups from participation in the political process. In the United States, the excluded groups have most often been racial minorities. The poignancy of the remarks from many minority residents of the riot-affected areas was also paradoxical—they abhorred the rioting and destruction of their neighborhoods, while at the same time expressed their frustration and exasperation with their status as outsiders in the U.S. political system. Peter Bachrach and Morton Baratz (1970:105) maintain that in a restrictive political system, one where those outside of the system find it difficult to push their demands for change onto the system's agenda, excluded groups may find it necessary to threaten violence or actually use violence to get their voices heard. While there is much debate about the utility of violence as an agenda-setting tool, there is little debate about the limited access racial minorities have to the power centers of the U.S. political system.

Cobb and Elder (1972:14) define *agenda* as "a general set of political controversies that will be viewed at any point in time as falling within the range of legitimate concerns meriting the attention of the polity." In any given governmental structure, the number of potential policy issues far exceeds the capabilities of political decision-making institutions to process. Consequently, issues or their proponents must compete for a spot on the agenda (Cobb et al. 1976). Notwithstanding the importance of agenda setting, there has been a lamentable lack of research on the topic in general, but specifically, an almost total absence of research on the influence of racial minority groups on the agenda-setting process (McClain 1990; Wolman and Thomas 1970). More often than not, problems of importance to racial minority citizens in the United States, or that disproportionately affect minority communities, are not perceived as important by the dominant population, or to the governmental administration. The more than a decade of neglect of the problems of U.S. urban centers, which are residence to a sizeable portion of the nation's racial minority groups, is a glaring example of the "attitude of unimportance." Thus the overarching question, "where do new public policies of concern to African-American, Latino, American Indian, and Asian citizens come from?" requires more exploration. Moreover, the role of racial minority groups in setting the public policy agenda also requires investigation. Do minority citizens have access to the policy process? If so, to what extent are they able to influence public policy? If not, what are the barriers? This book is an attempt to continue to fill the gap in the public policy literature on the role of racial minority groups in the policy process.

AGENDA SETTING AND NONDECISIONS

Cobb and Elder, the pioneers of agenda-setting research, distinguish between two types of agendas—the systemic or public, and the institutional, governmental, or formal. The systemic (public) agenda "consists of all issues that are commonly perceived by members of the political community as meriting public attention and as involving matters within the legitimate jurisdiction of existing governmental authority" (1972:85). It consists of all items which (1) receive widespread attention or at least awareness; (2) are believed to require some type of action by a large share of the public; and (3) are believed by the public to be an appropriate concern of some governmental unit and to fall within the bounds of its authority (Cobb et al. 1976:127). The institutional, governmental, or formal agenda is "that set of items explicitly up for the active and serious consideration of authoritative decision makers" (Cobb and Elder 1972:86). Consequently, any list of issues established for consideration by any governmental body at any level of government will constitute an institutional agenda.

One pivotal component of the agenda-setting process is what E. E. Schattschneider (1975:69) refers to as the "mobilization of bias"—some issues are organized into politics while others are organized out. Bachrach and Baratz (1970:43) argue that political systems generate a "mobilization of bias," which they define, drawing from Schattschneider, as "a set of predominant values, beliefs, rituals, and institutional procedures ('rules of the game') that operate systematically and consistently to the benefit of certain persons and groups at the expense of others." They raise the possibility that through the "mobilization of bias" some individuals would limit decision making to relatively noncontroversial matters by influencing and controlling the political arenas in which the issues surface.

Bachrach and Baratz (1963) argue that the primary method of maintaining a particular mobilization of bias is nondecision making. They define *nondecision making* as "a means by which demands for change in the existing allocation of benefits and privileges in the community can be suffocated before they are even voiced; or kept covert; or killed before they gain access to the relevant decision-making arena" (1970:44). Some issues are blocked from the agenda by a combination of factors—dominant values, accepted rules of the game, existing power relations among groups, and instruments of force. These items, alone or in combination, effectively prevent some items from developing into full-fledged issues which call for a policy decision.

Nondecision making occurs in several forms. The first form is through the use of direct violence or physical force as a means of preventing demands for change in the political status quo from entering the political process. An example would be white terrorization of black citizens to prevent them from raising issues of equal rights. A second form is less extreme than the first but just as direct and is nondecision making through the exercise of power, for example, sanctions against the initiator of a potentially threatening demand. Bachrach and Baratz see these sanctions as being "negative or positive, ranging from intimidation (potential deprivation of valued things or events) to cooptation (potential rewards)" (1970:44).

A third and more indirect form of nondecision making evokes an existing bias of the political system to squelch a threatening demand or budding issue. They argue that a demand for change in the political system may be blocked by branding it as "socialistic, unpatriotic, immoral, or in violation of an established rule or procedure" (ibid.:45). The most indirect form of nondecision making is the fourth form, which involves "reshaping or strengthening the mobilization of bias in order to block challenges to the prevailing allocation of values" (ibid.).

Another prominent element of agenda setting is the process of problem identification/problem structuring of the policy issue. How a policy issue is structured and identified in this initial stage will determine the direction and content of the public discourse, and the proposed solutions as it moves through the remaining stages of the policy process. John Kingdon (1984) notes that the treatment of a policy issue on the agenda will be affected by the way in which a problem is recognized and defined, and the category in which it is placed. For instance, Paula McClain and David Pijawka (1986), in a study of utility perspectives toward decommissioning nuclear generating stations, recognized that the utility industry's success, through the mobilization of bias, in defining decommissioning as purely a financial problem had eclipsed the alternative identification of decommissioning as an issue of risk to individuals and hazardous waste disposal off the public agenda. Thus, the policy prescriptions address the financial ability of utilities to pay for decommissioning, taking the form of building future decommissioning costs into the rate structures. Issues of public safety, residual radiation levels, and long-term storage of nuclear waste are not addressed. In another area, Mark Moore (1988:57) suggests that the success of defining drunken driving as a problem of alcoholism rather than nonalcoholics who overindulge and drive has kept the focus away from potential policies aimed at this latter group.

THEORETICAL APPROACHES TO AGENDA SETTING

Barbara Nelson (1984:21) divides the literature on agenda setting into three approaches to explain the causes of expansion and shifts in the content of governmental agendas: (1) organizational behavior, (2) issue careers and issue cycles, and (3) economic logic. The organizational approach is concerned with the decisions made by officials within the context of their official capacities (Walker 1977, 1983; Gray 1973). More specifically, it centers on the importance of career patterns and the influence of professional associations on agenda setting.

The issue careers and cycles approach emphasizes the appearance and definition of a problem and is grounded in the interest group literature of political science (Bentley 1949; Truman 1951; Lowi 1964, 1979; Schattschneider 1975; Salisbury 1969; Dahl 1956, 1961, 1967). The grounding in interest group literature stresses the conflictual nature of agenda setting. The quest for a position on the governmental agenda is one where contending groups compete with other groups for governmental attention.

Along the same lines, Elaine Sharp (1990), following Anthony Downs's (1972) slightly different definition of issue attention cycles, suggests that agenda setting is more than the initial breakthrough of an issue on the formal agenda. Agenda setting in many policy areas, according to Sharp, "might best be viewed in terms of the long-term rise and fall of governmental attention to issues that already have attained some official standing on the formal agenda." Therefore, issues are not plainly either on or off the agenda at any given time, but in many instances, issues are permanently on the formal agenda, but the extent of the notice they receive waxes and wanes over time (Sharp 1990:1).

The economic logic approach, exemplified by public choice theory, is not concerned with determining which policy issues will be acted upon. Instead, it applies the logic of rational self-interest to governmental behavior (majoritarian voting with logrolling) and its negative consequences (uncontrollable public spending and economic inefficiency) (Buchannan 1975; Buchannan and Wagner 1977). While these three approaches to agenda setting stem from different scholarly foundations, they are not mutually exclusive.

In contrast to Nelson's three approaches, Donley Studlar and Zig Layton-Henry (1990) divide the agenda-setting literature into two major theoretical approaches—pluralism and elitism. The pluralist approach emphasizes the role of the public, interest groups, and the media in developing the political agenda. The elitist approach to agenda setting, on the other hand, sees the major initiatives coming from government officials and policy communities.

Nelson and Studlar and Layton-Henry approach the development of their agenda-setting categories from two different perspectives. Nelson's categories focus on the normative logic of agenda setting, institutional issues and structures, and the participants. Studlar's and Layton-Henry's categories are grounded in questions of the distribution of resources, control of power, and accessibility to decision makers. Recognizing the differences that exist in perspectives, one could, nevertheless, view Nelson's issues and careers approach as being similar to Studlar's and Layton-Henry's pluralist category, while her organizational and economic approaches could be analogous to their elitist category.

MODELS OF AGENDA SETTING

Building on the pluralist notion of agenda setting and working with the issue cycles and careers approach identified by Nelson (1984), Cobb, Jennie Keith-Ross, and Marc Ross (1976) developed three models of agenda setting. These models are the outside initiative model, the mobilization model, and the inside access model, and are built on modifications in the four basic characteristics of issue careers: initiation, specification, expansion, and entrance (1976:127–128).

In the *outside initiative model* the generation of the issue in a general form comes from groups outside of the governmental structure. The general issue is then translated into more specific demands and expanded to a broader number of groups, thus gaining attention on the public agenda. Entrance is achieved when the issue receives attention from decision makers and moves from the public (systemic) to the formal (institutional) agenda. When decision makers or individuals with direct access to decision makers posit issues on the formal agenda, but need to expand the base of support for the issue by raising it to the public agenda, Cobb, Keith-Ross, and Ross (1976:132) indicate that the *mobilization model* is in force. Public support is essential to legitimate the policy issue; thus, entrance is achieved when the problem is moved from the formal agenda to the public agenda. The *inside access model* represents the initiation of policy issues within a governmental agency or within a group which has effortless access to decision makers. In this model, the issue is only expanded to those groups necessary to place the requisite political pressure on decision makers to move the problem forward. At no time is expansion to the public a consideration and no effort is made to place it on the public agenda. Entrance in this model is, as Cobb, Keith-Ross, and Ross (1976:136) note,"not spectacular and public."

Kingdon (1984), in the second major work on agenda setting, examined the process from within the federal governmental bureaucracy—an elite theory perspective. Building on Michael Cohen, March James, and Johan Olsen's (1972) garbage can model, he found that in order for issues to squeeze their way onto the decision agenda, three policy streams must converge. These streams are the policy (the realm of identification and emergence of the issue), the politics (the appearance of a favorable political climate), and the participants (policy entrepreneurs, lobbyists, and legislative and agency specialists, who generate proposals and push the issue). Given the mercurial nature of the political climate, "windows of opportunity" for particular issues open only briefly, and it is at this moment that the three policy streams intersect and burst through the window.

PLURALISM AND MINORITY GROUP ACCESS

Regardless of the number of categorizations of the approaches to agenda setting, the theoretical approaches narrow to two well-trod and utilized theories of political science—pluralism and elite theory. The pluralist approach assumes that policy making in the United States is pluralist, meaning that there is a supposed "free enterprise" system of policies with a number of interest groups competing for power and influence (Peters 1986:42). These groups are assumed to be equal in power and access to the policy process. The dynamics are such that some groups will win at times, while other groups will win at other times. However, all groups will have a chance to influence the outcome and no group will be systematically excluded from the decisions (ibid.:43).

The elitist approach, on the other hand, makes assumptions that directly counter those of the pluralist model. As C. Wright Mills argues, the existence of a power elite that dominates the policy process is presumed. The interests of this power elite, which are those of the upper and middle classes, consistently dominate the policy process. The interests of the working and lower classes are purposely not represented (ibid.), and if working and lower class individuals do organize for input into the process, their participation is only token (Schattschneider 1975). The policy agenda, therefore, is not the result of a competitive interaction between equal groups but is the use of power by an elite group of individuals.

Several questions may be raised about the utility of these models for examining minority group access to the policy agenda. On the surface, it would appear that the pluralist model provides greater access for racial minorities, whereas the elitist model, as its name implies, draws its policy initiatives from a body in which few minority citizens have membership. However, is the pluralist approach to agenda setting an appropriate window through which to view minority group influence on the policy process? This question has been debated extensively in the literature on black politics and could serve as a foundation from which to address the question of the ability of racial minorities to influence the public policy process.

The pluralist paradigm is the reigning model within political science and has been used extensively in studying racial and ethnic politics (Dahl 1961;

Eisinger 1980; Wilson 1960). Dianne Pinderhughes, in an excellent and comprehensive re-examination of pluralist theory, argues, however, that based on the very axioms of the Dahlian notion of pluralist theory, pluralism is not an appropriate paradigm through which to view the political activity of blacks. She states that three principles "summarize the process by which racial and ethnic groups find ready entrance into the American political system according to pluralist theory: interest diversification, interest incorporation, and racial and ethnic democracy" (1987:14).

Interest diversification implies that there is little need for racial and ethnic groups to organize around group-based issues. Groups move rapidly away from racially based positions to issues that are more diversified in their appeal—socially, economically, and politically. Race and ethnicity are obscured as other issues take precedence (ibid.:14).

Interest incorporation suggests that once groups realize their subjective interests, members achieve political incorporation through bargaining. Once a group recognizes its interest in the political process, political organization of that interest leads naturally to political representation and incorporation (ibid.:14–15). Finally, in the absence of persistent group identity and with political representation dependent upon the realization of interests—racial and ethnic democracy—little political hierarchy or inequality based on group status will occur.

Pinderhughes's analysis of racial and ethnic life in Chicago led her to conclude that "the existence of a pattern of racial interaction . . . contradicts the principles of the pluralist model." Drawing on the analysis of Marguerite Barnett (1976), Pinderhughes concludes

> that racial status is characterized not by diversity, incorporation, and democracy, but by hierarchy and collectivism. . . . Blacks are in all locations within the country subordinate to whites as a race, regardless of the ethnic status of whites. Second, blacks are treated as a group; no individual achievement ameliorates the status of an individual or elevates the position of the group as a whole. (ibid.:38)

Other examinations of black politics have drawn similar conclusions (Holden 1973; Morris 1975; Barker and McCorry 1976), which are summarized by Hamilton's (1981:168) declaration, "The political situation of black Americans always posed a special problem for the pluralist system." John Manley (1983:368) recently suggested that "pluralism . . . fails to account for the reality of political and economic inequality in the United States." Some scholars have reached similar conclusions about the utility of pluralist theory as a framework for understanding the political behavior and activities of Latinos in the United States (Marquez 1989; Garcia and de la Garza 1977; Hero 1992).

MINORITY GROUP AMERICANS AND AGENDA SETTING

In view of the limitations of pluralist theory to explain racial minority group political behavior, how well do present theories of agenda setting, most of which are grounded in a pluralist foundation, explain or account for minority access to the policy process? There has been little research on the impact of minority Americans on the agenda-setting process. What does exist presents a mixed, yet dismal, picture of access to and impact on the process. One of the few studies on the influence of blacks on the federal policy process (Wolman and Thomas 1970) cautions that pluralism is not entirely adequate for explaining black access to the policy-making process. They conclude from their study of black influence on housing and education policy that black groups essentially do not possess effective access to the major centers of decision making (ibid.:886, 890). They suggest, however, that the lack of access is the result of a severe lack of resources on the part of blacks and the decision to concentrate most of their activity on the local level. The channels of access to decision makers do appear to be open but the assumption of pluralism, that individuals will form groups in order to accomplish their policy outcomes, is defective. Blacks are not as likely to organize to achieve policy outcomes as are "producers, of goods and services" (ibid.:895) to protect their preferred positions relative to the "have nots" in society (Lowi 1964).

A symposium on the topic of racial minority group influence on the agenda-setting process published in *Policy Studies Review* (McClain 1990) presented mixed conclusions. Although there were successes, the weight of the evidence fell on the side of minimal influence of minority groups on the policy agenda-setting process. The reasons for the failures could be broken down into two broad categories—cultural differences in problem definition, and lack of strong minority group organization. This book builds on the symposium using many of the same authors, but with entirely new contributions. Moreover, several new authors and contributions were incorporated in this expanded edition. The chapters in this book approach the subject of minority group access to and input into the policy process from a multiplicity of perspectives and across distinct policy areas. Clearly, this topic deserves further exploration and this volume will contribute to the developing body of literature.

STRUCTURE OF BOOK

The book is organized into three sections, each concerned with minority group access to the agenda-setting process in several distinct contexts and at different governmental levels—international (Britain), national (United States), and state (North Carolina, Texas, and Arizona). Moreover, different minority groups are investigated—nonwhites in Britain, and African-Americans, Alaskan Natives, and Latinos in the United States.

The first section, International Perspective, presents a study on the influence of nonwhites on the political agenda in Britain by Donley Studlar. If the literature on agenda setting in the United States is sparse, Studlar indicates that there are even fewer agenda-setting studies in British political studies. Therefore, to study agenda setting within the British context necessitates the use of frameworks developed on a federal system of government (United States) to examine behavior which occurs within a parliamentary system. Studlar begins by admitting that nonwhites in Britain have an extremely limited capacity to influence the political agenda. Liberal white allies are the key element in setting the political agenda on race-related issues in a direction favorable to nonwhite interests. The chapter examines the importance of policy borrowing for generating issues of concern to nonwhites in Britain.

The access of racial minorities to the national policy arena is the focus of the second section. Four different policy areas are addressed in the chapters. Charles Henry examines the issue of full employment legislation from the New Deal era to the late 1970s, principally examining the debate and circumstances surrounding the Hawkins-Humphrey Bill. Henry analyzes this area through the concept of political innovation, and concludes that full employment legislation has failed primarily because political innovation was replaced by technical innovation.

The political situation in South Africa is of growing concern to individuals worldwide, but in particular to African-Americans. Frederic Solop traces the emergence of the anti-apartheid movement in the late 1980s as an outgrowth of the black civil rights movement of the 1950s and 1960s. Solop discusses the tactics used by the anti-apartheid movement to become a participant in the debate on U.S. relations with the white South African government.

My own chapter looks at the situation of black urban violence and the context of the public discourse that occurs at the national level. The argument is stressed that the powerful notion of the "public idea" dictates the form in which the issue is raised to the political agenda. Where black urban violence is concerned, the present conceptualization of the problem ensures that nothing of consequence will be accomplished. Thus, in order to change the policy prescriptions, the "idea" behind the present conceptualization of the problem must be transformed and the issue re-raised on the political agenda.

While most agenda-setting research focuses on the initiation phase of the policy-making stage, Fae Korsmo, in the last chapter of this section, focuses on what she calls the evaluation and revision stage of the agenda-setting process. The 1991 amendments to the Alaska Native Claims Settlement Act (ANCSA) are examples of the agenda-setting evaluation process. Using three theoretical frameworks, Korsmo shows how different Alaska Native groups viewed the 1991 amendments to ANCSA. Her analysis suggests that, under some circumstances, minorities can set their own policy agenda.

The third section focuses on agenda-setting or policy initiatives of minorities at the state level. Cheryl Miller directs attention to the agenda-setting possibilities for black state legislators through the formation of black legislative caucuses. Using empirical data on black legislative caucuses in seven southern states, she discovered five issue areas that are common in the seven states' black caucuses—economic development; increasing the number of black appointed officials; enhancing minority colleges and universities; reforming the judicial system; and providing human services. Within these five areas, Miller examines the varying degrees of success the caucuses have had in placing various issues on their respective states' policy agenda.

Texas is the setting and Mexican-Americans the actors in Benjamin Marquez's chapter on the Industrial Areas Foundation (IAF) in Texas. He poses two questions: (1) has the IAF been able to articulate the needs of the poor and translate them into a viable public policy agenda; and (2) has the IAF been able to change the economic conditions facing the poor Chicano in Texas? Marquez evaluates several IAF organizations in several Texas cities in an attempt to answer the two questions.

Are there programmatic instruments that facilitate the access of minorities to the agenda-setting process? Carl Meacham probes this question through a study of the State of New York Minority Internship Program, which was created in 1987 to increase the pool of minority public policy employees. This chapter evaluates the outcomes of that program, with input into the agenda-setting process as a primary concern.

The final chapter in this section, by Francesca Schmid Thomas, focuses on minority health care, principally AIDS. Recognizing the barriers that exist to minority input into the agenda-setting process, Thomas studies one group, Cultural Communities United in Health and Wellness (CCUHW), that is comprised of American Indian, Mexican-American, Asian Pacific, and African-American health professionals in Phoenix, Arizona, and the alternative methods of mobilization used by the CCUHW.

The last chapter in the book, by the editor, presents a concluding view of the influence of racial minorities on the policy agenda-setting process. Since this book blends the agenda-setting activities of several minority groups, internationally and domestically, we hope that it will begin to fill the void in knowledge about the influence of racial minorities on the public policy agenda-setting process.

I

INTERNATIONAL PERSPECTIVE

2

Ethnic Minority Groups, Agenda Setting, and Policy Borrowing in Britain

Donley T. Studlar

> It is necessary to identify and distinguish between the reasons for the introduction of legislation, and those influences which help shape and form its content.
>
> (Sooben 1990:56)

Agenda-setting studies in countries other than the United States are rare. Despite the broad comparative theoretical focus developed by Roger Cobb, Jennie Keith-Ross, and Marc Ross (1976), few comparativists have taken up the challenge. In British political studies, for instance, there are, in general, relatively few agenda-setting studies (Solesbury 1976a; Solesbury 1976b; Richardson and Jordan 1979; Stringer and Richardson 1980; Flickinger 1983; Hogwood 1987; Goodin 1982; Sochart 1988). Nevertheless, there has long been disproportionate attention to the question of agenda setting on ethnic and race-related policies[1] (Hindell 1965; Katznelson 1973; Studlar 1974, 1985, 1986; Kirp 1979; Young 1983; Benyon 1984; Layton-Henry 1984; Bulpitt 1986; Messina 1989; Studlar and Layton-Henry 1990). The reason for this disparity is the insecure foothold race-related policies seem to have on the political consciousness and actions of political elites. Indeed, several of the above studies argued that there was a conscious or unconscious (cultural) conspiracy to keep race off the political agenda, one of the few well-developed examples of a mobilization of bias toward nondecision making in a political system, especially on the central level (Schattschneider 1960; Bachrach and Baratz 1962; Crenson 1971).

This chapter has been aided especially by the contributions of Zig Layton-Henry and Lynn Murnane. All matters of fact and interpretation are the responsibility of the author.

Another thread in the policy literature on British race relations, albeit one that has not been explored systematically and theoretically, is that of policy borrowing or lesson drawing, especially from the United States. A recent survey of the policy convergence literature (Bennett 1991b) indicates that race relations legislation of the 1960s is one of the areas in which the United Kingdom has borrowed from the United States (Lester and Bindman 1972). Various other studies of subsequent anti-discrimination legislation as well as urban aid have mentioned, at least in passing, that U.S. experience has had some influence on British developments (Rose et al. 1969; Edwards and Batley 1978; Sooben 1990; McCrudden 1983). In view of the resurgence of interest in the politics of agenda setting in U.S.-based public policy research (Cobb and Elder 1981, 1983; Downs 1972; Jones 1977; Walker 1977; Eyestone 1978; Kingdon 1973, 1984; Nelson 1984; Peters and Hogwood 1985; Durant and Diehl 1989; Baumgartner and Jones 1991; Bosso 1987; Petracca 1990) and the development of comparative policy-borrowing research (Waltman 1980; Wolman 1990; Rose 1990, 1991, 1992; Bennett 1991a; Bennett and Howlett 1991; Robertson 1991; Robertson and Waltman 1992), it is appropriate to attempt to apply some of this theoretical literature to the well-documented agenda-setting and policy formulation dilemmas of British race politics, with particular focus on the role of minority group "black" access to the agenda and participation in policy formulation. First, we shall generally discuss how agenda-setting theory can aid understanding of the role of nonwhites in British public policy, especially in problem recognition and issue definition. Next, we shall discuss the theoretical relevance of the policy-borrowing or lesson-drawing literature to this policy area. Then we shall briefly survey the evidence concerning agenda setting and policy borrowing in race-related policy. Finally, we shall draw some conclusions about whether minority group access to the political agenda or lesson drawing in policy formulation is a more important influence in British race-related policy.

AGENDA-SETTING THEORY

We define *agenda setting* as the process through which political institutions and actors confront political issues and consider making policies to cope with them. Agenda setting can be a complex phenomenon. Indeed, the dominant metaphor in recent agenda-setting studies has been the "garbage can model of choice," in which streams of problems, policies, and politics flow independently until the right combination of them leads to a "policy window" in which decisions can be made (Kingdon 1984;

Cohen et al. 1972; Durant and Diehl 1989). Since these concepts were developed in studies of agenda setting in the United States, one must be cautious in applying them to other polities, especially since parliamentary democracies usually feature more specific party policy commitments, better executive-legislative coordination, and greater stress on less publicly visible interest group–executive contacts, among other things. In short, most other liberal democratic polities probably lean more toward the organization end of what has been called "organized anarchy" (Cohen et al. 1972) than does the United States. This is not to deny that there exists a "policy primeval soup" (Kingdon 1984) in each.

Although they use overlapping terms, there is not complete agreement among analysts about the major concepts, dimensions, and processes of agenda setting. Broadly, the agenda-setting literature can be divided into two major theoretical approaches, which resemble the pluralist and elitist schools of thought (Nelson 1984; Petracca 1990). The pluralist approach emphasizes the role of the public, interest groups, and the media in developing the political agenda (Cobb and Elder 1972; Downs 1972; Jones 1977; Eyestone 1978). In contrast, the elitist approach to agenda setting sees the major initiatives coming from government officials and policy communities; other elements largely act as veto groups (Walker 1977; Kingdon 1984; Nelson 1984; Durant and Diehl 1989). Perhaps because the research stems from a U.S. base, neither orientation rates political parties highly in the agenda-setting process. Cobb, Keith-Ross, and Ross (1976) provide a bridge across these two approaches by positing three models of agenda setting—outside initiative, mobilization, and inside initiative. The first is mass to elite, the second elite to mass, the third elite to elite only.

Despite these two broad approaches, there is substantial overlap in how theorists from the two conceptualize agenda setting. William Solesbury (1976a) posits three stages of agenda setting: (1) commanding attention, (2) claiming legitimacy, and (3) invoking action. Barbara Nelson (1984) has four stages of agenda setting: (1) issue recognition, (2) issue adoption, (3) setting priorities among issues, and (4) issue maintenance (substantive decision points). The last stage is divided into initial maintenance and recurring maintenance. For Charles Jones (1977) the different agenda statuses are (1) problem definition, (2) proposal, (3) bargaining, and (4) continuing. Cobb and Charles Elder (1972) and Cobb, Keith-Ross, and Ross (1976) posit four stages of agenda setting: (1) initiation, (2) specification, (3) expansion, and (4) entrance. Their "initiation" stage appears to be close to Nelson's "issue recognition," Jones's "problem definition," and Solesbury's "commanding attention." What Cobb and his associates call "specification" and "expansion" are similar to what Solesbury calls "claiming legitimacy," Jones "proposal" and "bargaining," and Nelson "issue adoption" and "setting priorities among issues." Likewise, "invoking action" (Solesbury), "issue maintenance" (Nelson), and "entrance" (Cobb et al.) also resemble each other.

Nelson (1984), Jack Walker (1977), Jones (1977), and Brian Hogwood and Guy Peters (1983) recognize the need to distinguish agenda setting in policy innovation from agenda setting in policy succession. Walker presents a topology of agenda items in the U.S. Senate as varying between two poles, required and discretionary, and four categories along these poles: (1) periodically recurring problems, (2) sporadically recurring problems, (3) crises (pressing problems), and (4) the chosen problems. Hogwood and Peters study agenda setting in the U.S. federal bureaucracy.

There is general recognition among agenda theorists that a distinction needs to be made between a formal (government, institutional, official) agenda and a systemic (popular, public) agenda (Cobb and Elder 1972; Cobb et al. 1976; Eyestone 1978; Nelson 1984; Ripley 1985). In addition, Robert Eyestone (1978), John Kingdon (1984), and Nelson (1984) refer to "specialized" or "professional" agendas among members of policy communities and the attentive public, issues which may not have reached either the formal or public agendas. If politicians give an issue rhetorical attention only, Cobb and Elder (1972) call it part of the pseudo-agenda. Randall Ripley (1985) has attempted to relate Cobb, Keith-Ross, and Ross's models of agenda setting to different types of public policy (Lowi 1964). Anthony Downs's (1972) formulation of the issue-attention cycle has been adapted and tested several times subsequently (Peters and Hogwood 1985; Benyon 1984; Bosso 1987).

A salutary distinction between agenda analysis and alternatives analysis is made, even if not always maintained, by Cobb, Keith-Ross, and Ross (1976), Kingdon (1973, 1984), and Robert Durant and Paul Diehl (1989). The latter have attempted to synthesize and theoretically reformulate the agenda-setting literature, with a particular focus on developing a set of categories useful for both foreign and domestic policy, incremental and nonincremental change. They generate a topology of agenda procedures based on biological analogies. Yet their discussion of the applicability of this topology emphasizes the generation of alternatives for decision, especially in the foreign policy arena, rather than problem recognition and definition, our main concerns.

Given the long-standing concern with the agenda status of race-related issues in British politics, there is considerable material to draw upon. The rest of the paper will focus on domestic race-related policies, that is, we shall not consider agenda setting and formulation on the question of immigration although there is no doubt the two subjects are closely related. We are especially interested in problem recognition and issue definition on the governmental or formal agenda. Once on the formal agenda, and indeed even before it, issues are discussed in terms of policy alternatives.

POLICY-BORROWING THEORY

Until recently, little was heard about direct policy borrowing by one country from another. For some time, of course, there have been policy diffusion studies, usually quantitative and focusing on crossnational or crossprovincial patterns of adopting similar policies in certain areas (Collier and Messick 1975). Policy diffusion research is further linked to the policy innovation literature. The spread of policy innovations across countries or across federal units within a country is an important and measurable component of the policy diffusion literature (Walker 1969; Gray 1973; Savage 1985). But aside from broad institutional and cultural variables which help account for patterns of policy adoption, these studies normally contain very little specific information about how one country comes to emulate the policies of one or other countries, or indeed how closely the policies resemble each other. Similarly, studies of policy convergence concentrate on the broad similarities and differences among the policies of different polities (Kerr 1983). Even when careful comparisons of the policies of two polities are done, the directions of influence and how the countries came to resemble each other are often neglected (Waltman and Studlar 1987). In short, the research traditions embodied in policy diffusion, policy innovation, and policy convergence studies can aid policy borrowing investigations but are not synonymous with it. What, then, is policy borrowing? The general area of policy borrowing is also called policy transfer, policy emulation, policy copying, and lesson drawing. Richard Rose (1991, 1992) prefers the term *lesson drawing* as indicating a more general process of weighing nonimmediate experiences, even in the same political unit, in making policy. Lesson drawing can be negative as well as positive. "A lesson is thus a political moral drawn from analyzing the actions of other governments" (Rose 1991:7). But he then goes on to say that concern with the transferability of a program is an important aspect of lesson drawing. Particular elements of policies in one country may be grafted onto policies in a similar area, or even a different area, in a second country. For the broad exploratory purposes in this paper, we shall use the terms lesson drawing, policy borrowing, and policy transfer as interchangeable.

Although the general issue of policy borrowing by the British from the United States has been bruited for sometime (Rose 1974), probably the first systematic study of policy borrowing, especially in the United States—United Kingdom vein, was that of Jerold Waltman (1980), in which he examined how the income tax and old age pensions came to be adopted in the United States. More recently, Hal Wolman (1990) has looked at two-way policy transfers from the United States to Britain in urban policy, David Robertson and Waltman (1992) at education and manpower policies, Rose (1990) at potential British policy borrowing from Germany in youth training schemes, and Colin Bennett (1991a; see also Bennett and Howlett 1991) at Canadian and British borrowing from the United States in freedom of information and data protection policies.

The conceptual basis for the upsurge of interest in policy-borrowing studies rests in the idea that policy ideas must come from somewhere. The amount of high-level political, economic, and bureaucratic contacts among countries, especially capitalist democracies, plus the availability of cross-national data on a variety of topics and increasing contacts of countries through international organizations, should encourage policy learning and policy borrowing by those involved. The appearance of similar problems on the political agenda of countries generates a search for alternatives to deal with the problems; one relatively easy place to search is in the political experience of similar countries. This is not to say that policies are easily transferred from one country to another. Differences of conceptualization, institutions, political cultures, policy styles, previous policy commitments, and international position, among others, may inhibit successful policy borrowing (Neustadt 1970; Rose 1974, 1990, 1992; Kirp 1979; Waltman and Studlar 1987; Richardson and Jordan 1982). But even the attempt at policy borrowing is noteworthy. Furthermore, policy borrowing can help set agendas and specify alternatives.

NONWHITES, AGENDA SETTING, AND FORMULATION OF POLICY

Today, as in the past, nonwhite resources for affecting the British political agenda are few and limited in scope. Although nonwhites remain a weak group politically, they do have some capacity to affect the political agenda. The major problem is that most of their resources for getting issues on the political agenda are double-edged and are likely to rebound against them in alternative selection. Donley Studlar and Zig Layton-Henry (1990) present a thorough assessment of these variable resources, including growing numbers (currently approximately 5 percent of the total population), citizenship rather than guest worker status, concentration in urban areas, and connections to political parties, especially Labour. On the other side, the elitist nature of British political culture, the lack of cohesion of nonwhite groups, the relative decline of race as an issue on the central government agenda, the unitary nature of British government, and the generally unfavorable treatment of nonwhites in the popular media mitigate against agenda access and policies in line with particular nonwhite desires.

Nonwhites do have what has come to be called the "race industry" lobbying on their behalf. This refers to a policy network of private research organizations and lobbying groups who have extensive contacts within the political parties, with the Race Relations and Immigration Subcommittee of the Home Affairs Select Committee, and in such quasi-governmental agencies as (in the past) the National Committee for Commonwealth Immigrants, the Community Relations Commission, and the Race Relations Board and (in the present) the Commission for Racial Equality and Community Relations Councils. On occasion in the past, nonwhite groups such as the Campaign Against Racial Discrimination or Equal Rights have been successful in pressure group activity to urge the government to put forward anti-discrimination legislation in a form which they preferred (Hindell 1965; Rose et al. 1969; Lester and Bindman 1972; Heineman 1972). Over the longer term the multiethnic Runnymede Trust, assisted by research from such organizations as Political and Economic Planning and the Policy Studies Institute, has been influential on behalf of racial and ethnic minorities. Sporadic urban violence has also been important in agenda setting for the inner cities, although there is considerable dispute over whether such violence can validly be termed racial in nature (Banton 1985; Benyon 1984).

Nevertheless, the actual initiative for most British government agenda setting on race-related issues has lain with the government itself rather than with outside groups. Based on experience since the 1960s, government policy initiatives on race are more likely to appear during a Labour government, and may even be heavily dependent on the particular views of the home secretary. Even then, they tend to have a long gestation period, are often amended in the legislative process, and may have severe problems in enforcement (Hindell 1965; Rose et al. 1969; Lester and Bindman 1972; Edwards and Batley 1978; Sooben 1990; McCrudden 1983; Russell 1990). In at least one instance, the Race Relations Act of 1976, the nature of the legislation seems to owe much to attempting to reconcile anti-discrimination provisions in race with those of a Sex Discrimination Act passed the previous year (Ashford 1981; Gregory 1987; Sooben 1990).

British governments, both Conservative and Labour, have also shown considerable capacity to resist policy initiatives by consultative groups both inside and outside government. The lack of a persistent, broadly encompassing nonwhite lobby group since the demise of the Campaign Against Racial Discrimination in the late 1960s has hampered nonwhites' attempts to place their particular issues on the governmental agenda (Banton 1985; Fitzgerald 1988). Although some attempts at a more coordinated policy of ethnic monitoring have been made by Conservative governments since 1979, the financial stringencies of the 1980s and the disinclination of these governments to take interventionist action on behalf of racial and ethnic minorities have led to such issues being removed from the central government agenda, barring urban violence (Benyon 1984).

Even more than previously, central government has peripheralized race-related issues by assigning them to local governments (Bulpitt 1986; Russell 1990; Nelson 1991), but constant battles over central government restrictions on the finance and powers of local authorities have not made the era a propitious time for successful coordinated local government agenda setting on race. Nevertheless, in some areas the local politics of race has allowed concentrated nonwhite groups to have some impact on agenda setting on such issues as multicultural education, racial discrimination in public housing, official respect for differing religious practices, and police-nonwhite relations. Studies of policy making at this level, however, suggest that even here nonwhite access to the agenda is uneven and may be countered by other groups (Tomlinson 1986; Jacobs 1986; Ben-Tovim 1989; Messina 1989; Saggar 1991; Nelson 1991; Ball and Solomos 1990). As the general election of 1992 approached, the Labour party once again brought forward some modest proposals for changing British race relations policy, but whether this attempt at central agenda setting will be pursued with vigor is debatable (Messina 1989; Russell 1990).

In summary, then, nonwhites have an extremely limited capacity to influence the political agenda in Britain. Even then, they need the aid of sympathetic white allies, both inside and outside government. In fact, the liberal white allies are probably the key element in setting the political agenda on race-related issues in a direction favorable to nonwhite interests. Utilizing Cobb, Keith-Ross, and Ross's (1976) models of agenda access, Studlar (1986) argues that domestic race relations acts in Britain closely resemble the mobilization model; governmental actors are the key initiators, in consultation with affected interests. Minority groups may have some impact on setting the agenda, but it is a subordinate one.

Once an issue reaches the governmental agenda, however, the next question (analytically if not always practically) is: what alternatives exist for policy formulation? In the case of British race-related policies, the alternatives rarely come from the minority groups themselves. Their contribution is to call attention to the problem, and perhaps to lobby for particular alternative "solutions." Until the last quarter century, however, British government officials were rarely confronted with race-related problems on their home territory. Even today, race relations expertise is not cultivated by many bureaucrats or politicians; as noted above, the race relations industry is kept at arm's length by most governments. Evidence on the adoption and implementation of particular race-related policies by British governments suggests that officials have relied heavily on the example of the United States in formulation of such policies.

Policy borrowing or lesson drawing has been most prevalent from the United States for obvious reasons. The common language, the greater U.S. experience in dealing with race-related problems, and the frequent visits by bureaucrats, politicians, industrialists, trade unionists, academics, and policy researchers from one country to the other ease the inevitable problems of communication. In this instance, even though we are dealing formally with a domestic problem, it is fair to say that there is a transnational policy network which is of some importance in agenda setting in Britain and of even greater significance in generating alternatives for policy formulation. British lesson drawing from the United States is preeminent in this international policy network. Even British nonwhite interest groups and their white allies have taken their cues from the United States. The book *Colour and Citizenship* was a self-conscious attempt to emulate Gunnar Myrdal's *An American Dilemma*, a brief visit from Martin Luther King in 1964 inspired the formation of the Campaign Against Racial Discrimination, and visits by Black Muslims from the United States led to the development of the Racial Action Adjustment Society and other black consciousness groups (Rose et al. 1969; Heineman 1972; Banton 1985).

The most obvious influence of the United States on British agenda setting is the sudden announcement and development of the Urban Programme in 1968. In contrast to the incremental nature of movement toward the governmental agenda of most race-related initiatives, the Urban Programme was quickly announced by Prime Minister Harold Wilson in a speech in Birmingham in the spring, and government officials scrambled to prepare and implement the strikingly brief legislation (Edwards and

Batley 1978; Deakin 1974). Early 1968 was a difficult time for the government, with its restrictions on Kenyan Asians immigrating to Britain and Conservative front bencher Enoch Powell's "rivers of blood" speech. Although counterbalancing these fears of racial strife was undoubtedly an impetus behind the Urban Programme, Wilson's own words suggest that he was mindful of what had occurred in other countries, particularly the contemporary urban racial disturbances in the United States, and that he was anxious to prevent similar developments in the United Kingdom.

In other instances, the experience of the United States, as interpreted by British researchers and policy makers, was influential in the formulation of policy, even if not in agenda setting *per se*. Both the Race Relations Acts of 1965 and 1968 owed much to lesson drawing from the United States. The 1965 act redeemed a Labour election manifesto pledge to legislate against racial discrimination. Never having acted in this area previously, however, both the Labour party and permanent government officials sought guidance from the United States, where the civil rights movement of the time had recently brought about the 1964 Civil Rights Act outlawing racial discrimination in a wide variety of activities. Even earlier some U.S. states had acted against racial discrimination. These acts, and especially their coverage and enforcement mechanisms, were the subject of much study and debate, especially by those favoring the legislation, in the course of formulation not only of the 1965 act, but also of its successor in 1968.

The major issues of coverage were whether to legislate against private acts of discrimination in housing and employment as well as those in "public places," narrowly defined. The major issue of enforcement was the relative role of conciliation mechanisms through a government agency versus individually brought cases of criminal law, or as Gregory (1987) puts it, the "administrative agency model" versus the "individual complaint model." Keith Hindell's (1965:394) account of the making of the first Race Relations Act notes that the Martin Committee, which drafted proposals for the National Executive Committee of the Labour party, "drew attention to the American practice of dealing with discrimination by using administrative means and incorporating some element of conciliation." Later, the Lester group, with some of the same membership as the Martin Committee, lobbied to change the government's draft proposals on the basis of an intensive study of practices in the United States and Canada. Finally, Shirley Williams moved an amendment at the committee stage of the bill in the House of Commons based on her own interpretation of how much access to the courts alleged victims of racial discrimination should have (Hindell 1965).

In the wake of what was widely thought to be a weak law in 1965, the Street Report, sponsored by the National Committee for Commonwealth Immigrants and the Race Relations Board, and published by Political and Economic Planning, specifically examined civil rights laws in the United States and Canada, including those below the central level of government. The recommendations of this report served as the foundation for the legislation of 1968 (Rose et al. 1969; Lester and Bindman 1972; Sooben 1990). As the account co-authored by Anthony Lester, a major participant in the transnational policy community, makes clear, there was also a major transatlantic meeting of industrialists and trade unionists where the "lessons from America" about how race relations law worked in employment were extensively debated and, in the process of amending the legislation in the House of Commons, one clause was referred to as the "Colorado Compromise" because its provisions were based on those applying in an anti-discrimination statute in that part of the United States. With the passage of the Race Relations Act of 1968, British law moved from its usual preoccupation with universal individual rights to a concern with selective governmental intervention on behalf of groups of people subject to discriminatory behavior because of their ascriptive characteristics (Lester and Bindman 1972).

The widespread perception of the Race Relations Acts as ineffective, however, and the opening of a policy window in the form of another Labour government with the same civil libertarian home secretary, Roy Jenkins, who had shepherded the 1968 bill through Parliament led to a further initiative in 1976, the third Race Relations Act. As noted previously, the form of this legislation was modeled on the Sex Discrimination Act of the previous year, an act which was brought forward after Jenkins had visited the United States and learned how the concept of indirect discrimination worked there (Gregory 1987). This policy instrument then became incorporated into British race relations law in 1976.

Philip Sooben's (1990) careful study of the origins of this legislation indicates that Jenkins and others closely involved with the development of the 1976 act looked to the experience in the United States for policy guidance. Ethnic monitoring and positive action to remedy identifiable patterns of ethnic disadvantage were encouraged. Encouragement, however, did not mean mandatory policies; instead, it was left to individual government agencies, including local authorities, to pursue ethnic monitoring and positive action in employment and contracts as they saw fit. The results were predictably variable; debate raged over whether to include an "ethnic question" in the census, local governments engaged in racially sensitive policies according to the context of local political forces, the meanings of "positive action" and "positive discrimination" were end-lessly debated, and the Commission for Racial Equality has been both ineffective and controversial, and the Home Office's role as coordinator of race relations policy has been extensively criticized (Sooben 1990; Young 1983; Layton-Henry 1984; Nixon 1982; Gregory 1987; Booth 1988; Russell 1990; Nelson 1991). Whatever the intent of the law, the inclination of British courts is still to think in terms of the negative liberty of individuals and to avoid group-related remedies (McCrudden 1983). In short, there is nothing yet in Britain resembling court-ordered affirmative action in the United States.

Race-related policy in the field of central aid to local areas affected by immigration and racial settlement patterns has also been influenced by the example of the United States. Three programs developed in the 1960s owed something as well to the ideas of area-based policies to deal with poverty and social disadvantage, an important trend in both the United States and Britain at the time (Wolman 1990; Edwards and Batley 1978). In the latter case, an area-based approach was a departure from the previous emphasis upon universality in British social programs (Deakin 1974).

The first race-related policy of this sort was Section 11 of the Local Government Act of 1966, which provided for central government grants for personnel to deal with problems identified with particular areas of "immigrant" settlement. Although still extant a quarter century and several changes of government later, the impact of this section has been modest because of limited funds and even the refusal of some local governments in ethnic minority areas to apply for support (Young 1983; Nelson 1991). But it remains the only government aid program specifically dependent on the ethnic makeup of a territory.

In contrast, the Urban Programme and its later extension, the Commu-nity Development Projects (CDPs), were not exclusively ethnic-related although they were largely inspired by the aim of aiding such areas (Edwards and Batley 1978; Deakin 1974). The origins of the Urban Programme have already been described; the specific working elements of both programs were developed with close scrutiny of similar policies already being implemented in the United States, the Model Cities and Community Action initiatives (Edwards and Batley 1978; Marris and Rein 1972; Deakin 1974). In fact, both front bench parliamentary debates and bureaucratic planning made explicit the connections made and lessons drawn in regard to the programs (Deakin 1974).

The major differences between the approaches of the two countries are the modest financing of the British programs and the closer incorporation of the British CDPs into local government authorities. The implications of the latter structure have been much debated, reflecting either coaptation or responsibility, depending on one's operating assumptions (Edwards and Batley 1978; Russell 1990; Nelson 1991; Ashford 1981; Jacobs 1986; Deakin 1974). When the Labour government attempted to move toward more specifically ethnic group–oriented aid, the proposed legislation, the Local Government (Ethnic Groups) Grants Bill of 1979, was aborted by the parliamentary defeat of the government on other grounds and its subsequent replacement by the Conservatives (Fitzgerald 1986). When the Conservative government thought it had to enact some modest urban aid initiatives in the wake of the 1981 riots, however, it too sent officials to the United States to study developments there (Wolman 1990). Race-related policy in the field of education has been somewhat different, with less explicit policy borrowing in the early years but more attention to developments in the United States and elsewhere more recently (Kirp 1979; Little 1974; Tomlinson 1986). As the nonwhite school-age population has grown in Britain, multicultural education has become more of a concern. Despite the Conservatives' 1988 Education Act, many educational decisions are still made at the local level, where lesson drawing from abroad is less likely. As previously noted, the policy of the Conservatives has been to maintain the existent government components of the race industry but to introduce no legislation specifically oriented toward British minority groups and to pass off responsibility for minority concerns to local authorities. After the urban disturbances of 1980, 1981, and 1985, some local governments have been especially active in attempting to improve the lot of disadvantaged ethnic minorities, but there are severe limitations to what they can do in the face of central government reluctance (Benyon 1984; Russell 1990). The Conservatives see their approach as an integrationist strategy, perhaps best summarized in their 1983 election poster of a black man with the slogan, "Labour says he's black; Conservatives say he's British." Their critics, on the other hand, see the policy as one showing insensitivity to minority needs. How much the Conservatives have taken their cues on race-related policy from the United States in the era of Reagan and Bush remains to be researched. As Dave Russell (1990) notes, however, there are fundamentally different conceptions of what "equal opportunity" means, in both countries. In short, there are competing definitions of the problem as well as debate over alternative policies.

Nevertheless, there is abundant evidence that earlier decisions about the direction of race policy in Britain were heavily influenced by official attention to events and policies in the United States. Once central government agreed to put race-related issues on its agenda, it consistently looked to the United States to provide guidance for policy alternatives and policy formulation. Attention to developments in the United States has also been a characteristic of the House of Commons Select Committee on Race Relations and Immigration (since 1979, a subcommittee of the Home Affairs Committee) (Sooben 1990; Drewry 1985). Whether British officials interpreted U.S. developments correctly and whether similar approaches were appropriate in the somewhat different policy environment in the United Kingdom are interesting questions that will not be fully addressed here. Differences in the scope of race-related legislation, the role of the courts, and the policy style of the bureaucracies have been noted elsewhere in this conjunction (Rose 1988; Kirp 1979; McCrudden 1983; Rose 1992). For our purposes, it is sufficient to demonstrate that, once a race-related issue became part of the central government agenda, the search for solutions focused considerably, although not exclusively, on the United States. Lesson drawing was attempted, even if policy borrowing was not exact.

CONCLUSION

This overview of race-related policies in Britain shows that nonwhite access to the British political agenda remains minimal and problematic. While overt hostility toward nonwhites may have diminished over the years, indifference to their situation is still the norm, among both elites and masses, but especially the latter. Thus it takes unusual circumstances for nonwhite concerns to become part of the ongoing public or governmental agenda.

In Walker's (1977) topology, nonwhite problems remain sporadically recurring and crisis problems, not periodically recurring or chosen problems. Some attention must be paid to them, but, after a flurry of activity, interest in the issue subsides. Maintaining race-related issues on the agenda is a continual struggle for those who are interested in doing so. Few political leaders choose to pursue nonwhite problems, and nonwhites are not sufficiently integrated into the bureaucracy to claim periodic attention. Thus, some governmental and public attention is required, but there is still a large element of discretion present. Substantial difficulties occur in problem definition and alternatives specification.

A major contributor to this lack of consensus on problem definition and alternatives specification is the attitudes of nonwhites themselves. On domestic issues such as law and order and housing, splits between Afro-Caribbeans and Asians, as well as among Asian-descended groups, are evident. East London Bangladeshis want greater protection by the police, London Afro-Caribbeans want greater protection from the police. Asians tend to be private landlords, Afro-Caribbeans tend to be renters. Gross public opinion findings show a surprising degree of consensus between white and nonwhite attitudes on what the most important issues are (Studlar 1986; Studlar and Layton-Henry 1990). Such findings, however, only touch the surface and mask the greater differences, even within the nonwhite group, on how issues are to be defined.

These mass divisions are also reflected on the elite level. Asian-descended groups are, in general, more cohesively united behind their leaders than Afro-Caribbean ones, but there are several different Asian groups, varying in education, occupations, culture, religion, and residential location. Most British nonwhites have made individual and group accommodations to the society in which they live.

The government has encouraged this process by refusing to take responsibility for many of the problems faced by nonwhites in Britain. The Conservatives' economic cutbacks, more stringent controls on local government, and general refusal to do much about nonwhite concerns have discouraged the voicing of demands. Treating black activism as part of the extremist Left has allowed the Conservative government to readily stereotype and dismiss it. Without overt government persecution of nonwhites on a massive scale, the well of public sympathy for their problems is not likely to run very deep. With Western liberalism as embedded as it is in British political culture (Studlar 1974), group-centered egalitarian issues, unless they are class-defined, have difficulty in gaining access to the public or formal agenda.

Whichever theoretical schema one adopts, racial issues have only a niche of low and sporadic agenda status in British politics. In Solesbury's (1976a) terms, nonwhites have only a limited capacity to command attention for their issue concerns, and even when attention is received, the legitimacy of issues (changing police behavior, for instance) may be denied. Action is thus even less likely to be invoked. In Nelson's (1984) terms, race-related issues are recognized, at least in a general sense, but are usually at either the issue adoption or issue priority stage, on both the formal and systemic levels. In Durant and Diehl's (1989) topology, conscious policy change in areas of nonwhite concern is usually gradualist, that is, transformative and protracted. Insofar as there is any recurring maintenance for racial issues, it is due to the activities of the Home Affairs Subcommittee on Race Relations and Immigration and bureaucratic processes usually hidden from public view, such as consideration of changes in implementation of the Local Government Act of 1966. Similarly, using Jones's (1977) schema, nonwhite access to the agenda has had plenty of difficulty in getting to the problem definition stage, much less beyond it to the proposal, bargaining, and continuing agendas. Lacking powerful bureaucratic, parliamentary, and interest group sponsors, nonwhites do not benefit from the normally easier agenda access of policy succession (Hogwood and Peters 1983).

Aside from a small number of race-conscious liberal politicians and activists, the discovery of nonwhite problems has never really generated optimism about the capacity of the British polity to cope with them. Both political decision makers and the public have more commonly simply wanted the problems to go away without government or public commitment to alter them. Serious and active consideration of race-related problems is rare and is even harder to maintain.

The dominant preference is still to offload as many racial issues as possible onto a central government bureaucracy fragmented in its responsibilities for such issues and to a local authority structure increasingly bereft of financial capacity to deal with the problems. Police, education, housing, ethnic recordkeeping, and even employment are usually handled in this manner.

However much allowed in the nominal constitution, rapid political change rarely occurs in the United Kingdom (Studlar 1984). Even a more unified, issue-focused nonwhite group, with a more sympathetic public and major political leaders willing to champion their cause, would find it difficult to effect major policy change. The struggle for policy space in a putative Labour government, for instance, might make it difficult to create a policy window for nonwhites (Ben-Tovim 1989; Kingdon 1984; Messina 1989). It is extremely difficult for a small, distinctive minority to have its views heard except where these views substantially overlap with those of the dominant groups and institutions in the polity. That is the continuing dilemma for any ethnic minority, and especially nonwhites, in their attempt to obtain agenda access in Britain.

The search for lessons from abroad to apply to race-related policy is unusual behavior and results from dissatisfaction with current policy (Rose 1991; Robertson and Waltman 1992). In this case, a large part of the search was due to the inexperience of Britain with race-related policies. Once agenda access for racial issues has been obtained in Britain, there has been extensive lesson drawing by cabinet ministers and civil servants, interest groups, parliamentary committees, and individual M.P.s. Where were they to look? English-speaking countries with large white majorities but also a more substantial history of attempting to cope with such problems, such as the United States and Canada, were an easily accessible source. As seen especially with the three Race Relations Acts, policy dissatisfaction continued, and policy makers continued to look to the same places abroad for additional lessons. There has been a similar long-term lesson-drawing phenomenon in urban policy.

Policy borrowing is more likely to occur in technical areas rather than in softer areas more subject to cultural differences (Wolman 1990; Robertson and Waltman 1992). The fact that anti-discrimination legislation and urban policy are social rather than technical in nature would seem to make them less likely candidates for transfer. But the core values and policy goals were not at issue; the search abroad was to acquire suitable instruments (administrative techniques) to realize the goals (Bennett and Howlett 1991; Robertson and Waltman 1992).

We can find little evidence that anti-discrimination legislation and area-based urban policy initiatives were placed on the political agenda because of lesson drawing. The extant policy studies emphasize the relevance of British experience and commitments in putting anti-discrimination legislation on the agenda. Although the urban initiatives of the Great Society in the United States may have had some influence in the more modest British proposals reaching the agenda, the weight of the evidence indicates that area-based approaches to dealing with deprivation were current in British political thinking as well, and the problem of poverty and what social policies could relieve it were a major thrust in both countries in the 1960s. Robertson's (1991) contention that lesson drawing is more important at the agenda-setting than at the alternative selection stage may be due to the particular policy area he was studying, plant closing notification legislation, and/or the fact that the separation of powers makes policy borrowing more contentious in the United States. The unitary nature of the British polity may make lesson drawing a less contentious process there (Wolman 1990). Furthermore, policy makers in the United Kingdom have been quite willing to acknowledge publicly that they are engaged in lesson drawing from the United States, in contrast to what Bennett (1991b) argues is the usual tendency for policy borrowers to be less forthright about the process than policy lenders.

The emphasis of lesson drawing on race-related policy by Britain from the United States has been on learning what policy instruments were more likely to work once the decision to face a problem had largely been made. This makes the long debate over what combination of enforcement models to use in anti-discrimination policy more understandable. Similarly, although the evidence is less clear, the penchant of the British government for clear lines of responsibility and ultimate central control may have led to the deliberate rejection of the U.S. form of community development. Finally, even though British urban policy is less ethnic or race-specific than in the United States, even Conserva-

tive governments have never completely abandoned financial aid to
nonwhite areas.

This evidence indicates that, in terms of policy types, domestic race-related policy in Britain lies closer to regulatory policy (Race Relations Acts)
and distributive policy (urban aid) than to redistributive policy (Lowi
1964; Ripley 1985; Wolman 1990). Small-scale solutions and small commitments of resources—laws, personnel, finance—are emphasized.
Changing the orientation of British legal thinking to allow better enforcement of race relations law, for instance, has not been attempted; that would
mean a major challenge to deeply held institutional values (McCrudden
1983; Gregory 1987). In contrast, similar civil rights and urban development policies in their country of origin, the United States, tended to be
more redistributive or social regulatory in character, at least initially on
the federal level, but the judiciary there was more prepared for a politically
controversial role (Dye 1992; Smith 1975; Ripley and Franklin 1991;
Tatalovich and Daynes 1988). Policy typologies, however, need much
more extensive comparative research before firm conclusions are drawn
about these matters (Freeman 1985; Heidenheimer 1985).

Even considering their handicaps in resources for agenda setting in Britain,
ethnic minorities are more likely to be able to influence the political agenda
than they are the latter stages of the policy process. When it comes to
alternative selection, minorities lack the expertise and cohesion to be able to
exert other than a very diffuse impact. Indeed, evidence suggests that lesson
drawing from the United States has been a major influence on the shape that
race-related legislation has taken in the United Kingdom. Even if they have
allies who have a role in policy formulation at this point, ethnic minorities
themselves are unlikely to be part of the transnational policy networks which
enable policy borrowing to take place.

Whether lesson drawing in race-related policy has led to successful
transfers of policy and effective implementation remains a question for
future exploration. As Rose (1976, 1990, 1992) has argued, often the
wrong lessons are learned, and the barriers to effective policy transfer are
considerable. Race-related policy in Britain is not immune to these difficulties.

NOTE

1. The terms *ethnic* and *race* are defined as follows. "Ethnic" refers to a self-identifi-
cation of cultural distinction from the nearby population. "Race" refers to a distinction
imposed by outsiders usually on the basis of skin color, that is, black-white.

II

UNITED STATES—NATIONAL PERSPECTIVE

3

Political Innovation and Economic Rights: The Case of the Hawkins-Humphrey Bill

Charles P. Henry

The major public policy conflict of the early 1960s revolved around the issue of civil rights (Garrow 1978; McAdam 1982; Lawson 1991; Whalen and Whalen 1985). With the passage of the Civil Rights Act of 1964 and the Voting Rights Act of 1965, the domestic policy agenda began to shift to issues of economic rights. By the early 1970s, the various groups pushing for a change in focus from political and civil liberties to economic rights consolidated their forces behind the Hawkins-Humphrey full employment bill.

Full employment legislation was not new to the political arena. The Employment Act of 1946 is generally regarded as a landmark in political innovation. Thirty-two years later, the passage of the Full Employment and Balanced Growth Act of 1978 marks the rebirth of innovative (redistributive, nonincrementalist) policy under new leadership in a changed environment. By examining the case histories of these two bills this study will analyze political innovation as it relates to full employment. It will also contend that both bills failed to achieve their ultimate goal of guaranteed full employment largely because technical innovation was substituted for political innovation. Finally, this study will suggest modifications to the criteria we use in categorizing policy innovation.

WHAT IS INNOVATIVE POLICY?

Scholarship on political innovation is at the very vanguard of social science research. The evolution of research from formal institutions to political behavior has been accompanied by a transition in the policy research from the legislative process to the implementation process. Yet, the initiation of new policy—the very substance of the political process—is seldom given equal attention.

In part this lack of attention to innovation results from the dominant mode of thought in policy making—incrementalism. Bargaining, logrolling, and coalition building came to define the parameters of political discourse. In the competition among interests to assert their program preferences, the overriding goal of policy is lost. If policy implies a consensus and a course of action, it is often lost in the conflicting objectives of narrow programs. Are job training programs, for example, consistent with programs designed to reduce inflation by increasing unemployment? Is our priority to reduce inflation or increase employment? Is it possible to do both? If not, how do we decide which priority is more important?

In part the lack of attention to innovation results also from the dominant mode of thought in policy analysis—empiricism. Positivist conceptions of social science envision the generation of accurate data as their *raison d'etre*. Ends are treated as "given" and the main task of social science is to separate facts from values (Rein 1976; Nelson 1977; Hawkesworth 1988; Goodin 1982). If welfare, for example, reduces people's willingness to work we must make welfare contingent on accepting a job, for example, workfare. However, if the job is low paid and dead end, it defeats the very values we are attempting to instill by requiring a job. If the job is rewarding and leads to advancement there is no need to offer welfare. Thus, even if we accept that facts can be separated from values there is no logical way to derive an "ought" from an "is" proposition (Rein 1976:42).

In fact, policy analysis is the ideal place to unite fact and value. It should provide a theory of intervention based on a value premise and informed by the practical consequences of action. That is, public policy should rest on an agreed-to moral or ethical principle and the cost of intervention should be known or predictable. Innovative public policy provides the greatest challenge for policy analysis precisely because it raises new value premises or challenges old ones and it is difficult to predict the consequences. Given the uncertainty in regard to consequences, the principles underlying an innovative policy must be strong for it to succeed. It is generally recognized that such policies have been rare in the United States[1] (Lowi 1964:677–715).

How do we decide whether a policy is innovative as opposed to routine? Grover Starling has suggested three criteria. First, an innovative alternative builds on a new combination of available knowledge concerning properties of the social system. This definition excludes both branching alternatives and totally new scientific discoveries. Second, an innovative alternative must be the product of a mental effort above the average. This definition excludes routine technical adjustments. Third, an innovative alternative must be productive by either reducing the cost of delivering already authorized services or delivering new services for which the cost is justified. Obviously, there is a problem in measuring noneconomically oriented innovative activity. Using these criteria, Starling identifies approximately 100 legislative actions during the period from 1949 to 1972. He indicates that the Employment Act of 1946 qualifies as an important and innovative policy but was not adopted during the period he investigates (Starling 1979:211–222).

Nelson Polsby, in *Political Innovation in America*, uses this act as one of eight case studies in "the politics of policy initiation." His criteria for choosing policies are: (1) that they are relatively large-scale, highly visible phenomena; (2) that they break in some way from previous governmental responses; and (3) that they have lasting institutional or societal effects (Polsby 1984:8). Polsby recognizes that his selection criteria limit him to crisis-like events in the national arena. Furthermore, he does not examine the obstacles to innovation, that is, nonevents.

Given his criteria, Polsby's examination of the Employment Act of 1946 is curious to say the least. While admitting that the act represented "a larger ideological controversy over the efficacy—and appropriateness for the United States—of planning," he chooses to focus almost entirely on one aspect of the act—the creation of the Council on Economic Advisers. In doing so, he ignores the most innovative and controversial aspects of the legislation.

POLITICAL INNOVATION IN THE NEW DEAL ERA

The entry of the United States into World War I, in April 1917, marked the beginning of government experiments in centralized economic planning. In order to fight a war, government and business had to work together for a year and a half. As the war ended these habits of cooperation persisted as Herbert Hoover, first as secretary of commerce and then as president, actively promoted industrial planning through trade associations. In response to the Great Depression, Hoover created a Reconstruction Finance Corporation to promote business growth[2] (Gross and Singh forthcoming:8). However, all the president's measures operated within the guidelines of a balanced budget, pushing mass purchasing power even lower. The result was unemployment estimated at 25 percent of the work force in 1933.

The ensuing "crisis in capitalism" created by the Great Depression not only produced a realignment in party politics through the election of

Franklin D. Roosevelt, but also a willingness to innovate. On entering the White House, Roosevelt declared his intention to save capitalism through "pragmatic planning" and immediately expanded Hoover's Reconstruction Finance Corporation.

Early in his administration FDR set up a National Planning Board which functioned as a research and coordinating group for the New Deal's scattered brain trusters. Despite congressional and corporate hostility to planning, Roosevelt eventually transformed this group by executive order into the National Resources Planning Board within the Executive Office of the President. The same 1939 executive order also transferred the Bureau of the Budget from the Treasury Department to the Executive Office of the President and gave it a highly professionalized planning staff (Gross 1974; Bailey 1950).

Despite these planning innovations and the many other programs of the New Deal, unemployment in 1939 remained at an unacceptably high 17.2 percent. But the situation changed dramatically in September 1939 when Germany invaded Poland and World War II began. With official entry of the United States into the war effort the GNP grew from $90.5 billion in 1939 to $125 billion in 1941 and $212 billion by 1945. Reported unemployment in 1944 dropped to 1.7 percent, the lowest rate of unemployment in recent economic history.

The shift in attitude created by the war was remarkable[3] (Rein 1976; Goodin 1982). Employers welcomed the illiterate and unskilled as they were quickly trained on the job. Women were given the opportunity to work as day care centers were created on a scale never before seen. In response to pressure, blacks were brought into the war effort as some racial barriers in industry fell. The war effort had a number of consequences directly relevant to our study. It gave the president almost dictatorial power to conduct the war. Moreover, his need to coordinate and plan was greater than ever. The most visible aspect of this need was the establishment of the Office of War Mobilization in the Executive Office of the President. Finally, as the war wound down, demobilization and reconversion assumed increasing importance. Would the United States return to its pre-war condition of depression and unemployment as spending slowed and millions of troops returned to the labor force?

Roosevelt's first response to this question came in his January 11, 1944, State of the Union message: "We have accepted, so to speak, a second Bill of Rights under which a new basis of security and prosperity can be established for all. . . . Among these [is] the right to a useful and remunerative job in the industries or shops or farms or mines of the Nation." As the 1944 election grew nearer, Roosevelt's "guarantee of full employment" after the war drew increasing attention including a promise from Governor Thomas Dewey, the Republican presidential nominee, to make full employment through private enterprise the first objective of national policy. Roosevelt countered by promising to provide a quantifiable number of jobs—60 million (Gross 1974:4).

These election year promises took shape in a bill introduced by Senators James Murray and Harry Truman entitled "The Full Employment Act of 1945" (S. 380). Bertram Gross of the War Contracts Subcommittee, under the chairmanship of Senator Murray, was largely responsible for drafting the bill. As Stephen K. Bailey recounts in his classic study of this bill, Gross and his assistants were allowed an unusually wide scope of initiative in planning and carrying out the legislative campaign[4] (Bailey 1950:66). The bill contained three major political innovations. First, it transformed FDR's promise of "the right to a useful and remunerative job" into policy by assigning the federal government the responsibility of guaranteeing good jobs to everyone able and willing to work for pay. Second, the legislation established the president as the nation's chief economic planner and required him to transmit to Congress every year a comprehensive domestic economic program with specific goals for the number of needed jobs and specific measures to produce an economic level guaranteeing job rights. Third, it created a Joint Committee of Congress to review the president's program and present its conclusions in a congressional resolution to be voted on by the Senate and the House (Gross 1985).

If not to be rejected outright, these innovations had to be presented in a form that would win crucial moderate support. The National Resources Planning Board's concept of full employment had been set forth in 1943 in a "Second Bill of Rights." This "Bill of Rights" included civil liberties and state and local planning as well as comprehensive federal policy making. Roosevelt's version of this "Second Bill of Rights" emerged in 1944 and omitted both civil liberties and state and local planning. He focused solely on the right to job opportunity and excluded mention of any other economic rights. At the same time Congress was considering a full employment bill, the drafters of the United Nations Charter rejected the idea of economic rights by setting up a commission to study the subject and limiting the charter commitment to "promoting" full employment.[5]

Neither the economists nor political scientists who dealt with the bill pursued the economic rights concept. Perhaps they could not relate human rights to the conceptual basis of either neoclassical or Keynesian thought. Another consideration was the vehement reaction to the "subversive" National Resources Planning Board that led to its demise. In any case, the sponsors of the bill overemphasized compensatory fiscal policy and concentrated on economic advice and projections of foreseeable trends. This shift to a more technical approach to full employment set the stage for later linkages to inflation and helped undercut the moral arguments which had the passion to arouse mass support. Sponsors also sought to cloak the president's new power as economic planner by assigning the Bureau of the Budget the task of helping the president carry out his new responsibilities rather than creating a new planning agency. This strategy helped assure the support of the bureau's conservative staff.

Finally, to help offset the president's new responsibility, Congress was given a new agency to strengthen its role in economic policy. These innovations, and a strong populist attack on those business people who benefit from depressions, helped to confuse the opposition. However, opponents rallied and after a year of intense debate and the substitution of several weaker versions, a Senate-House conference committee drafted a compromise that became the Employment Act of 1946.

The substitute bill introduced in the House by Representative William Whittington had rejected the fundamental principles of the Senate bill, replacing them with a policy aiming for a "high" level of employment, production, and purchasing power. Moreover, it provided for a Council of Economic Advisers (CEA) who would consult with economic groups, issue regular reports on economic trends, and make recommendations to the president whenever inflation or unemployment threatened. Nelson Polsby sees the creation of the CEA as the major policy innovation emerging from the Employment Act of 1946. The CEA is viewed as a compromise between government planners influenced by liberal Keynesian economic theory and conservative politicians who did not understand Keynes and labeled planning as communism. Thus, the result was an institutional role for the economists, but one that was limited to recommendations subject to congressional approval.

While Polsby's viewpoint is correct in a sense, it misses the forest by focusing on a tree. The president retains his wartime role as "Economic Planner-in-Chief" and the Truman Council under Leon Keyersling moved from countercyclical policies to GNP "growthmanship." In the *Modern Corporate State*, Arthur S. Miller contends that the Employment Act of 1946 laid the legal foundations for the corporate state in the United States. Bertram Gross states that the political idea of using high and appealing rhetoric to justify total growth now survives as conservative or military Keynesianism. "The simile that a 'rising tide raises all boats'—heard often during the Reagan Administration—suggests that rising output will by itself raise poor people from poverty or overcome institutionalized discrimination against women and minorities" (Gross 1974). Thus, Polsby's focus on the creation of the CEA and its promotion of "growthmanship" under Walter Heller in the Kennedy Administration misses what was lost in the original battle over economic rights. "Growth" replaces "rights" as the government's primary economic responsibility.

The major loss in the final version of the full employment legislation was not the president's role as economic coordinator but rather the guarantee of a job. Gone is Roosevelt's right or entitlement for all those who come to work. Without this right the concept of full or even high employment becomes unenforceable. It is this right to earn a living that must come of age over a period of years. Without public support this concept could and would be interpreted as a tolerable level of unemployment by the CEA, Joint Economic Committee, or any of the economic experts that found an institutional home in Washington after World War II.

POLITICAL INNOVATION IN THE GREAT SOCIETY ERA

At the peak of the civil rights movement in 1963, the historic March on Washington had two major themes—"jobs and freedom." Supported by labor and religious groups, civil rights leaders and organizations were successful in promoting passage of the most effective civil rights bill to that date—the Civil Rights Act of 1964. The following year witnessed passage of the Voting Rights Act and liberal support for further reform seemed to wane. As inner city violence flared in 1965 and again in 1967, resistance to black demands hardened.

The demand for jobs and economic rights was now fully joined as Martin Luther King, Jr., stated that blacks had moved "from issues of personal dignity to programs that impinge upon the basic system of social and economic control. At this level, Negro programs go beyond race and deal with economic inequality, wherever it exists" (King 1967:17). Conservative spokesperson William F. Buckley, Jr., accused black leadership of advancing state omnipotence, socialization, and inflation rather than black interests. He argued that the black community was just as divided as the white community on nonracial issues like jobs and national health insurance. Vernon Jordan of the Urban League responded that racial issues had not been settled with the civil rights laws of the 1960s. According to Jordan, "race is an inescapable element" of real world issues of concern to all, like jobs, housing, education, and health, "because a black child born today is simply by virtue of his color, is less likely to partake of the rewards and responsibilities of our society than a white" (Copley News Service 1978).

The policy response to black economic demands was a series of piece-meal job programs, including paraprofessional programs, new careers approaches, and public service employment (sub–civil service jobs)[6] (Starling 1979:211). The 1960s also witnessed a massive rise in welfare programs, some of which were designed to discourage job seekers. None of these programs were coordinated with each other and none struck at the roots of structural unemployment.[7] With the defeat of the New Deal coalition as represented by Hubert Humphrey in 1968, President Nixon moved in two new directions. One was to attempt a basic reform of the welfare system through guaranteed minimum incomes but at below sub-sistence levels. This approach drew little black support. Moreover, national public opinion polls consistently showed that the American people op-posed guaranteed minimum incomes but supported guaranteed jobs by roughly a two-to-one margin[8] (Levison 1980:192–195). The other direc-tion can be summed up in Daniel Moynihan's famous phrase—"benign neglect."

Nixon Administration officials went beyond "benign neglect" to a direct attack on Great Society programs like the Office of Economic Opportunity (OEO). Nixon was able to carry out such offensives largely because of the relative lack of support for targeted programs for the disadvantaged as compared to the more broad-based programs of the New Deal. Vincente Navarro has recently pointed out that New Deal–type programs like Social Security, Medicare, and unemployment in-surance retained popular support even in the 1980s while Great Society–type programs such as Supplemental Security Income, Aid to Families with Dependent Children, food stamps, and Medicaid have been subject to severe cutbacks by the Reagan Administration (Navarro 1985). Sensing the need for a broad-based, comprehensive attack on unemployment, black leadership made full employment the central policy demand of the 1970s.

Black political mobilization during the 1960s had produced record numbers of black elected officials, which led in part to the establishing of a Congressional Black Caucus (CBC) in 1970 (Henry 1977). This innovative legislative group responded to the Nixon Administration with a host of policy proposals directed at extending the concept of equality into economic areas. With the support of the CBC in general and Representative John Conyers, Representative Yvonne Burke, and Senator Edward Brooke in particular, Representative Augustus Hawkins of California introduced a bill in 1974 meant to fulfill FDR's promise of full employment made thirty years earlier. He was assisted in drafting the bill by Bertram Gross, the author of the Employment Act of 1946, and by academics associated with *Social Policy* magazine. The severe recession of 1975–1976 served to popularize the bill and make it an issue in the 1976 presidential campaign. Both candidates Fred Harris and Morris Udall made full employment a central element in their campaigns.

The original Hawkins bill was entitled "The Equal Opportunity and Full Employment Act." Its major provisions were as follows:

- The president was required to develop a full employment and national purposes budget that would necessitate a greater use of the national labor supply.

- Full employment was defined as "a situation under which there are useful and rewarding employment opportunities for all adult Americans willing and able to work."

- Local reservoirs of public and private employment projects were to be developed by Local Planning Councils in cooperation with Community Job Boards.

- A Job Guarantee Office was created giving priority to job development through the private sector.

- A Standby Job Corps was created for those who temporarily were unable to find suitable jobs.

- The congressional Joint Economic Committee was given an expanded role in reviewing and initiating the implementation of the Full Employment and Production Program.

- A National Commission for Full Employment Policy Studies was created to conduct research on full employment as it relates to inflation.

- Any person deprived of his or her job rights was given the opportunities to sue through the United States District Courts (Hawkins 1975:15).

Once full employment gained national attention, a bill of such far-reaching dimensions was bound to generate intense opposition from traditional opponents of planning and federal intervention in the economy, such as business groups and the Republican party. What is surprising, however, is the opposition coming from sections of the labor community and many liberal economists as well as a Democratic president. What follows is a very brief case history of the legislation highlighting major changes and the opposition of key political actors.

LEGISLATIVE CHANGES FROM BIRTH TO ENACTMENT

Stage I on the legislative process involved the writing of contending drafts of the legislation during the winter of 1973. Scholars were heavily involved at this stage, especially through full employment conferences at UCLA and Columbia. Bertram Gross and Russell Nixon, who died in December 1973, were major forces in the development of the legislation. This work culminated with the introduction of the Equal Opportunity and Full Employment Act of 1976 by Representative Hawkins in the House on June 19, 1974, and by Senator Humphrey (selected because of his chairmanship of the Joint Economic Committee) in the Senate on August 22.

On March 20, 1975, the House Equal Opportunities Subcommittee (chaired by Hawkins) issued a greatly amplified substitute print of the Hawkins bill (H.R. 50). It strengthened the provisions in the original bill dealing with specific, useful, and abundant government employment programs (Job Guarantee Office, Standby Job Corps, and Local Planning Councils) and the right to administrative and judicial redress of violations of employment rights, and added anti-inflation provisions. Moreover, it provided an emergency implementation provision which required the president to implement the act completely within thirty-six months of enactment, as well as achieve 3 percent unemployment within eighteen months of enactment. To do this, the president was authorized to request $15 billion or more from Congress. During this second stage, academicians were still very much involved, most notably through a special edition of *The Annals* on "Planning for Full Employment" in March 1975. However, the bill was still largely ignored by the general public.

Stage III encompasses House action on the bill beginning in the winter of 1975 through October 1978. On March 10, 1976, the Equal Opportunities Subcommittee issued a substitute print which constituted a merger with the Humphrey-Javits planning bill. Leonard Woodcock, president of the United Auto Workers, had argued that the two bills were complementary. The amalgam provided a national economic planning bill which made full employment the primary goal. However, other labor factions—namely George Meany and the craft unions—wanted more changes in the bill. They objected to the provision giving individuals the right to sue for employment, perhaps sensing that it might undercut union control of hiring and bring more minorities and women into the labor force than some union leaders were willing to accept. Moreover, Humphrey requested changes to make the bill a palatable Democratic presidential vehicle. These included elaborate anti-inflation provisions and an extension of time allowed to meet the 3 percent unemployment goal from eighteen months to four years.

On September 16, 1976, the Education and Labor Committee issued a substitute print to meet the criticisms of presidential candidate Jimmy Carter and freshman House Democrats. Greater emphasis was placed on curbing inflation, and the quality and quantity of last-resort federal jobs were diminished. Despite these changes, it was not until November 14, 1977, that now President Carter embraced a still weaker version of the original bill. The new draft raised the *acceptable* overall unemployment rate from 3 to 4 percent within five years. A "bailout" clause was added that gave the president the right to request Congress to alter these goals for the third and subsequent years that the bill was in effect. As an economic conservative, Carter never accepted the premise that structural unemployment was a problem. Moreover, like his economic advisers, including CEA chair Charles Schultze, Carter believed inflation was the major priority and that full employment threatened to increase inflation levels. Only Secretary of Labor Ray Marshall, among Carter's advisers, was convinced that a strong full employment bill was needed.

On March 16, 1978, the House approved H.R. 50 after four days of debate and consideration of fifty amendments. Although stringent anti-inflation and budget-balancing amendments were proposed, only mild ones lacking specific numerical goals were adopted. The House adopted the Senate version on October 15, 1978.

Senate action (Stage IV) on the bill stretched from the summer of 1974 to the fall of 1978. On March 16, 1976, a substitute S. 50 was introduced (same as the March 10, 1976, House Education and Labor substitute), with slight differences in age-group categories to meet unemployment goals. *Adult* was here defined as eighteen years plus, in contrast to the House version, which defined an adult as sixteen years plus. On January 10, 1977, a substitute was introduced for the same reasons as the September 16, 1976, House Education and Labor substitute. Likewise, Muriel Humphrey and a bipartisan group of twenty-six senators introduced a February 23, 1978, substitute that paralleled the December 14, 1977, House Education and Labor Committee substitute.

By May 4, 1978, the Human Resources Committee reported its version of S. 50. The overall unemployment goal was 4 percent within five years of enactment. Although it required the president to propose an annual inflation goal, along with specific policies consistent with attaining full employment, it did not contain specific numerical goals or a timetable. On June 28, 1978, the Banking, Housing, and Urban Affairs Committee reported its version of S. 50. It contained an overall unemployment goal of 4 percent within five years of enactment, required a balanced federal budget, reduction of the federal share of the GNP, and an inflation goal of 0 percent within five years of enactment. The considerable differences between the bills reported by the two Senate committees—especially on inflation goals pushed by Senator William Proxmire—led to two months of negotiations in which few differences were settled.

By this time, a conservative-led filibuster became a real threat given the scheduled October adjournment by Congress. Opponents of the legislation had filed some 430 amendments that could be called up to stall the bill. Only concerted pressure on President Carter and Senate Majority Leader Robert Byrd led the latter to appoint an ad hoc committee to work out a timetable for floor consideration of the legislation. This innovative strategy produced a last-minute compromise, which was essentially the Banking Committee's version. Led by Orrin Hatch of Utah, this version contained the inflation goal of 0 percent within ten years of enactment.

On October 13, 1978, the Senate approved the bill. The overall unemployment goal was set at 4 percent within five years of enactment. The inflation goal was 3 percent by 1983 and 0 percent by 1988. Senator Edmund Muskie's amendment for reducing the federal proportion of the GNP "to the lowest possible level, consistent with National needs," was adopted instead of Senator Proxmire's amendment which attached specific percentages to the reductions of 21 percent by fiscal 1981 and 20 percent by fiscal 1983. Also adopted was an amendment proposed by Henry Bellmen of Oklahoma which gave the Budget Committee discretion (if the president changed the timetable) to include in its subsequent budget resolution a new date for achieving the bill's unemployment goals.

Amid much ceremony at the White House, President Carter signed the Full Employment and Balanced Growth Act of 1978 on October 27 (Stage V). He proclaimed that: "Success in fighting inflation is critical to success in fighting unemployment."

DISCUSSION

Both Hawkins and Humphrey saw the right to earn a living as a human right. The success of the civil rights movement and increasing black political power made the possibility of guaranteeing this right a greater probability than at any other time during U.S. history. They also saw a full employment economy as a preferable alternative to programs like affirmative action, which tended to divide workers and had no meaning for those without jobs[9] (Humphrey 1975:21). Using the language of the civil rights movement, early drafts sought innovative ways of providing "economic equal opportunity." As the bill gained national attention, opponents chipped away at many initiatives and raised the specter of inflation.

By grounding their legislation on human rights, Hawkins and Humphrey were acknowledging that fact and value are linked. The fact of unemployment involves more than simple technical adjustments to the economy. It involves a principle or moral proposition that moves beyond matters of personal preference to make a claim about things that are more generally or universally good. For example, the original Hawkins-Humphrey legislation contained a statement of personal rights and attempts to place legal appeal machinery at the disposal of the jobless. While these provisions were dropped, primarily at the insistence of labor groups, the intent to establish personal legal rights is clearly reflective of the civil rights movement. If one refused to acknowledge any "moral" basis for the law, the majority could claim to rule the minority only by the license of numerical strength (might).

In proposing a full employment philosophy to include *every* adult American, Hawkins and Humphrey were reconceptualizing the standard definition of the work force, which excludes older workers, housewives, retirees, welfare recipients, veterans, those discouraged from seeking employment, the physically and mentally handicapped, and others. This innovation has a direct racial component that was recognized by Vernon Jordan in his testimony on the bill. He stated that "the labor force has become split-level, with an upper-tier who have good jobs, union membership, decent salaries, and fringe benefits." The lower tier, composed of disproportionate numbers of Vietnam veterans, blacks and other minorities, and young people, have none of these (Jordan 1973:7).

Of course, economists have long recognized the distinction between cyclical unemployment—people who temporarily lose their jobs because of declines in economic activity—and structural unemployment—people who suffer chronic unemployment because their skills are not demanded by employers. While New Deal innovations like unemployment insurance aided the former, they did nothing for the latter. What changed over time was the increasing number of youth and minorities in the latter category. Lyndon Johnson's Great Society efforts to aid the chronically unemployed were not coordinated and lacked the popular support of the earlier programs. Many critics saw these programs as rewarding undeserving people whose chronic unemployment was their own fault[10] (Hawkesworth 1987). Thus, former Treasury Secretary John Connally could state in 1972, "Let's not be concerned about 6% unemployment among minorities, teenagers and women"[11] (Bullock 1978:16).

A final innovation in the original Hawkins-Humphrey legislation attempts to affect political structure. Perhaps in response to the growing centralization of power in the presidency that began with Franklin D. Roosevelt, the new legislation conferred major planning functions on local councils set up by local governments[12] (Baumer and Van Horn 1985). Labor and public interest groups opposed such decentralization. At the federal level, Hawkins-Humphrey attempts to restore the Congress as co-equal with the president in setting forth guides to budgetary policy. The influence of the CEA is to be balanced by a stronger Joint Economic Committee.

In terms of theory on political innovation, our analysis of Hawkins-Humphrey and, to a lesser extent, the Employment Act of 1946 raises a number of questions about Polsby's approach. In one sense, our analysis of Hawkins-Humphrey affirms his view that there is a type of policy innovation that builds over many years, is researched thoroughly, and arouses ideological conflict. However, by focusing on only one aspect of the 1946 legislation, the Council of Economic Advisers, Polsby misses what for some was the most significant part of the legislation. It was FDR's promise of jobs, rather than the CEA, that inspired the actions leading to the 1978 legislation. In fact, the failure of monetary and fiscal policies recommended by the CEA to meet the problem of black unemployment (roughly twice the national average since World War II) led Hawkins and his colleagues to revive the original intent of the Full Employment bills of 1944, 1945, and 1946. A theory of political innovation must include those elements that are initially rejected but later resurrected in another political environment. Moreover, it must not neglect the symbolic impact of legislative proposals on public attitudes. Finally, a close look at truly innovative initiatives tends to upset our notions of traditional allies. In the case of Hawkins-Humphrey, labor support was split, liberal economists opposed the bill, and several civil rights and public service groups favored more piecemeal (patronage or client-based) employment programs. Furthermore, several large corporations—attracted by the provisions for national economic planning—endorsed the original bill. If we are to uncover the possible sources of political innovation, our job is made easier if we can eliminate certain political actors. By the same token, innovative ideas may be found in alternatives presented by opponents, for example, the CEA.

The passage of Hawkins-Humphrey was widely regarded as only a symbolic act. This reaction was largely due to the fact that the legislation itself created no new jobs. However, there are a number of important consequences which could lead to further policy initiatives. First, Hawkins-Humphrey explicitly commits the national government to the right to full opportunities for useful paid employment. Second, the act establishes for the first time specific quantitative goals and timetables for the reduction of unemployment and inflation, with priority given to unemployment goals. Third, the president, Congress, and Federal Reserve Board are called upon to work together to develop a comprehensive and consistent national economic plan for meeting the act's goals. Fourth, the act was a fundamental advance in social legislation which sought to define those traditionally outside the labor market as useful, productive citizens with fundamental rights. Fifth, the bill's supporters saw full employment as a basic change in economic policy that would address structural unemployment and move the nation out of stagflation. Sixth, and finally, black leadership played the key role in initiating and pushing the bill to passage. This marks a coming of age in legislative politics and a new sophistication in building political coalitions (Gross 1974).

Had the act been in effect in 1969 when the newly elected Nixon Administration decided to induce a recession to lower inflation, they would have had to proceed differently. The president's *Economic Report* would have had to set a "goal" for the increase in unemployment and specify the policies it intended to follow to achieve it. The president would have to demonstrate that no less destructive policy was possible and that reducing inflation required a deviation from full employment. This executive report would then be subject to ten hours of mandatory debate in Congress in which alternatives could be proposed (Levison 1980:182–183).

IMPLEMENTATION AND REBIRTH

The first budget and annual report prepared in accordance with the Hawkins-Humphrey act, for 1979, did frame basic economic policy in terms of achieving 3 percent unemployment by 1983 and established full employment as a serious objective of economic policy. Yet, the president's 1979 *Economic Report* was short on proposals for carrying out the objectives declared in the report and Representative Hawkins argued that Carter had ignored the inflation-unemployment mandate of the Full Employment and Balanced Growth Act. In response, CEA Chairman Charles Schultze stated that the administration was shifting its public service employment efforts toward reducing structural unemployment.

In January 1980, President Carter exercised the "bailout" provisions of the 1978 act. In his second *Economic Report* he contended that the "4 percent unemployment rate and the 3 percent inflation rate by 1983 is no longer practicable" and extended the timetables. Hawkins and his supporters accused the president of following the same policies as the Nixon-Ford Administrations. Carter's final *Economic Report* in 1981 eliminated any schedule for attaining the act's targets (Roth 1981).

In 1985, as the new chairman of the House Education and Labor Committee, Representative Hawkins attacked the Reagan record in job training and his clear violation of the 1978 law. The president's *Economic Report* neither mentioned the word "unemployment" nor set any date for reducing the then current 7.5 percent to 4 percent. In fact, the president did not even bother to use the "escape provision" in the 1978 statute allowing him to propose a lower goal.

By contrast, black leaders from Jesse Jackson and the Congressional Black Caucus on down have made full employment a permanent part of their political agenda[13] (Clark and Franklin 1983:4–8; Farmer 1984:4). Moreover, the moral argument for full employment was given a major boost by the first draft of the U.S. Catholic bishops' pastoral letter on "Catholic Social Teaching and the U.S. Economy." The bishops state, "The most urgent priority for the U.S. domestic economic policy is the creation of new jobs with adequate pay and decent working conditions" (U.S. Catholic Bishops Conf. 1984:358). They correctly link unemployment to increased levels of crime, family quarrels, divorce, child abuse, infant mortality, mental illness, and welfare dependency. Predictably, as he had done with black leaders, Buckley castigates the bishops' letter as one of "striking intellectual slovenliness." Labeling them the "Humphrey-Hawkins bishops," he contends that the real problem has to do with the spiritual malaise of the unemployed (Buckley 1984). This malaise, Buckley says, was promoted by the anti-poverty programs of the 1960s.

While it is relatively easy to counter Buckley's arguments linking increased illegitimacy with increased welfare payments, it is more difficult to deny that his tendency to blame the victim is not shared by large numbers of Americans. These perceptions largely account for the failure of both Democratic and Republican administrations to implement the 1978 Hawkins-Humphrey legislation. Labor groups, which were economically marginal during the New Deal, were now middle class and worried about inflation. Moreover, the novelty of Keynesian economic theory had been supplanted by a narrow economic view that linked reduced unemployment to high inflation.

These problems were directly confronted in a bill introduced on March 6, 1985, by Representative Charles Hayes of Illinois. Entitled the Income and Jobs Action Act, the bill was aimed at fulfilling the objectives of the 1978 legislation. However, the Hayes bill significantly expanded a number of provisions in Hawkins-Humphrey. For example, the new bill included the right to an adequate standard of living for all those unable to work for pay. It also counted as unemployed the millions of part-time workers and the jobless outside the "official labor force." Finally, it recognized the need for realistic planning to help declining industries and to provide for conversion of military spending to peacetime production.

On June 1, 1987, Hayes and Hawkins came full circle and introduced an Economic Bill of Rights Act. This legislation finally proposed endorsement of Roosevelt's eight-point bill of rights as national policy. It required the president each year to set forth a detailed legislative program to carry out the national policy; it set forth a minimum, short-term legislative program and it established a Commission of Economic Rights (CER) to monitor compliance and suggest changes. Obviously, the CER would have a much different institutional role than the CEA. On July 3, 1987, President Reagan introduced his own economic bill of rights. It essentially mandated a balanced federal budget and gave presidents the power of a line-item veto. Both the Hayes-Hawkins proposal and the president's "bill of rights" were largely ignored by the media. None of these measures was enacted. During the presidential campaign of 1988, Jesse Jackson, Michael Dukakis, and Paul Simon flirted with the full employment concept but then retreated.

CONCLUSION

The return to a focus on "economic rights" as compared to "balanced growth" reflects a return among the bill's proponents to arguments based on moral obligation rather than technical innovation. Growth implies progress for all but does not commit the government to provide jobs for the unemployed. Today, the desire of women and minorities to obtain jobs is seen as the special interests of narrow groups rather than a moral obligation for society. It seeks to bind citizens together through ties of moral commitment rather than through the bonds of commercial dependence. The proponents of this legislation are not willing to let the marketplace set the parameters of their moral concern. With Madison, they believe that "justice is the end government" (Arkes 1981; Steinberger 1985).

If we accept the strength of the moral argument for full employment, why hasn't the legislation discussed above been more productive and lasting in its effects? In other words, full employment legislation meets all of the criteria set forth by Starling and Polsby for innovative policy except the latter—its ability to reduce unemployment. This study suggests that there are two obstacles preventing the implementation of this innovation. The first obstacle involves a value conflict, not over the value of work itself, but rather over whose responsibility it is to provide jobs. This debate is conducted at the level of ideology that tends to either critique or defend existing political practices and seldom seeks to develop systematic normative principles of relatively enduring and universal application. The persistence of such ideological conflict often leads to a tendency to search for technical innovations to solve political problems rather than principled ideological solutions. Inequalities in the distribution of influence and power destroy the rationality of the policy process by failing to make available to weak groups the resources they need to enter into the bargaining arena. Thus, the question of rights is reduced to the protection of people from material injuries.[14]

The second obstacle to implementation involves the proponents of the bill themselves. As black leadership shifted its focus from political and civil rights issues to economic injustice, it found compelling the economic rights arguments in the New Deal struggle for full employment. It sought to broaden the base of support for the targeted programs of the Great Society by returning to the more inclusive policies of the New Deal. However, traditional New Deal allies like labor were divided in their support for such innovative policy. Moreover, class divisions emerged among blacks as the major civil rights organizations gave more priority to affirmative action than basic job programs. During the 1980s, Republicans were successful in portraying as special interest groups all proponents of such innovative policy as full employment. Thus, the moral or ethical core of the rights argument was undermined.

NOTES

1. In his widely used categorization scheme, Theodore Lowi distinguishes policies as distributive, redistributive, or regulatory. Only the few policies labeled as redistributive, including the Employment Act of 1946, would qualify as innovative. Yet Lowi's analysis tells us nothing about the process of generating such ideas or their impact on political structure.

2. Polsby states that President Hoover had little sympathy for ideas like economic planning. However, he notes that Herbert Stein believes "Hoover was much more interested in issues of planning and economic data gathering than is generally believed" (102n). Bertram Gross confirms this latter view of Hoover, noting that in 1922 he worked with Franklin D. Roosevelt "to set up the American Constitutional Council to 'stabilize' construction as a form of cartelization."

3. It is generally acknowledged by policy scientists that public preference is not stable and that the individual is not always in the best position to predict his or her own future interest.

4. Although Gross had only been working in Congress since 1942, he had played a major role in developing several important pieces of legislation including the Civilian

Supply Bill, a Joint Committee on the Organization of Congress, the Contract Termination Bill, the Surplus Property Bill, and the Office of War Mobilization and Reconversion Bill. I am indebted to Professor Gross for his assistance in preparing this part of the chapter.

5. The commission's study resulted in the 1948 Universal Declaration of Human Rights, which set forth a broad range of political and economic rights, including the "right to work." Eleanor Roosevelt was a key figure in the commission's deliberations and borrowed freely from her husband's economic bill of rights. Under the Eisenhower Administration, U.S. representatives at the United Nations insisted on two separate covenants that would give force to the declaration. Under the Covenant on Civil and Political Rights, member states were to ensure civil and political rights, a Human Rights Committee would monitor enforcement and an optional protocol allowed the committee to hear individual as well as state complaints. In contrast, under the Covenant on Economic, Social and Cultural Rights, each member state would be expected "to take steps . . . to the maximum of its available resources with a view to achieving progressively the full realization of the rights recognized in the present Covenant." There was no follow-up committee or optional protocol for this covenant.

6. Grover Starling refers to such new programs as branching. That is, longitudinal study shows that the development of public policy is not unlike the growth of a tree; branching out from a few seminal ideas or themes are multifarious variations that lead to further variations.

7. Structural unemployment refers to job loss caused by factors like skill requirements or location, while cyclical unemployment involves periodic layoffs in major industries and is traditionally viewed as a byproduct of capitalism.

8. Andrew Levison cites a variety of polls covering a period from 1956 to 1975 that show an overwhelming number of Americans were opposed to a guaranteed minimum income but supported a guaranteed job program. For example, in December 1968 Gallup found 79 percent against the former, while in 1969, 64 percent were for the latter.

9. Humphrey stated that without a new departure along the lines suggested by the many sponsors of this bill, many of the government's so-called affirmative action programs may turn out to be negatives. Sociologist William J. Wilson has consistently attacked black leadership for promoting affirmative action, which benefits the middle class, while ignoring full employment legislation. However, any fair assessment of the Congressional Black Caucus effort to pass Hawkins-Humphrey would suggest that Wilson's criticism is better directed toward labor leadership and the Carter Administration.

10. In reality, laid-off workers in states with high unemployment benefits use up the amount their employers paid into the system in about one month. After that, they benefit from federal grants and the taxes paid by other employers. M. E. Hawkesworth contends that differing conceptions of individuality and human rights are the source of severe, intense policy conflicts.

11. Official unemployment statistics exclude millions of people by using the artifact of the "labor force" rather than the total labor supply. Using the latter 1987 figures would include over 7 million for job seekers (the official unemployment), over 5 million part-time employees (seeking full-time work), over 1 million discouraged jobless (outside the labor force), and over 5 million jobless waiters (outside the labor force), for a total of over 18 million plus dependents.

12. These local planning councils are modeled on those set up for the Comprehensive Employment and Training Act (CETA). The record of such councils is mixed at best.

13. To a lesser degree, full employment was a part of Jesse Jackson's 1984 presidential campaign.

14. A revision of the criteria set forth by Starling and Polsby for innovative policy might include: (1) policy based on moral values that challenge old values or raise new values; (2) policy that recognizes some problems are not amenable to technical solutions; (3) policy that cuts across the self-interest of powerful groups; (4) policy that recognizes its open-ended, evolutionary character; and (5) policy that recognizes costs and injury may be nonmaterial as well as material.

4

African-Americans Confront Apartheid

Frederic I. Solop

South Africa! Once a land teeming with resources offering abundance to all her people, now a corporate haven offering safe profit margins to the extractors and misery to indigenous workers. South Africa! Home of apartheid, mother to struggle. South Africa! Politics of hate and politics of resistance. South Africa!

Since the early twentiethth century, African-Americans have identified with black South Africa's struggle with apartheid. While Africa, as the motherland, was a beacon of liberation to many, including Marcus Garvey and the United Negro Improvement Association, black South Africa's struggle against white rule has historically resonated with the experiences of many African-Americans. In sympathy with the resistance movement in South Africa, a U.S. anti-apartheid social movement, largely based within the African-American community, emerged in the 1960s. And just as black South Africa has experienced periods of great tragedy and tremendous exhilaration, the U.S. anti-apartheid movement has had its moments of success and failure. This chapter represents one segment of African-American politics: mobilization against apartheid and the struggle for a voice within the conversation of U.S. democracy. In the following pages, I present a framework for understanding minority politics in the United States. I then proceed to use this framework to analyze the struggle of African-Americans to confront apartheid through the use of institutional and noninstitutional political mechanisms.

MINORITY POLITICS IN THE UNITED STATES— A FRAMEWORK

It is well accepted that governmental systems manage conflict (Schnattschneider 1960). Generally speaking, conflict management strategies can be located on a continuum that extends between absolutely open to absolutely closed governmental systems. Open governmental systems possess the capacity to respond to new problems and offer citizens the ability to use institutional mechanisms of participation (e.g., elections, interest groups, political parties) to further their interests. Institutional mechanisms of participation are relatively less effective within closed political systems. Within closed systems, citizens must step out of the mainstream and employ noninstitutional mechanisms (e.g., social movements, protest politics, rioting) to promote their goals. The structure of citizen mobilization is thus heavily influenced by the nature of prevailing opportunities for influence (Piven and Cloward 1977; Tarrow 1988).

Opportunities are not equally distributed throughout society. In fact, opportunities to influence the making of public policy vary depending upon one's relationship to the power structure. Some groups, by virtue of their resources, values, sex, color, or ethnic origin, enjoy regular access to the power structure. Other groups never enjoy this privilege. For most interests in society, the reality is somewhere in the middle. Access fluctuates as the structure of prevailing opportunities changes over time.

African-Americans, like other minorities in the United States, have traditionally stood outside the institutional political system. Unlike other minorities, however, their position outside the mainstream system seems almost to be cast in stone. The history of black enslavement in the United States is well known; triangular trade relationships underwrote the colonial economy, and the long history of violence and abuse against African-Americans is all too familiar. African-Americans were originally defined as worth three-fifths of a white person in the U.S. Constitution, the Dred Scott decision and the Missouri Compromise legally defined African-Americans as the property of white men to be used and abused at the white man's discretion, and slavery was integral to the conditions which led to the deaths of almost 500,000 people in the American Civil War. Race is a dominant issue in U.S. politics even today, as evidenced by the recent confirmation hearings for Clarence Thomas, President George Bush's nominee for the Supreme Court (Edsall and Edsall 1991).

History has defined an "outsider" status for the African-American struggling to promote his or her interests within the U.S. political system. The civil rights movement bears witness to this condition. Civil rights required the mobilization of massive numbers of people to participate in protest politics to bring about achievements in this area. Since the civil rights movement and its legislative offspring—the Voting Rights Act of 1965 and Title VII of the Civil Rights Act—African-American legislators now preside in the halls of Congress and African-American voters form significant voting blocs in some election districts. But racism still exists in the United States, and institutional linkage channels rarely pacify interests fundamental to African-Americans. The challenge for African-Americans today lies in combining the institutional access they have achieved with the continued use of noninstitutional channels to promote their policy agenda. Exploration of anti-apartheid movement dynamics in the United States highlights this ongoing search for a balance.

HISTORY OF ANTI-APARTHEID SENTIMENT IN THE UNITED STATES

South Africa has been a concern of African-American activists throughout the twentieth century. Marcus Garvey and W.E.B. Du Bois took up the issue in the early 1900s. In fact, the National Association for the Advancement of Colored People (NAACP), founded in 1910, provided advice to black South Africans working to establish the African National Congress (ANC) in 1917. The ANC later emerged as the primary organizational vehicle for black South Africans to oppose the apartheid system. Paul Robeson, scholar and African-American activist, established the Council on African Affairs, the first anti-apartheid organization in the United States, in 1937.

This first wave of anti-apartheid activism in the United States was primarily a response to two conditions. First, some African-American activists identified with the liberation struggles of indigenous peoples in Africa. These activists proffered an internationalist perspective of racial relations and pursued unity among black people throughout the world struggling against colonial and other oppressive regimes.

Second, African-Americans were responding to the cozy friendship that existed between the U.S. and South African governments. According to Donald Easum (1975), this relationship was traditionally founded upon the pillars of economic and military support. An open door, free trade policy and the promise of higher-than-average profit ratios created a favorable climate for U.S.-based corporations in South Africa. Furthermore, the South African government was developing an industrial economy, and the promise of another partner in the world market economy helped to create a tight alliance between the United States and South Africa.

Militarily, South Africa is strategically located at the Horn of Africa, a major shipping route. Control of this area had severe repercussions for geo-strategic positioning. Also, the South African regime persisted as a bulwark against communism and Soviet influence on the African continent throughout the 1930s, 1940s, 1950s, and 1960s. Finally, South Africa contained rich resources of strategic minerals like titanium, useful for development of sophisticated military machinery.

Deeply disturbed by the United States—South African alliance, and simultaneously inspired by liberation movements successfully casting off colonial oppression in African nations like Ghana, Guinea, Mali, Zaire, Senegal, and Nigeria in the 1950s, African-American activists joined with white liberal forces to establish the African-American Institute in 1952, the American Committee on Africa in 1953, and the African Studies Association in 1957 (Danaher 1985). These organizations helped activists to accumulate resources and create public awareness of African-related issues. The American Committee on Africa, in particular, worked tirelessly through the 1950s and 1960s to recruit popular figures such as Martin Luther King, Eleanor Roosevelt, Pablo Casals, and Jackie Robinson to speak out against colonial oppression in Africa and, especially, apartheid in South Africa.

MOBILIZATION AFTER 1960

The Sharpeville Massacre of 1960 helped to crystallize U.S. anti-apartheid sentiment into a social movement better able to mobilize public support and action. In March 1960, South African police fired into a crowd and murdered black South Africans protesting pass laws, which restricted movement within the country. This incident inflamed racial relations in South Africa and sparked mass demonstrations. The South African government declared a state of emergency and banned major anti-apartheid organizations including the ANC and the Pan-African Congress (PAC). As one author noted, "It was the Sharpeville massacre, in which seventy blacks lost their lives, which changed the terms of the debate overnight" (Coker 1986:5).

The Sharpeville Massacre became a symbol among activists in the United States of the violence and immorality upon which apartheid is founded. One and a half weeks after the Sharpeville Massacre, the American Committee on Africa (ACOA) ran an advertisement in the *New York Times* entitled "The Shame of South Africa." They solicited emergency donations for the African Defense and Aid Fund. Also, in 1960, the committee tried to expand the scope of mobilization by initiating a fund-raising drive for the victims of Sharpeville and organizing a conference on South Africa featuring Oliver Tambo, president of the ANC. Additionally, ACOA launched a boycott against South African goods.

George Houser, founder of ACOA, assembled a conference in 1962 with the specific objective of transforming the domestic civil rights agenda of African-Americans into an international program. From this conference, the American Negro Leadership Conference on Africa (ANLCA) was born (*New York Times*, "Leading" 1962). Civil rights leaders such as Martin Luther King, Whitney Young, A. Philip Randolph, and Roy Wilkins, representing the Southern Christian Leadership Conference, the NAACP, the Congress of Racial Equality, and the Urban League, were in attendance at the founding conference (White 1981:83–101; Houser 1976:16–26).

Simultaneous to the reawakening of concern for African affairs among African-American leaders, anti-apartheid sentiment was erupting at the United Nations. Member nations had been passing resolutions which condemned racial discrimination in South Africa as a violation of human rights for quite some time. Now, with the highly publicized massacre at Sharpeville and the defiance of the South African regime to world opinion, third world member-nations were trying to move the United Nations to take an increasingly more forceful position against apartheid.

The definition of the issue shifted, especially in the General Assembly, during the post-Sharpeville period. Whereas apartheid had previously been defined as an internal human rights issue, the United Nations now declared that apartheid posed a threat to internal peace (Özgur 1982). Third world nations successfully prodded the United Nations to endorse a liberationist position as the solution to apartheid in South Africa. This position endorsed the legitimacy of the internal, black South African movement to overthrow the South African regime (Özgur 1982). In November 1962, the U.N. General Assembly called for diplomatic and economic sanctions against South Africa (Resolution-United Nations General Assembly 1761, 1962) and established the Special U.N. Committee on Apartheid as a monitoring agency. Also in 1962, the U.N. Security Council called for member nations to support a voluntary embargo against sales of military items to South Africa.

With a strong organizational base and legitimacy derived from U.N. edicts, African-Americans continued to build a fledgling anti-apartheid movement throughout the 1960s. Movement building required that the base of anti-apartheid sentiment be broadened to include new constituents. By the late 1960s, the anti-apartheid movement included members (black and white) of religious and student communities. The principal vehicle for appealing to these communities was a shift in strategy from pursuing movement goals via conventional political channels to challenging economic linkages which bolstered the South African economy and thereby underwrote apartheid politics.

By 1965 a campaign against the financial community's credit arrangements with South Africa took hold in the United States. The first stockholder resolution involving financial relationships with South Africa was raised in 1967 by James Foreman, former director of the Congress on Racial Equality, at the national meeting of Morgan Guaranty Trust. Morgan Guaranty Trust was one of the banks participating in a consortium of financial institutions which held a $40 million credit arrangement with South Africa (*New York Times*, "Morgan" 1967).

George Houser, the director of ACOA at the time, had this to say about the implications of the stockholders' tactic:

> Considerable publicity was given to the annual stockholders' meetings of both Chase and First National City Banks. Some depositors and stockholders went to the meetings, or gave their proxies to ACOA representatives, to protest the loan to South Africa. This was the beginning of an effort which rapidly expanded to include investments not only in banks but in large American corporations doing business in southern Africa, particularly South Africa.
>
> Of all American institutions, the churches were the most receptive to this campaign. They were subjected to pressures, particularly from their black membership, to withdraw their investments from those corporations involved significantly in South Africa. This led to organized efforts within the denominations to look into their investments, and to take actions which could influence corporate policy. (Houser 1976:23)

Resolutions dealing with credit arrangements were expanded to include corporate responsibility for any economic relationship with South Africa. By the end of the 1960s, sustained campaigns against the investments of corporations, universities, and colleges in the South African economy were being waged. The tactic of lobbying government officials for economic sanctions was almost fully replaced with campaigns to challenge the right of institutions to invest their monies without regard for public consequences.

The primary actors in the anti-apartheid movement during the 1970s continued to be civil rights and African-American activist groups, stockholders, religious groups, and students (Solop 1990). As the movement grew new organizations, including the Interfaith Center on Corporate Responsibility and the Washington Office on Africa, were founded to offer better coordination of movement efforts.

Some elements of the anti-apartheid movement became frustrated by the seemingly moderate approach of using stockholder resolutions to challenge corporate activity in South Africa. They wished to make a more direct assault against corporate operations. This frustration is best symbolized by a highly publicized campaign which directly attacked corporate policies at the Polaroid Corporation. This campaign was orchestrated by workers at a Polaroid plant working in collusion with the ACOA during the early 1970s and was called the Polaroid Revolutionary Workers' Movement (PRWM).

In reaction to public attention, Polaroid had announced that it would initiate a pilot project to improve black South African salaries, job opportunities, and education for its employees (*New York Times*, "Polaroid" 1971). The PRWM launched a public campaign to expose the duplicity of this policy. They argued that Polaroid's pilot program ultimately supported the continuation of apartheid because it failed to address underlying problems facing blacks in South Africa (e.g., their inability to participate in political and legal structures). The PRWM intended to initiate a worldwide boycott of Polaroid products. While the PRWM was unable to ever mount an effective international boycott against Polaroid, the controversy drew substantial attention from the mass media.

The significance of this campaign lies in the entrance of more militant members of the African-American community into the corporate responsibility debate and a shift in the debate about corporate responsibility beyond the church position of responsibility through reform. This campaign raised the issue of total corporate disengagement from South Africa as the solution to ending apartheid (White 1981).

This shift in the debate coincided with uprisings in South Africa during 1976, which brought renewed international attention to the apartheid regime. The depth of the problem with apartheid was made apparent when Steven Biko, a popular leader of the Black Consciousness Movement, was illegally detained, then tortured and murdered by the South African police in 1977. It was against this background that Jimmy Carter entered the White House with a commitment to human rights as the underlying principle of U.S. foreign policy. A window of opportunity for the anti-apartheid movement was opening.

The election of President Carter and Carter's subsequent appointment of Andrew Young as ambassador to the United Nations were interpreted by the African-American community as symbols of greater access to the foreign policy-making process. African-American expectations also rose as the number of African-Americans in Congress expanded and as more liberal representatives were elected to Congress.

These developments renewed expectations within the civil rights community for governmental relief, and encouraged leaders concerned with apartheid issues to pursue an "inside" strategy more closely associated with the power of member interests rather than the "outside" strategy that challenger interests must follow. African-American leaders appealed to President Carter to "leave no stone unturned" in the fight against apartheid (*New York Times*, "Black Leaders" 1977).

The insider strategy of the African-American community is typified by the role played by the Congressional Black Caucus (CBC) on African issues. In 1976, the CBC organized the Black Leadership Conference on Southern Africa. This meeting brought together 120 African-American leaders from major civil rights organizations, business, labor, religion, civic associations, and public office. One of the more important developments of this conference was the African-American Manifesto, which represented a consensus within the black community for condemnation of U.S. political and economic support of apartheid and South Africa (White 1981).

Another important development which emerged from this meeting was a new organization: TransAfrica. TransAfrica was initiated as *the* African-American lobby organization for African and Caribbean issues. Randall Robinson was appointed executive director of the organization. TransAfrica's expressed purpose was to "influence the U.S. Congress and Executive branch of Government to fashion progressive and enlightened policies toward the black Third World" (TransAfrica 1986).

Despite the institutionalization of African-American concern for apartheid, some activists continued to pursue an outside strategy: more militant, grassroots, anti-apartheid efforts continued throughout the late 1970s and into the early 1980s. Campus-based protests reignited between 1977 and 1978. The focus of these efforts was to pressure colleges and universities to divest portfolios of investments in businesses operating in South Africa.

In 1977, anti-apartheid protests were held at the University of Massachusetts, the University of California at Berkeley (400 arrested), and at Smith College. Protests continued in 1978 at Stanford University (294 arrested), Ohio University, Princeton University, Brown University, Miami University in Ohio, Harvard University, Williams College, Rutgers University, Tufts University, Philip Exeter Academy, University of Michigan, Hampshire College, Brandeis University, and Columbia University. Between 1977 and 1979, twenty-six higher education institutions divested approximately $87 million of stocks in corporations involved in South Africa—and campus divestments were on the upswing as the 1970s ended. The *New York Times* reflected on student anti-apartheid campaigns in 1978 with the headline "South Africa is New Social Issue for College Activists."

COMBINING OUTSIDER AND INSIDER POLITICS

Ronald Reagan entered the White House in 1981 and his agenda priorities for South Africa policy were quite clear. Reagan favored friendly persuasion, also known as "constructive engagement," rather than confrontation, as a way to move South Africa toward reform. The appointment of hard-line conservatives like Jeane Kirkpatrick and Chester Crocker to Reagan's foreign policy team sharply curtailed any influence the African-American leaders may have hoped to have over the foreign policy process. Anti-apartheid bills raised in Congress could not even be passed out of committee during the early Reagan years.

Despite the failures of conventional, insider politics during this period, campus and community-based anti-apartheid efforts continued. Between 1980 and 1983, eighteen colleges and universities divested more than $69 dollars in stocks from businesses operating in South Africa, including partial divestments at Harvard University, Rutgers University, Oberlin College, and Williams College. Four states plus twelve cities and counties also passed either divestment or selective purchasing agreements during the early 1980s (The Africa Fund 1986).

Responding to the rise of state-sponsored violence in South Africa in 1984, recent legislative defeats of anti-apartheid bills,[1] and the general anti-minority mood pervading the Reagan era, TransAfrica organized a national campaign to redefine the South Africa issue as a national civil rights concern and to focus national attention on the social agenda of African-Americans. TransAfrica tapped into the protest energy manifest at the grassroots level and refocused that energy into pressure for national anti-apartheid sanctions legislation. Thus, TransAfrica, the institutional voice of African-Americans on foreign affairs, explicitly sought to use the outside tactic of protest politics as a lobbying force to indirectly influence insiders in Congress. Importantly, this combination of outsider and insider politics was a throwback to the strategy of the civil rights movement.

TransAfrica's campaign was wonderfully orchestrated. Beginning in late 1984 and continuing for an entire year, the campaign featured civil disobedience and celebrity arrests at the South African Embassy in Washington, DC. The "Free South Africa" campaign involved traditional civil rights leaders, labor leaders, religious leaders, legislators and other public officials, movie stars, and other celebrities protesting apartheid and getting arrested, every day, at the embassy.

The celebrity arrests captured the gaze of the national media and by the first week of December, the Free South Africa campaign extended protests to South African embassies in New York City, Boston, Chicago, Los Angeles, Houston, and Seattle (*New York Times*, "Protests" 1984). Within five months, more than 1,800 people had been arrested at the Washington, DC, embassy, and another 1,000 had been arrested in South Africa protests around the nation (Metz 1986:379–395). Like the lunch counter protests spearheaded by students in 1960, civil disobedience flourished as a tactic for challenging political and economic complicity with apartheid in South Africa. "It seems as if we struck a chord," said Ceclie Counts of Trans-Africa (*New York Times*, "Protests" 1984).

The Free South Africa campaign revived the traditional civil rights coalition in the United States. As it did so, apartheid once again became a metaphor for the experience of African-Americans in the United States. Blacks in South Africa were denied a voice in public affairs, and African-Americans as well as other minorities in the United States were denied a voice within the Reagan Administration. Constructive engagement promoted, rather than challenged, apartheid; so too, Reagan's domestic agenda was perceived as advancing social and political inequality in the United States. Reagan's stubborn attachment to constructive engagement symbolized the disenfranchisement of African-Americans and the inability of African-Americans and other minorities to alter national policy. The Free South Africa campaign underlines the value of simultaneously pursuing insider and outsider politics as a necessary means for African-Americans to position and support their interests on the policy agenda.

As citizen pressure mounted and as violence proliferated in South Africa, economic sanctions legislation neared passage in Congress. An emerging consensus called for Congress to challenge President Reagan's policy of constructive engagement and to make an unequivocal statement of condemnation against apartheid. By late June 1985, both houses of Congress supported sanctions packages with bipartisan votes: 29–6 in the House Foreign Affairs Committee, 295–127 with fifty-six Republicans supporting sanctions on the floor of the House of Representatives; 16–1 in the Senate Foreign Relations Committee, and 80–12 on the floor of the Republican-controlled Senate.

The Reagan Administration responded by rhetorically condemning apartheid while continuing to implement constructive engagement and denounce sanctions legislation. But Congress was determined to condemn South Africa in no uncertain terms. The administration was savvy enough to know that, despite its ideological attachment to constructive engagement, it had to respond to the anti-apartheid consensus which was emerging in the United States.

Commenting on protests in the United States and the flurry of legislative activity, Secretary of State George Schultz made this comment:

We simply cannot afford to let Southern Africa become a divisive domestic issue—tearing our country apart, rendering our actions haphazard and impotent, and contributing to the ugliest and most violent outcome. (*New York Times*, "Schultz" 1989)

Increasingly, the Reagan Administration tried to nurture a public image of opposition to apartheid. Immediately prior to the congressional conference committee meeting to work out a compromise economic sanctions package, the United States also called for talks between Prime Minister Pieter W. Botha and Bishop Desmond Tutu.

On September 9, 1985, after the House passed the compromise sanctions package and just prior to the Senate commencing debate on the package, Reagan reversed his longstanding opposition to sanctions and imposed limited economic sanctions on South Africa with an Executive Order containing these provisions:

- A ban on sales of computers to South Africa security agencies.
- Barring most loans to the Pretoria government.
- A ban on importation of Kruggerands pending consultation with trading partners.
- A prohibition on most exports of nuclear technology.

In a national address, President Reagan said that "America's view of apartheid is simple and straightforward: We believe it is wrong. We condemn it. And we are united in hoping for the day when apartheid will be no more" (*New York Times*, "Reagan" 1985). Secretary of State Schultz followed up this policy with statements calling for political accommodation in South Africa. He also suggested that Nelson Mandela be freed from jail as a symbol of good faith by the Pretoria government.

Although President Reagan maneuvered to co-opt congressional interest in shaping U.S. foreign policy relations with South Africa, Congress was not to be deterred. On June 10, 1986, the House Foreign Affairs Committee favorably reported out a bill designed to strengthen Reagan's sanctions. The bill, authored by a leading African-American legislator, Representative William Gray (D-PA), received a 27–14 vote in the committee with three Republicans joining the Democratic forces.

Anticipating a confrontation with the White House, Senator Richard Lugar, the Republican chair of the Senate Foreign Relations Committee, warned President Reagan that he would personally lead the fight to override a presidential veto (*New York Times*, "Lugar" 1986). Despite the warning, Reagan vetoed the comprehensive sanctions bill on September 26, claiming that the bill would hurt those it was intended to help—the black majority in South Africa. The House voted to override Reagan's veto on September 29 by a 313–83 vote, with eighty-one Republicans voting to override Reagan. The Senate similarly voted for an override on October 2, 1986, 78–21, with thirty-one Republicans voting against their president. The final law (P.L. 99–440) contained provisions for a comprehensive economic sanctions package.

With passage of this legislation, African-Americans, working in conjunction with other constituencies, handed President Reagan his greatest foreign policy defeat and simultaneously realized a longstanding concern within their community. Throughout the twentieth century, African-Americans struggled to condemn apartheid in South Africa. For most of this period, the struggle took place on the margins of the political system, to no avail. During the early to mid-1960s and during the Carter years, this struggle took place within the institutional setting of the government, to no avail. Finally, within the mid-1980s, simultaneous pursuit of insider and outsider politics led to policy success. African-Americans had arrived at a position where their institutional representatives could be effective if supported by widespread consensus and mobilization within the African-American community.

AFRICAN-AMERICAN POLITICS BEYOND ECONOMIC SANCTIONS

Although the African-American community wielded sufficient power to raise anti-apartheid sentiment to the policy agenda and to successfully push for a comprehensive economic sanctions package, the consequence of this success has been a widespread perception that something has been done about apartheid. This perception has had a deleterious effect on the ability of the U.S. anti-apartheid movement to continue to mobilize public attention. The movement has declined in strength since the Free South Africa campaign of 1985. Not coincidentally, stronger divestment packages, such as the Dellums bill calling for a near-total ban on investments and trade with South Africa, have been unable to successfully move through the halls of Congress since 1986.[2] In fact, by August 1991, the tide of sentiment had clearly shifted. It was during this period that President Bush repealed all U.S. sanctions against South Africa. There was barely an audible whimper of protest heard from Congress or from the remnants of the anti-apartheid movement.

Does this mean that the anti-apartheid movement, and, by extension, the African-American community, failed to achieve its goals? The answer to this question is mixed. Yes, the U.S. anti-apartheid movement failed in its ultimate goal of totally dismantling the apartheid regime in South Africa. But, no, the anti-apartheid movement did not fail in persuading Congress to send an unequivocal signal to South Africa that business as usual (i.e., apartheid) will not be tolerated by the United States. By all accounts, economic sanctions levied by the United States and other nations against South Africa had severe effects, and would have continued to impose damage as time continued to pass (Love 1988).

Perhaps the greatest success of this period was that the African-American community, historically on the fringes of the U.S. political system, was able to pull together the vestiges of the old civil rights coalition and to expand the scope of its concerns into a broad-based social movement. It was able, in the 1980s, to combine the power of an outside political strategy using old-time pressure and protest politics with an inside political strategy of mobilizing African-Americans and other sympathizers who occupy strategic locations within the power structure. Ultimately, through this dual approach to politics, the African-American community was able to influence the complexion of policy.

The battle over U.S. foreign policy toward South Africa provides additional insight into the state of African-American politics in the United States. It is interesting that five years after comprehensive economic sanctions were legislated against South Africa, the presidency regained control of the policy area and sanctions legislation was repealed. This suggests the inability of the African-American community to influence the policy process over the long haul. As long as African-Americans, and minority communities in general, remain largely in the position of "outside initiators," their policy successes, if they come at all, will be brief and fleeting. Within the context of the enduring salience of race in the United States and the ubiquitous presence of racism, this is not so much an argument for minority communities to buy into the structure norms of the U.S. political system (Ginsberg 1982) as much as it is an argument for the need to change them.

NOTES

1. The House of Representatives, for the first time, had just voted favorably on an economic sanctions package. This package failed to successfully proceed through the Senate.

2. One additional anti-apartheid measure was adopted since economic sanctions were instituted by Congress. In 1987, Representative Charles Rangel sponsored a tax measure which prohibited corporations from deducting the taxes paid to the South African government from their U.S. taxes.

5

Urban Violence: Agendas, Politics, and Problem Redefinition

Paula D. McClain

Over the last several decades, whenever one speaks of urban centers the discussion is prefaced with the word crisis—the crisis of civil disorders, crisis of urbanization, fiscal crisis. The urban crisis of the 1990s is violence. Many cities are overwhelmed by the extent and increasing frequency of the violence. In 1991, four of the nation's largest cities, San Diego, CA, Dallas, TX, Phoenix, AZ, and Los Angeles, CA, recorded record-high homicides. New York City, Chicago, and San Antonio all recorded their second-highest homicide totals, and while not the highest, Detroit experienced a 5 percent increase over its 1990 homicide level. Among smaller cities, Washington, DC, experienced one of its most violent years in history in 1991 with recorded homicides of 490, up from 483 in 1990. Since 1988, Washington has had the dubious distinction of being the "homicide capital" of the United States. Other cities setting homicide records in 1991 include Milwaukee, WI, Oakland, CA, and Minneapolis, MN (Daniels 1992).

Violent crime and fear of victimization are central themes in presidential campaigns, with politicians using urban violence as a symbol of the risk of criminal victimization to which citizens, primarily white suburban residents, are exposed. Although this tactic often strikes a responsive chord among a large segment of the electorate, the reality is that the risk of criminal victimization is race-specific, with the risk to blacks, who principally reside in urban centers, being substantially higher than the risk to whites. Blacks are six times more likely than whites to be victims of homicide (Rose and McClain 1990), and two-and-one-half times more likely than whites to be victims of rapes. For robbery, the black victimization rate is three times that of the white rate, and the black rate for aggravated assault is one-and-one-half that of the white rate (Rose 1981; Silberman 1978). The Federal Bureau of Investigation (FBI) recently indicated, based on 1987 data, that a nonwhite male born today has a 1 in 38 chance of being murdered, while the risk to the aggregate population is 1 in 177 chances. For men already twenty years of age, nonwhites have a 1 in 41 chance of being murdered, while whites have a 1 in 224 chance (*Arizona Republic*, "Non-White" 1989). In 1991, there were an estimated 24,703 murders, a U.S. all-time high, with contributing agencies providing data on 21,505 of the victims. Of the latter figure, 50 percent of the victims were black (FBI *Uniform Crime Reports* 1991:14).

On the other side, in 1991, blacks represented slightly more than one-half, 55 percent, of those arrested for murder and non-negligent manslaughter (ibid.:16); yet they were only 12 percent of the population. Moreover, the FBI data indicate that based on incidents involving one victim and one offender, 93 percent of the black murder victims were slain by black offenders. These statistics raise the question of what is to be done to ameliorate these occurrences.

Scholars argue constantly over the importance of particular policies and policy areas for one specific group or another. However, rarely do we examine, much less debate, the more mundane, yet critically important topic of issue definition and problem structuring related to particular policy areas. The discourse centers on the policies that have been developed, but rarely do we question whether the underlying theoretical framework or causal theory is the correct conceptualization of the problem. This latter concern, I contend, is the problem with the debate surrounding urban violence.

This chapter is an attempt to generate debate concerning the conceptualization of urban violence, particularly homicide, for policy formulation purposes. Given the nature and structure of urban violence, is the present conceptualization of the problem for policy purposes the most appropriate or correct conceptualization? Finally, an argument is developed to reconceptualize urban violence for purposes of policy development that, hopefully, will move us in a direction to begin to reduce the levels of violence present in a large number of urban communities.

URBAN VIOLENCE AND THE "IDEA"

Urban violence, while local in character but national in impact, is viewed, nonetheless, as a local matter to be controlled by local policy makers through local governmental institutions. The basic function of urban governments is service delivery (Yates 1976). Services such as police and fire protection, public education, and garbage collection are delivered on a daily basis. While national public discourse may center on crime-related issues, crime control is the purview of local police agencies, and the assumption is that local government machinery will do what it deems appropriate for its particular area.

Local governments, however, and their abilities to respond to policy problems, are often determined and defined by forces beyond their control. Urban violence is one area in which the identification of the problem has determined the direction and types of policy responses possible. Conceptualizing the problem as one of crime and crime control localizes the issue and assumes that crime is unaffected by forces other than those in the particular city in which it occurs. Moreover, it prestructures policy agencies' responses to the problem. Citizens also view the problem, as Wesley Skogan (1990) submits, in less than concrete terms but more in terms of the mere "anticipation of disorderly behavior or the possible consequences of growing disorder for the community, rather than a specific criminal incident." The impression of the magnitude of this growing disorder is not dispelled by the violent crime statistics in many urban centers. Table 1 shows the actual numbers of murders, rapes, robberies, and assaults committed in fifteen large urban centers in 1989. These statistics, coupled with the anticipation of disorderly behavior, result in the call for local police authorities to address the problem. The context of the public discourse at the national level contributes significantly to the definition of the problem as simply one of crime control.

This narrow conceptualization of urban violence as crime and the solution as punishment is promulgated by neo-conservative scholars such as James Q. Wilson and Charles Murray. Both assume an economic view of crime, that is, as Murray (1984) states, "Crime occurs when the prospective benefits sufficiently outweigh the prospective costs." Murray and Wilson theorize that if the risks associated with committing crime are increased, crimes will decrease. They argue that there is a deterrent effect in increasing the penalties for criminal behavior. Wilson (1983:121) contends that the argument that deterrence does not work denies the "plainest facts of everyday life." People, he argues, govern their lives by rewards and penalties; thus, increasing the penalties for criminal behavior will bring about a change in the behavior patterns of those who commit crimes. This particular "public idea" has dominated the agenda-setting process for several decades. This dominance should not be a surprise since, as Jack Walker (1977) identified, an item's appeal as an agenda item is increased if the source of the problem is readily identified and if an uncomplicated solution is easily devised. Moreover, the conservative ideology of the Reagan and Bush Administrations has created

Table 1
Number of Violent Crimes in 15 Large Urban Centers, 1989

City	Population	Murder	Rape	Robbery	Assault
New York	7,369,454	1,905	3,254	93,377	70,951
Chicago	2,988,260	742	N/R	31,588	37,615
Detroit	1,039,599	624	1,424	11,902	11,006
Philadelphia	1,652,188	475	784	10,233	6,562
Los Angeles	3,441,449	877	1,996	31,063	43,361
Washington, DC	604,000	434	186	6,541	5,775
Houston	1,713,499	459	1,152	9,820	8,097
Baltimore	763,138	262	541	7,966	6,849
New Orleans	528,589	251	388	5,449	4,115
Memphis	651,081	141	781	3,781	3,327
Atlanta	426,482	246	691	6,796	9,119
Dallas	996,320	351	1,185	9,442	10,250
Cleveland	523,906	144	837	4,045	2,939
St. Louis	405,066	158	330	4,220	7,936
Newark	313,839	107	376	5,310	4,547

Source: Federal Bureau of Investigation, *Crime in the U.S.—1989* (Washington, DC: U.S. Government Printing Office, 1989), pp. 69–117.

an environment of public discourse in which the punishment perspective is, as Donald Schon (1971:123) would agree, an idea in "good currency." It is too early to tell if this particular identification of the issue will continue under the Clinton Administration. The control policies emanating from this identification of the problem from the national level are "easily devised" and are packaged as the panacea that resolves the problem of urban violence. The solutions are in the form of death penalties for drug dealers, longer prison terms, relaxation of constitutional protections for individuals accused of crimes, and various and sundry crime control proposals.

Clearly, the views of Wilson and Murray are not universally accepted, particularly since they identify as the root cause of all of the problems of the urban poor the liberal social policies of the 1960s and 1970s. Their remedy, therefore, as Murray (1984:223) has rigidly argued, "is to repeal every bit of legislation and reverse every court decision that in any way requires, recommends, or awards differential treatment according to race." Nevertheless, the neo-conservative identification of the problem simply as one of crime and crime control, and its control of the agenda-setting process, preclude the development of prevention and interdiction policies aimed at preventing individuals (black urban residents) from becoming victims of violent crime. It is clear from the public discourse and the structure of the agenda that the goal is to punish those who commit crimes, rather than the broader goal of reducing the levels of criminal violence and lowering the risk of victimization for those who are the true victims of urban violence. I do not suggest that punishment is not an essential part of the broadened goal of reducing urban violence, but merely argue that it represents a short-sighted and simplistic view of the structure and gravity of the situation, and is not and should not be the only approach to this serious problem.

Yet intertwined in the national public discourse, and explicitly central to the Wilson and Murray arguments, is the interaction between the concept of the "underclass," with its overt racial implications, and the conceptualization of urban violence as a crime. The use of the term "underclass" as a euphemism for deviant aberrant behavior by undeserving urban black citizens implies, as Herbert Gans (1990:272) cautions, that these individuals should "be selected for separation from the rest of society." Gans further suggests that acceptance of the belief that urban blacks are undeserving dictates that government's responsibility relative to these people is limited to strengthening the mechanisms—for example, the courts and other punitive agencies and institutions—to more successfully isolate the underclass and protect the remainder of society (ibid.:275–276). These crime control policies clearly address that separation.

Policy makers capitalize on the anxiety over the anticipation of disorder among the polity and propose policy solutions to assuage the public's anxiety. A conservative political ideology, which is at the core of the interaction of the concept of the "underclass" and the conceptualization of the problem of urban violence, defines the agenda and pushes many current policy proposals in this area. As Charles Lindblom (1968:23) so deftly observes, the importance of ideology in policy analysis is that it produces some agreed-upon assumptions that policy makers believe are true, and therefore accept. But, if the ideology is far removed from the facts of the policy problem, it cripples policy analysis. As Lindblom suggests, "[Ideology] may generate agreed-on policies that nevertheless do not work" (ibid.).

While ideologically correct in the twelve-year conservative political environment of the Reagan and Bush Administrations, the problems the policies were designed to alleviate continue to get worse. If one conceptualizes the problem incorrectly, error will occur in the formulation process. This error, which Howard Raiffa (1968) refers to as a Type III, is constructing a solution to the wrong problem. Such is the case, I suggest, of urban violence. It is possible, and highly probable, that the reason policies aimed at curbing the rise of violent crime, particularly homicide, have not had an effect is that the situation has been politicized to such an extent that ideology has determined the conceptualization of the problem. The American polity, as well as our policy makers, have conceptualized the issue of urban violence (homicide) in a way that ensures that whatever policy initiatives are developed will not address the problem as it exists.

RACE AND THE CURRENT CONCEPTUALIZATION OF URBAN VIOLENCE

Race has been and is an essential fabric of U.S. politics and public policy. From slavery to the present, the raising of the specter of "menacing blacks" has proven to be a successful tactic used by politicians to generate fear among white voters and bring them to the polls. While there is extensive documentation of the uses of race in a variety of ways in American politics since before the founding of the United States, the concern for the issue of urban violence is in its more recent usage and current representation in the political arena.

Thomas and Mary Edsall (1991:13) trace the use of race by the Republican party, in subtle and not so subtle ways, to undercut Democratic strength in the South, thereby "position[ing] itself just where the overwhelming majority of white Americans stand on racial policy: in favor of the principle of equality, but opposed to the enforcement mechanisms developed by the courts and the federal regulatory system." They argue the Republican party has successfully used opposition to busing, to affirmative action, to quotas, and to housing integration in order to devise a common ground of opposition to the federal regulatory structure, thus forging an alliance of a traditionally Democratic working-class electorate with the traditional constituency of the Republican party, business interests and the affluent (ibid.:13).

Barry Goldwater's campaign of 1964 was characterized, among other things, by his opposition to the Civil Rights Act of 1964, although congressional Republicans provided the strong support and needed votes for the various pieces of civil rights legislation when Southern Democrats opposed civil rights for blacks (ibid.:61). The use of code words, however, as a surrogate for blacks did not become prominent until Richard Nixon's campaign of 1968. In the wake of the civil disturbances in urban areas in the mid-1960s, Nixon adopted a strong law-and-order position in his campaign rhetoric during the 1968 presidential race. This strong stance against the violence in urban environments committed by blacks, coupled with the increasing opposition among whites toward school integration and open housing, and the presence of George Wallace as a third party candidate in the race, provided Nixon with an opportunity. He was able to espouse a view "that staked out a position of comfort to racial conservatives, while remaining publicly committed to racial equality" (ibid.:76). When Nixon spoke of law-and-order the translation was, "blacks are out of control and need to be contained."

During the 1980 election, Ronald Reagan's appeal to race resentment among whites was more direct and less subtle. Reagan continually told the story of the "welfare queen" in Chicago who collected payments under "80 names, 30 addresses, 12 Social Security cards whose tax free income alone is over $150,000" (ibid.:148). Translation—black welfare cheats are draining the tax dollars of middle- and working-class whites. Food stamps also were a mechanism to allow "some fellow ahead of you [to] buy T-bone steak while you were standing in a checkout line with your package of hamburger" (ibid.:148). Translation—blacks are living better on government subsidies at the expense of working middle- and working-class whites. Reagan made it explicitly clear that "the target of his planned assault on government would be the means-tested programs serving poor constituencies, heavily black and Hispanic, that had become the focus of much public hostility to government" (Ibid.:148).

The use of code words to appeal to the racial fears and prejudices of the white electorate was the centerpiece of George Bush's 1988 presidential campaign. Willie Horton became Michael Dukakis's running mate and the message was clear—blacks are threatening the well-being of white America. As Edsall and Edsall state, "The focusing of public attention by the Bush campaign on the prison furlough of Willie Horton tapped not only voter resentment over the prisoners' rights, prison reform, and criminal defendant's rights movement, but tapped these concerns through a particularly threatening and dangerous archetype: of the black man as the rapist of a white woman" (ibid.:19). The symbols used by the Bush campaign, Willie Horton among them, conjured up the image of black crime as a major and everyday threat to whites, obscuring the reality that the principal victims of black crime are other blacks. However, the fear of whites to the supposed victimization of blacks is strong and was successfully exploited by Bush. (David Duke in his unsuccessful run for the governorship of Louisiana utilized the same tactics to play to the fears of the white electorate and make blacks the scapegoats for all of Louisiana's problems.)

PRESENT CONCEPTUALIZATION OF VIOLENT CRIME

Our current approach to homicide and violent crime, as it has been raised to the agenda, evolves from the use of race in U.S. politics and the image of white victimization by black criminals. The politicization of the problem of urban homicide as blacks preying on whites is a nondecision—the mobilization of bias to regard the phenomenon as black against white. The consequence has been to push the development of policies that do not help the true victims of urban violence, urban black residents, but that clearly confront the racial overtones of black-on-white crime. The underlying interaction of race and crime has produced an identification of the problem which uses the legal definition as the basic conceptualization of the problem for policy formulation purposes. Homicide is defined as a criminal act and therefore is deemed a criminal justice problem. From this perspective, the emphasis is placed on the perpetrator and the institutions involved in solving the problem are the police, prosecutors, prisons, and parole system. Thus, the policy recommendations call for the death sentence, more police, longer jail terms, mandatory sentencing for firearms crimes, and stricter furlough and parole standards. The emphasis is on punishment and the assumption is made that if the individuals who perpetrate these crimes are locked up, the crimes will not occur. Unfortunately, given the structure of the problem, there are others already in the queue ready to replace those who are arrested and incarcerated. Moreover, the policies only take effect *after* someone or a number of someones have been murdered. This narrow definition of urban violence fits neatly with a conservative ideological identification of the problem but ensures that the situation will only get worse in our urban centers, and many more life-years of black citizens will be lost.

Clearly, there is a politics of homicide. Agenda setting is a more precise way of saying what Peter Bachrach and Morton Baratz (1962) said so well long ago—hegemony of a few over the issues to be or not to be acted upon and the content of the policy directives. In short, nondecision making is explicitly present in the nation's approach to the problems of urban homicide. Theodore Lowi would contend that the nondecision represents the recognition by policy makers that the institutions (criminal justice) have failed to address the problem—"Success in one era renders institutions incapable of processing the demands of the next era" (1971:ix). But when faced with the quandary, society has the choice of "waging war on its dilemmas or on those who present the dilemmas" (ibid.). In this instance, those who present the dilemma are poor urban black residents. He goes on to say that when institutions fail, there is disorder.

In order to develop policies that will address urban violence, the "idea" surrounding the structure and nature of urban violence, particularly homicide, must be raised in a different form and the public discourse restructured. The prevailing idea of urban violence must be challenged and U.S. society persuaded to perceive and approach the problem differently. As Mark Petracca (1986) observes, redefining an issue may be critical in placing an item on the agenda. Given the difficulty of raising issues to the agenda, in general, and the difficulty for the political underclass, in particular, the suggestion of recasting the "idea" is not made lightly, but made with the realization that unless it is changed urban violence will continue to increase. Moreover, the number of life-years lost by urban black political underclass individuals will be of such a magnitude that urban black communities will be decimated for decades to come.

STRUCTURE OF URBAN HOMICIDE

Since 1977, a colleague, Harold Rose, and I have been involved in a major study of black urban violence. We have viewed the first phase of the project, 1977 to 1988, as an exercise in problem structuring/problem definition. Our study is unique in a number of ways. First, it takes the position that what is important to study to gain an understanding of the factors that contribute to the high incidence of black-on-black homicide is not the homicide event itself, which is an isolated point in time, but the environmental backgrounds the victim and offender brought with them to the situation that resulted in death. We utilized the concept of environment at several levels—macro-, meso-, and micro-environmental—and utilized an ecological approach. Second, black homicide was studied in several urban environments—Atlanta, St. Louis, Houston, Pittsburgh, Detroit, and Los Angeles. Most of the previous homicide studies focused on one city; thus, the ability to generalize across urban environments was difficult, if not impossible. Third, the time frame for the study was from 1960 to 1985. The twenty-five-year time span provided an opportunity for longitudinal analyses that have been lacking in previous studies.

While space does not allow for a full explication of our findings, one thing is clear from the multicity approach to the study of homicide: homicide is a complex phenomenon; cities differ in their inhabitants' risk of victimization (likelihood of death) and the structure of victimization (relationship of victim to offender and whether single or multiple offenders and victims). The six cities studied were found to occupy different points on a continuum between traditional violence (motivated by anger) and nontraditional violence (motivated by gain). At the beginning of the time period (1960), Atlanta, Houston, and Los Angeles anchored the traditional-violence end of the continuum, while Detroit, Pittsburgh, and St. Louis were on the nontraditional-violence end. By the end of the period (1985),

Los Angeles had changed categories and joined Detroit, Pittsburgh, and St. Louis as centers where acts of nontraditional violence predominated.

We also observed a shift in the structure of victimization in some cities (structure of victimization refers to the relationship between the victim and offender and whether there were single or multiple offenders and single or multiple victims). In traditional violence, the victims have commonly been family members and acquaintances; in nontraditional violence victims are primarily strangers or of unknown relationships. But we observed a shift in the structure of victimization that implied that those who are victims of instrumental violence[1] are increasingly acquaintances. For example, in Detroit there was no substantial change over the study period in stranger victimizations (robbery-homicide), but there was a major change in the number of victimizations in which victims and offenders were acquaintances. The largest number of these individuals were under twenty-five, which may be attributed to the increased use of teenagers in drug distribution and to random shootings. In Detroit, as well as in other northern urban centers, we are witnessing the coming-of-age of a cohort socialized in an environment where instrumental violence has become entrenched; as a result, gratuitous, violent confrontations have become more commonplace. This situation is fueled by the changed demands of the mainstream economy, the lure of the irregular economy (i.e., drug trafficking), the strengthening of secular values, and the growing attractiveness of the street hustler as a role model.

In our sample generally, in those communities where young blacks had experienced less success in sustaining themselves in the regular economy, nontraditional patterns of victimization were most in evidence. Houston, which had experienced few negative consequences as an outgrowth of economic transformation, had moved much less slowly away from the traditional end of the structural spectrum than had those communities that experienced many negative consequences. Therefore, it appears that the continuing examples of elevated risk are indirectly dependent upon urban growth and the ability of young adult males to successfully find a satisfactory niche for themselves in the growth sector of the economy.

The economic and subsequent cultural changes have had an impact on the structure of victimization, thereby altering patterns of risk. We contend that blacks residing in large manufacturing-belt cities prior to 1940 were strongly bound by aspects of southern culture. Most violent altercations during this earlier period were basically associated with individuals engaged in a primary relationship.

During the years following World War II, southern migration to northern urban centers continued to escalate, but at the same time a large base population of northern origin was being formed. In this situation one would anticipate a weakening of selected elements of the traditional culture and the adoption of values prevalent in the environment in which individuals were socialized. Values and lifestyle practices vary through space and over time, and account for subsequent differences in the modal pattern of victimization. It is also clear that these two sets of influences operate in tandem and ultimately influence the magnitude as well as the character of victimization. Several generational cohorts are present in large nonsouthern cities, each having encountered varying social experiences in a range of environments. The complexity of those groups' experiences, in terms of time spent in varying environments, should serve to distinguish initially between the prevailing structure in southern and nonsouthern urban environments, as well as within individual nonsouthern neighborhoods. Therefore, the very general concept of the existence of a subculture of violence, as developed by Marvin Wolfgang and Franco Ferracuti (1967), is inadequate to explain levels of risk we identified as being supported by etiological differences based partially on location.

Location is simply a surrogate for a stage in the economy's developmental sequence and the manner in which identifiable subpopulations adapt to changing sets of circumstances. Thus, we labeled the subculture that originated in the rural South, largely involving primary relationships, as a *subculture of defensive violence*. Yet in the latter third of the twentieth century, we find that young adult blacks have been exposed to a substantially different worldview. This alternative worldview, initially manifested in manufacturing-belt cities, has now begun to spread across the landscape at varying speeds. This different worldview has led to the evolution of another subculture in which the resort to violence is commonplace. We have labeled this the *subculture of materialistic aggression*. In most locations, robbery-homicide tends to be the situation in which materialistic aggression is principally manifested, but there is growing evidence that as this subculture matures it expresses itself in a growing variety of ways.

What happens in the future relative to levels of risk most likely will be influenced by the emerging status of individuals born since 1970. The extent to which these individuals successfully negotiate the economy will play a critical role in risk abatement, but certainly not the only one.

RECONCEPTUALIZING URBAN VIOLENCE

During my spring 1989 sabbatical, I spent five months with the Homicide Division of the Phoenix Police Department. Long hours, mostly in the wee hours of the morning, were spent at homicide scenes—on a street, in a nightclub, or in a vacant lot. Regardless of the circumstances and location of the homicide, the variable that was constant across homicide events was the presence of the victim's body. Moreover, the tagging and removal of the victim's body was the last task after all the investigative work was completed. It was painfully clear, and frustratingly expressed by the detectives, that by the time the Homicide Division is called, someone is already dead. Moreover, by the time the police catch the offender (if they do, given the changing nature of the victim-offender relationship), two or three additional people may also have been murdered or assaulted. One faces a very grim reality investigating homicides, and these criminal justice officers want something to be done *before* the event, so that it becomes unnecessary for them to respond.

Another painful reality was that many of the black victims were people who were not involved in any criminal activity. They simply had the misfortune of sharing the same geographical space with individuals for whom human life meant nothing. They were in the proverbial "wrong place at the wrong time." As previously discussed, the predominant victims of urban homicide are blacks, and they are murdered by other blacks.

The only way we as a society are going to begin to ameliorate the situation is to reconceptualize the problem so that the policies developed address the risk of victimization that confronts urban black residents. The present conceptualization places the emphasis on the offender after the homicide has occurred. This particular orientation to the problem makes it virtually impossible to discuss or develop homicide-prevention strategies. If homicide prevention and the preservation of the lives of urban black citizens are reasonable policy goals, then an alternative conceptualization is in order.

The proposed reconceptualization views homicide not as a criminal act but as a cause of death (O'Carroll and Mercy 1986). The term *homicide* in this context refers to victimization, rather than perpetration. Additionally, this reconceptualization places homicide within the framework of a public health response, rather than a criminal justice response. The emphasis, therefore, is on prevention and interdiction rather than on punishment. And the time frame is before the event, rather than after.

James Mercy and Patrick O'Carroll (1988) argue that violence in general, and homicide in particular, have enormous public health implications. Several factors imply that homicide should be viewed from a public health perspective. First, as other causes of death decline in importance as a result of innovations in medical treatment, homicide is becoming more prominent as a leading cause of death. In fact, in 1985 the Centers for

Disease Control listed homicide as the number-one cause of death of black males fifteen to thirty-four years of age (O'Carroll and Mercy 1986). Second, there is the increasing recognition within the public health field of the importance of behavioral factors in the etiology and prevention of disease. For example, prevention of the three leading causes of death in the United States—heart disease, cancer, and stroke—has been attributed to behavioral modifications such as exercise, changes in diet, and non-smoking (Mercy and O'Carroll 1988). Public health perspectives and practices hold promise for beginning to address the seriousness of the problem of urban violence.

The primary objectives of public health are to preserve, promote, and improve health (Last 1980:3). The philosophy of public health has several dimensions directed toward attaining these goals (Mercy and O'Carroll 1988). First, public health emphasizes prevention of disease or injury from occurring or recurring. This parallels nicely the differences between homicide defined as a cause of death (preventable) and homicide defined as a criminal act (after the fact). Second, public health interventions are concentrated on those at greatest risk of disease or injury—those in greatest need of intervention (ibid.). This implies that homicide policies would focus on those at greatest risk of victimization—urban black residents—rather than exclusively on those who are the victimizers (as in the criminal justice approach).

Interdicting homicide risk among black Americans will require a set of long-term strategies. The U.S. governmental system and its citizens are not excited about long-term strategies; the system is only geared to accommodate short-run solutions. The polity wants to see results from its policies and programs, and if things do not change quickly, the commitment begins to wane. Any set of strategies devised will have marginal utility in the short run, but in the long run they may do some good. The desire for short-run results pushes the punishment (criminal justice) response to the problem. It is only in the area of public health problems (e.g., cancer and AIDS) that the political system is inclined to make long-term policy commitments, realizing that results will occur for and benefits will be reaped by future generations.

If homicide is reconceptualized within the context of a public health model, our policy options for attacking, and hopefully interdicting, the problem are substantially broadened. The current stream of criminal justice approaches is nicely subsumed under the public health approach as part of an overarching solution to urban violence, but it is not seen as the only approach. Moreover, in this proposed framework the criminal justice machinery can become an active participant in the development of prevention strategies, because the broadened definition of the problem allows these agencies to move beyond their arrest and punishment responsibilities, which a few agencies (e.g., the Phoenix Police Department) are beginning to see as essential to reducing levels of urban violence.

By adopting this conceptualization of homicide, we begin to focus on interdicting the development of behavior patterns and worldviews in at-risk children that put them in danger in later years of becoming victims of lethal violence. As Nancy Allen (1981) has argued, potential victims can be made aware of their own dangerous behavior patterns that make them susceptible to being murdered. The concern, therefore, is with helping people learn and practice alternative behavior patterns (Spivak et al. 1989). Furthermore, it means that we begin to recognize that other social problems (e.g., black teenage pregnancy) are connected to the issue of lethal violence. Homicide is a very complex phenomenon that will require a complex set of solutions. The public health model offers us a vastly superior policy framework for tackling the issue than does the narrowly focused criminal justice model.

CONCLUSION

Problem identification and structuring the debate on policy issues are very important aspects of the agenda-setting process. John Kingdon (1984) notes that the treatment of a policy issue on the agenda will be affected by the way in which a problem is recognized and defined and the category in which it is placed. Thus, in this instance, defining urban violence as a criminal justice problem narrows the scope of the debate and limits the range of potential policy options, while defining urban violence as a public health issue broadens the scope of the debate and expands the range of potential policy options. There is no pollyanna-like delusion concerning the difficulty in redirecting the public discourse on urban violence into a more fruitful direction, one that will lead, we hope, to the development of public policies that begin to address the problem, rather than the current debate that sees punishment of the perpetrator as the ends rather than the protection of the lives of the victims. Unfortunately, the issue, as presently conceptualized, is "good" politics, and politicians will continue to politicize urban violence, defining it as blacks preying on whites, to gain votes of suburban whites at the expense of an increasing number of the lives of urban black residents.

NOTE

1. Instrumental violence is defined as violence committed to secure a goal (e.g., money or other material goods). It is most often classified as felony homicide.

6

Evaluation, Tribal Sovereignty, and the Alaska Native Land Claims Settlement Act

Fae L. Korsmo

The rise of certain concerns to public or governmental attention, the set of events and activities we associate with agenda setting, occurs in all phases of the policy process, including the evaluation and revision of existing programs. Most literature on agenda setting focuses on innovation (e.g., Kingdon 1984; Polsby 1984). Little attention has been paid to the importance of problem definition and public access in policy evaluation.

For minorities targeted by specific policies or programs they consider ineffective, setting the agenda for change through re-examination can be a powerful instrument. Unfortunately, the resources required to define the evaluative framework, initiate the study, and use the results to motivate key actors to abandon the status quo can overwhelm even highly mobilized groups. If systemic bias blocks policy initiation, its potential to discourage major overhauls of existing programs is even greater (Bachrach and Baratz 1970).

In the case described below, a minority group seized the impending deadlines built into existing legislation to propose their own criteria for policy evaluation. They did not succeed in persuading Congress to adopt all of their proposed amendments. But, without the proactive stance of the Alaska Natives, the Indian, Aleut, and Inuit peoples who make up less than 15 percent of the state population, it is doubtful whether the 1991 amendments to the Alaska Native Claims Settlement Act (ANCSA) would have made it to the decision agenda.[1]

Alaska Natives participated in fashioning both the ANCSA legislation in 1971 and the amendments in 1988 because of the unique policy windows available: first, the discovery of oil in the late 1960s, and second, the 1991 expiration date set by ANCSA for native control over the

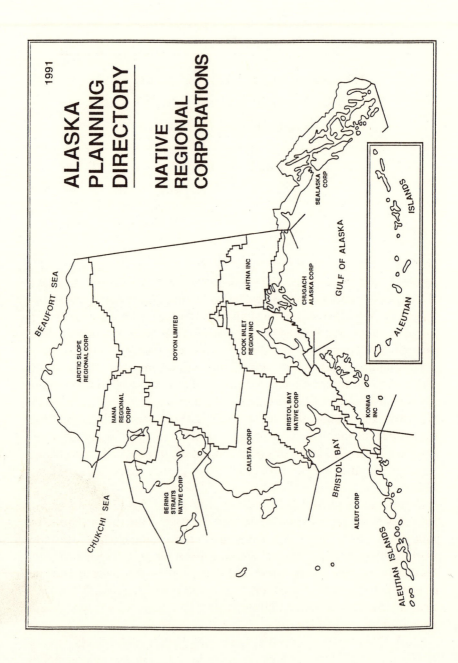

ALASKA
PLANNING
DIRECTORY
1991

NATIVE
REGIONAL
CORPORATIONS

corporations created to manage the land and assets from the settlement. The demand for oil gave great urgency to settling native land claims in the first instance. In the second instance, the danger that the Alaska Natives would lose control over the corporations and the land once the twenty-year period of protection expired mobilized several initiatives to extend those protections.

ANCSA compensated the Alaska Natives for lands taken (nearly the entire state of Alaska, or 360 million acres) and conferred fee simple title to the remaining 44 million acres to native-owned corporations. For twenty years native control of the village and regional corporations would be assured, but at the end of 1991 the corporations were required to replace the restricted stock with at-large shares on the open market. Natives feared that non-natives could easily buy up corporate stock and thereby acquire title to native lands. Although several amendments to ANCSA made in the 1970s and the 1980 Alaska National Interest Lands Conservation Act (ANILCA)[2] made it easier for the natives to protect their lands and stock, they did not alter the slated 1991 phase-out. In the early 1980s, Alaska Natives began to study and propose options to the approaching deadline. They lobbied Congress in the mid-1980s to extend the stock restrictions indefinitely unless a majority of shareholders in a native corporation voted to remove them. In addition, they wanted undeveloped lands placed automatically in a "land bank," free from taxation.

The amendments, signed into law in February 1988, lessened the fear of land loss, but not the fear of culture loss. Many natives, particularly in small remote villages, had wanted an amendment that would make it easy for the corporations to transfer land holdings to a tribal government, thus invoking the trust responsibilities of the federal government and assuring the land would be held in perpetuity. They hoped that the recognition of tribal government and perpetual title would give the villages more control over subsistence hunting and fishing on their lands. The tribal government amendment did not pass, however, striking a blow to the advocates of tribal sovereignty in Alaska.

Participants in the lobbying effort relied on different interpretations of ANCSA, its origins, intent, implementation, and value to the native community. Each description of ANCSA put before Congress carried with it implicit value judgments and explicit prescriptions for action. In the 1991 debate, evaluations competed for legitimacy. What had the settlement act done for the natives? Who had benefited? Different native groups came up with different answers. The evaluative search was disjointed, often bitter in tone. Disagreements among the Alaska Natives threatened to halt the entire process, while Alaska's congressional delegation demanded unity.

Some Alaska Natives thought it best to keep tribal sovereignty off the agenda, knowing the term's power to frighten legislators and constituents. Others made every effort to make it the primary focus of the agenda.

This chapter will trace agenda formation in the 1991 amendment process. Specifically, the case study will address three questions: (1) what potential exists for a minority group to set the agenda for program evaluation and change, to pose the valuative choices and criteria for success? (2) can the internal disunity and competition among minority group leaders play a positive rather than negative role in agenda setting? and (3) what constraints does a decision agenda hold for culturally distinct worldviews?

To answer these questions, I conducted open-ended interviews with representatives of Alaska Native groups, key congressional staff members, and former officials of the U.S. Department of Interior. Additionally, I prepared digests of testimony and submissions made to congressional hearings to locate the policy positions of various stakeholders. Finally, I examined the archives of the Alaska Native Review Commission, a major policy evaluation effort.

PLURALISM, ELITISM, AND ASSIMILATION

The link between evaluation and agenda setting combines perceptions of the past, problem definitions, and action programs for the future. A traditional policy sequences model (problem formation, formulation, adoption, implementation, and evaluation) allows the consequences of policy evaluation to influence the next policy cycle, beginning with problem formation (Nakamura 1987). But if policy evaluation is inherently political, the questions the evaluator poses will direct the activity toward specific policy actions (Weiss 1987).

Evaluations, formal and informal, use different views of reality to interpret the failures and successes of the past, prioritize problems, and suggest solutions. Each evaluation has its own "logic," or a system of ideas and norms that dictate standards according to which policy performance is criticized (Anderson 1978:23–24). According to John Kingdon's (1984) agenda-setting model, evaluations would probably flow in the problems stream, where quantitative indicators and critical feedback from existing programs supply the material perceived as problems. The other streams—policies (or solutions) and politics—go their own way until chance or purpose unites them. Commonly, an advocate for a particular program will link a problem and a solution at any opportunity, or "policy window." But evaluations link problems and solutions automatically. As in any ideology or system of thought, problem definition presupposes action for remediation.

Kingdon's model leaves out the mobilization of bias that limits the content of decision agendas. Whether the evaluative language accompanying proposals is called ideology or story telling, it must present a view of reality credible to policy elites to be placed on the decision agenda.

In the 1991 amendments, three evaluative logics competed for the decision agenda. First, *pluralism* sees politics as the interaction and competition of groups to achieve their goals. Power shifts among the different groups, so that no one sector remains dominant. This is the classic view of U.S. politics, articulated by David Truman and Robert Dahl in the 1950s. Second, in *elitism* power is concentrated at the top, with elites forming an interlocking structure of wealth and power. Third, an *assimilation* logic hardly admits power exists. Instead, individuals, not groups, employ their own rational and productive abilities to adapt to societal rules.

The retrospective views on ANCSA can be divided into these three categories. First, groups such as the Alaska Federation of Natives (AFN) and the leaders of the twelve regional corporations saw ANCSA as an ongoing settlement process that began as a compromise between unequal parties. Through amendments and adjustments, ANCSA became a viable mechanism for native participation and leadership in the Alaskan economy and polity. This view corresponds to pluralism, where organized groups have access to decision makers and change comes about in increments.

Other Alaska Native groups took a second approach. They saw ANCSA as a product of non-native greed, deception, and racism. According to groups such as the Association of Village Council Presidents (AVCP) and the United Tribes of Alaska (UTA), the for-profit corporate institution was forced on native villages without the villagers' consent, so it is no wonder the village corporations have had little financial success. Because people at the "ground level" were shut out of the process of negotiating ANCSA in the late 1960s and early 1970s, ANCSA lacks legitimacy, a perspective that corresponds to the elitist interpretation of politics.

Finally, non-natives represented in recreational hunting and fishing groups, the state government, and the Department of Interior believed ANCSA's purpose was to assimilate Alaska Natives, bring them into the mainstream as entrepreneurs and citizens of the State of Alaska, and eliminate any special rights they thought they had as tribal peoples. An alternative to reservations, ANCSA was not supposed to create separate institutions based on ethnicity or maintain distinct native cultures. Obviously, the natives wanted this solution also, because their leaders lobbied intensively for a settlement like ANCSA. This perspective corresponds to the assimilationist school of ethnic politics.

Pluralism, elitism, and assimilation contended for the decision agenda during the 1985–1987 lobbying efforts that led to the 1991 amendments. The discussion below examines each evaluative effort, then the process by which the evaluations entered the decision agenda.

PLURALISM: THE ALASKA FEDERATION OF NATIVES

The major interest organization representing Alaska Natives grew out of the land claims struggle of the 1960s. When Alaska became a state in 1959, most natives (then about one-fifth of the state's population) lived in small villages and settlements across rural Alaska where they used the land and water as their ancestors had—for subsistence hunting, fishing, trapping, and gathering. Shortly after statehood, Alaska's government began selecting and selling leases on these lands. The federal government also threatened intrusion: a nuclear bomb test near an Inupiat village and a dam that would flood several Athabaskan villages. In response to the increased threat, native villages filed land claims that amounted to 380 million acres by 1967, or a little more than the entire land area of the state (Arnold 1978:119).

As a part of the mobilization against encroachments, representatives from native associations across the state met in Anchorage in 1966 and formed an umbrella organization, the Alaska Federation of Natives. The conference called for a "land freeze" until all native claims were resolved. Before the year ended, Secretary of Interior Stewart Udall put a stop to further withdrawal of lands claimed by Alaska Natives until Congress could settle the claims (ibid.:113–114).

The AFN became the principal native voice in the congressional negotiations resulting in ANCSA. With the land freeze extended by Udall and the 1968 discovery of significant oil reserves at Prudhoe Bay, the AFN leaders had a certain leverage in blocking economic development. But they had only a short time to exercise their power. The House and Senate Interior Committees, the oil companies, and the State of Alaska were no champions of native rights. Under tremendous pressure, the AFN approved a settlement in December 1971: natives would surrender their claims to most of the state in exchange for title to about one-ninth of Alaska's land area, plus $962.5 million in compensation (Berry 1975; Arnold 1978).

The idea of for-profit corporations surfaced early in the discussions of a state task force, consisting largely of AFN representatives, created by Governor Walter Hickel in 1967 to resolve land claims (Governor's Task

Force 1968; Hensley 1991). Corporations, unlike reservations, could make their own land use decisions without interference from the Bureau of Indian Affairs. The AFN promoted the corporate form as a management vehicle for the land and funds (AFN 1969).

The final settlement created two types of corporations. The twelve regional corporations, whose boundaries would correspond to the areas of the existing twelve regional native associations, hold surface title to their areas and subsurface title to the mineral resources for the total settlement acreage. The village corporations, formed by approximately 200 existing villages, hold fee simple title to the surface estate only.

ANCSA had many flaws and ambiguities that became apparent during implementation. Congress had underestimated the time and money needed to get the corporations started, select the lands, and begin to turn a profit. Furthermore, federal agencies put up barriers to enrollment and land selections. While some of the problems were addressed in amendments passed from 1973 through 1980, fundamental flaws remained.

The AFN began policy review in 1981, ten years after the settlement. Now led by the representatives of the twelve regional corporations, the AFN focused on corporate success or failure.

Prior to formal review, however, one of the regional corporations, the Northwest Area Native Association (NANA), located in northwest Alaska, conducted a survey in 1976 and found the overwhelming majority of shareholders wanted NANA to take steps to continue native control of the corporation after 1991. As a result, NANA—within an overall lobbying effort by the AFN—fought for congressional measures that would keep non-native shareholders (who, for example, had inherited stock from native shareholders) from voting and give the native corporations and shareholder families the right of first refusal once stock was up for sale in 1991 (Shively 1991; Public Law 96–487). These and other provisions of the Alaska National Interest Lands Conservation Act of 1980 (ANILCA) provided some, but not enough, protection for the native corporations.

By 1981, ten years after ANCSA, the native corporations had received less than half of the land through interim conveyance and full title to approximately 3 million acres. The regional corporations had only marginal profits, with at least one in danger of going under (Williams 1981). Disputes over easements and overlapping claims, uncertain title, and the costs of creating corporations from scratch exposed the ridiculous assumptions behind ANCSA; in one generation, how could the native corporations stand up and fight the Fortune 500? Some speculated the settlement act was meant to fail (Lenz 1981). Whatever the intent of Congress, both the corporate leadership and the shareholders feared loss of control and land.

In 1981, the AFN commissioned a report on ANCSA by the Alaska Native Foundation. The report and subsequent discussions among the AFN leaders, lawyers, and consultants revealed three major problems that required immediate attention. The following paragraph paraphrases AFN's presentation of the problems to Alaska Native communities (AFN 1984).

First, the automatic cancellation of restricted stock in December 1991 and its replacement with ordinary stock gives the natives the option to sell their stock or pledge it as collateral for a loan. If enough natives sell their stock to non-natives, whether to individuals or corporations, natives will lose control over the corporations. Second, the loss of corporate control means loss of corporate-owned land. Third, ANCSA neglected to provide for certain populations, the children and the elders. Natives born after the enactment of the settlement did not receive stock, although they could inherit it. Without stock, the younger natives had no say in the management of the corporations or the use of native lands. The elders received few if any benefits from the settlement, because of the time it took to implement ANCSA. If elders do collect dividends from the corporations, they risk losing the benefits they receive from the state or federal government.

To address the problems, the AFN sponsored leadership retreats and workshops, and presented the proposals worked out at these sessions to the greater membership. While the AFN's mobilization of ideas can only be described as a top-down initiative, the organization was careful to elicit feedback from the villagers and incorporate their wishes into its proposals. As a result, delegates to a special March 1985 AFN convention approved eight resolutions on ANCSA amendments:

1. Each corporation can decide whether to allow dissenters' rights. That is, if a majority of shareholders in a corporation votes to keep certain stock restrictions, the corporation need not compensate the minority of stockholders who voted against the restrictions.

2. Eliminate the ANCSA provision that allows stock alienation after 1991; instead, extend restrictions indefinitely, reserving the option for each corporation to permit alienation, subject to shareholder vote.

3. Allow a corporation to buy stock from shareholders, for example, dissenters who voted against continuing stock restrictions, to alleviate the chance of a dissenter taking the corporation to court.

4. Offer corporations the options to issue special stock to elders and new stock to natives born after the December 1971 enrollment.

5. Prohibit stock transfer to non-natives who are not descendants of natives while corporate stock remains restricted.

6. Give corporations the option to grant voting rights to shareholders who are descendants of natives.

7. Provide automatic federal land bank protections for all ANCSA land against taxation, adverse possession, bad debt judgments, and bankruptcy.

8. Give the corporations the option to transfer land and assets to other native entities, including governments set up under the Indian Reorganization Act of 1934 (IRA), traditional council, nonprofit corporation, cooperative, or trust organization, without the burden of dissenters' rights. (*Alaska Native News* 1985; AVCP 1985a)

With regard to the latter option, the so-called "qualified transferee entity" or QTE, the AFN conceded to tribal advocates who wanted to separate the land and corporations, but at the same time tried to maintain maximum flexibility for the corporations (Kitka 1991).

ELITISM: THE STRUGGLE FOR TRIBAL RIGHTS IN ALASKA

Tribal advocates, such as the AVCP, the UTA, and the Alaska Native Coalition (ANC), were dissatisfied with the AFN's review process. They disagreed with the AFN's acceptance of the existing corporate structure and argued that ANCSA was invalid. As the basis for their argument, they relied on the history of contact with Russians and Americans as well as the principles of federal Indian law.

Tribal sovereignty is a complex concept that provokes emotional responses. The irony of tribal sovereignty is the implied dependence of native communities on the United States. Alaska Native leaders and key members of Congress (including the chairman of the Senate Interior Committee, Henry Jackson) rejected reservations during the ANCSA negotiations because they represented a policy failure. The Bureau of Indian Affairs had a bad reputation even in remote Alaska; adopting reservations as the settlement mechanism would have meant reliance on an unpopular federal agency.

Despite the problems associated with reservations, Indian country (as reservations, dependent Indian communities, or allotments) has some legal advantages over the ANCSA corporation idea (NARF 1985). As domestic dependent sovereigns, Indian tribes may choose the form of their tribal government, determine tribal membership, legislate, administer justice, exclude outsiders from tribal territory, and make some decisions over non-Indians on tribal territory (Cohen 1982:247– 250). According to Felix Cohen, the powers of an Indian tribe to govern itself are not delegated powers granted by Congress but inherent powers of a limited sovereignty. "Once considered a political body by the United States, a tribe retains its sovereignty until Congress acts to divest that sovereignty" (ibid.:231).

Cohen bases his assessment on case law, especially the decisions of Chief Justice John Marshall: *Johnson v. McIntosh*,[3] *Cherokee Nation v. Georgia*,[4] and *Worcester v. Georgia*.[5] Charles Wilkinson calls these "the Marshall trilogy" (1987:55–56). According to the Marshall-Cohen concept, tribal sovereignty is based on a political relationship between governments, not between a government and a race.

Other legal scholars do not agree with the Marshall-Cohen definition. Frederick Martone (1977) writes that tribes "possess only those powers of self-government granted by Congress. In the absence of a specific grant, an Indian has no power." A case from southeast Alaska demonstrates his point. In *Tee-Hit-Ton Indians v. United States*, 348 U.S. 272 (1955), the court held that the United States did not owe compensation for land held by the Tee-Hit-Ton Indians since Congress had not explicitly recognized Indian title.

Whether tribal powers are inherent or delegated by Congress makes a difference in Alaska, since neither Russia nor the United States signed treaties with the indigenous inhabitants and few reservations existed at the time ANCSA was passed. Do the Alaska Native governments, organized at the local level in some 200 villages around the state, possess the powers of self-government associated with tribal sovereignty? If so, do the governments organized under the federal Indian Reorganization Act (IRA) of 1934 have stronger rights than traditional councils? The Alaska state courts have ruled in some instances that Alaska villages do not constitute tribes,[6] while the federal courts have in other cases affirmed the existence of tribes in Alaska.[7]

Leaders of the tribal sovereignty movement in Alaska used the process of amending ANCSA to promote their cause. They supported AFN's eighth resolution, the amendment that would bypass complicated state law requirements and make it easy for a native corporation to transfer land and assets to another entity (a QTE, or qualified transferee entity, as the legislation came to be worded), such as a tribal government. But they also wanted more: explicit recognition of tribal sovereignty in Alaska.

The historical argument claims that Russia never had complete sovereignty over Alaska between the late 1700s until the sale to the United States in 1867. After the United States took control of Alaska, Congress began to adapt federal Indian law to the Alaska Natives, including the IRA, applied to Alaska in 1936. The IRA promised to restore self-government to the Indians of the lower forty-eight states and reduce their dependency on the federal government. In the extension of this law to Alaska, the natives were allowed to organize as tribal governments and form reservations. As a result, about seventy Alaska Native villages were recognized as IRA governments. However, only six IRA reservations were approved, due to disruptive communications between the natives and the Indian Service, local non-native agitation against reservations, and native dissatisfaction with the amount of land offered in exchange for extinguished title to the vast areas they used for hunting and fishing (Case 1984:83–129; Arnold 1978:86–88). In other words, the principle of the IRA—tribal sovereignty—was applied to Alaska, even though the implementation suffered.

The tribal advocates were appalled by what could happen in 1991. Below is a summary of their views on ANCSA:

ANCSA eliminated reservations, but not tribal government.[8] ANCSA came about as a result of land claims brought by the villages and filed with the Department of Interior. The blanket settlement of all claims through a legislative act required the approval of the Alaska Natives through the certified elections of village (tribal) members. Congress did not seek such approval. Instead, President Nixon interpreted the Alaska Federation of Natives (AFN) approval by majority vote at its December 1971 convention, with the delegates of the Arctic Slope Native Association voting "no," as native consent.[9] The AFN does not constitute a tribe and the Alaska Native villages did not approve ANCSA; therefore, ANCSA alienated tribal lands without consent (AVCP 1985b).

ANCSA extinguished aboriginal rights to hunt and fish, but Congress also made ANCSA subject to valid existing rights. While Congress intended this clause to protect the land uses of non-natives (e.g., trappers, miners, traders), it can be argued that native claims on file with the Department of Interior at the time ANCSA was negotiated constitute valid existing rights. Otherwise, Congress failed in its fiduciary duty to protect tribal property interests and assist Alaska Native villages in securing permanent possession of lands claimed by the tribal governments. This failure, however, does not extinguish the land rights, including the right to hunt and fish, of the Alaska Native villages.

Congress had no intention of keeping the land in native hands. Unlike most settlements of claims to aboriginal title, ANCSA conveyed ownership in fee simple to for-profit corporations, with native control of the corporations and land guaranteed for only twenty years. Even during the twenty-year period, native corporation lands have been subject to loss to pay for bad debts and through adverse possession and condemnation.

Because of ANCSA and its corporate model, Alaska Native lands do not enjoy the same protections as tribal lands in the lower forty-eight states. In addition, the individualistic, profit-oriented corporate model clashes with native values of sharing and communal ownership. The pressures to develop, make profits, and pay dividends contradict the longstanding priority placed on subsistence in remote regions; especially problematic is the regional corporations' incentive to harvest subsurface resources in areas used by villagers for subsistence hunting and fishing (Langdon 1986).

While the tribal advocates worked with the AFN in developing a set of legislative proposals, they also wanted an independent review of ANCSA. Two concerned individuals met in 1982 and tossed the idea around before they decided to call Thomas Berger, a respected advocate of native rights and a judge on the British Columbia Supreme Court (Sambo 1991). Earlier, Berger had been appointed by the Canadian government to conduct the Mackenzie Valley Pipeline Inquiry. His 1977 report, *Northern Frontier, Northern Homeland,* drew on two parallel series of hearings. One consisted of prepared testimony of expert witnesses. The other took place in the communities of the Northwest and Yukon territories, with nearly 1,000 people telling Berger in eight different languages what effects they thought the proposed gas pipeline would have on their lives. Through the Berger inquiry, Canada's Indian, Inuit, and Métis peoples transformed the choice of whether or not to build a pipeline into a native land claims issue (Gamble 1978:951).

Berger decided to accept the offer, initially made over the phone, then placed formally through the Inuit Circumpolar Conference (ICC) in 1983, to conduct an inquiry in Alaska. The ICC named Berger and his staff the Alaska Native Review Commission and charged them with examining five areas: (1) social and economic status of Inuit (including other Indian and Aleut groups in Alaska); (2) the history and intent of ANCSA; (3) historic policies and practices of the United States in settling claims by Native Americans and the place of ANCSA in this political perspective; (4) the performance of various regional corporations in fulfilling the spirit of ANCSA; and (5) the social, cultural, economic, political, and environmental consequences of ANCSA and its significance to the international Inuit community (AFN 1983:43).

Berger visited sixty villages throughout Alaska and held formal hearings in Anchorage. After gathering the views of rural Alaska Natives, he observed:

Alaska Natives wish to choose a form of landholding that reflects their own cultural imperatives and ensures that their ancestral lands will remain in their possession and under governance. . . . At every hearing, witnesses talk of the corporations, shares, profits, sometimes even of proxies, but then, emerging from this thicket of corporate vocabulary, they will talk of what they consider of most importance to them—land, subsistence, the future of the villages. (Berger 1985:18–19)

Berger, taking direction from the expressed concerns of the villagers, concluded, "An analysis of ANCSA will not be sufficient" (ibid.:19). Instead, he focused on the Alaska Natives' efforts to strengthen their subsistence economies and restore tribal governments. In light of these goals, ANCSA's negative impacts outweighed the positive.

The method Berger chose, listening to the views of anyone who offered them, made his a bottom-up evaluation. He was not a stakeholder in any existing policy, although his previous exposure to ANCSA included participation in a conference that was highly critical of the settlement act (Alaska Native Review Commission Papers). Because of his method and his anti-ANCSA predisposition, Berger's recommendations went beyond improvement of existing policy to structural change.

First, in the area of subsistence, Berger urged the federal and state governments to recognize the rights of tribes to regulate their own fishing, hunting, and gathering. For Alaskans living outside the handful of cities, subsistence means both survival and culture. Wage employment is seasonal and imported foodstuffs expensive. Kinship relations and social networks are affirmed and made meaningful through patterns of gathering, exchange, and distribution. ANCSA assumed that subsistence would decline as natives moved into the modern economy, but research has demonstrated that the more cash native families have from jobs, the more they reinvest in subsistence technology (Ellana 1980). Subsistence shows no sign of declining in importance.

The framers of ANCSA left it up to the state and federal governments to deal with the natives' subsistence needs, but twenty years later, subsistence regulations are mired in confusion.[10] Alaska passed a law in 1978 to give subsistence users a preference over sport or commercial users, but the new law with its accompanying regulations only resulted in attempts to repeal it. On the national level, Congress enacted the Alaska National Interest Lands Conservation Act (ANILCA) in 1980 to protect subsistence hunting and fishing in sparsely populated areas of the state. ANILCA authorized the state to continue fish and game management on federal lands as long as subsistence users were given preference. It also allowed native corporations to enter into agreement with the federal government to place undeveloped lands in the Alaska National Land Bank. Once in the Land Bank, the corporation's land is protected from adverse possession, taxation, and court judgments. Land Bank agreements could be made for ten years, with the possibility of renewal every five years.

When Berger conducted his hearings in 1984, the single proposed land agreement had been put on hold due to Department of Interior requirements that the land be subject to public access (Berger 1985:104). Interior's lack of interest in implementing the ANILCA Land Bank was matched by the State of Alaska's reluctance to develop and carry through a subsistence policy that met ANILCA requirements. To add to the difficulties, ANCSA's creation of for-profit corporations elevated the values of economic development and competitiveness above that of cultural survival. For example, the regional corporations hold subsurface rights to villages within the region. Their incentive to develop oil or mineral resources may clash with the subsistence needs of the villages (Langdon 1986:36).

According to Berger's summation of the testimony he heard in native villages, subsistence needed protection, just as the land needed to be kept in native hands. It came as no surprise that land loss through corporate failure, takeover, or taxation was the predominant concern among the 1,450 people who testified at the hearings. Unlike the AFN, Berger rejected the fine-tuning of ANCSA as a solution. He recommended the tribal model instead.

Berger sympathized with the tribal sovereignty movement as a rational response to intensified pressure on native life. He saw tribal governments as the best mechanism to protect land and subsistence, since they are immune from lawsuits, exempt from federal income tax and state property taxes, and composed of a perpetually renewed membership (with membership based on who you are, not on what you own) (Berger 1985:113–116).

The advocates of retribalization took Berger's published report, *Village Journey*, with them to Washington, DC. This book became the evidence for the QTE's necessity, yet it did not persuade Alaska's senators. Instead, it drew criticism; the Berger hearings had merely raised the unrealistic expectations of Alaska Natives, giving them hope in a model that had resulted in misery and poverty on the lower forty-eight reservations. *Village Journey* sits on the shelves of private and public libraries, but the tribal sovereignty movement continues in the villages of rural Alaska.

ASSIMILATION: INDIVIDUAL RIGHTS

In contrast to the tribal sovereignty position, the assimilationists praised ANCSA for moving Alaska Natives into the mainstream and rejecting the reservation system that had failed in the lower forty-eight. According to the assimilationists, ANCSA terminated any rights to self-government the Alaska Natives may have had. It was a clear and generous settlement of native claims, in which the natives were given the opportunity to adopt modern business methods and run their own corporations. Back in 1971, Congress did not intend to create any permanent racial institutions, and AFN's proposed amendments to ANCSA, with the indefinite extension of stock restrictions, would violate the spirit of the law. Furthermore, the transfer of corporate land to village and IRA governments would create a patchwork of sovereign jurisdictions, with their own courts and enforcement agencies, across Alaska. Finally, immunity from property taxes on undeveloped land would give the natives special privileges above other citizens of Alaska, a state where all are equal under the law (U.S. Congress, Senate 1986:52–67, 430–457).

Recreational groups, joined by the National Rifle Association, took the above line of argument, and the Department of Interior largely agreed. Among the assimilationists, however, Interior was the only one to conduct a formal evaluation (U.S. Interior Dept. 1984).

ANCSA required the secretary of Interior to submit to Congress in 1985 a report on the status of Alaska Natives, a summary of actions taken under ANCSA, and any appropriate recommendations. Interior awarded the task to a contractor, ESG, who focused on policy implementation, the social and economic well-being of the natives, and the health of the corporations.

The report found major implementation problems with the land settlement, including the Department of Interior's inefficiency in developing a suitable method for conveyance and its intransigence in proposing an 11,135-mile system of transportation and utility corridors that would cross native lands and other parts of the state (ibid.: III–58). The effects of such delays and controversies, ESG implied, were to deplete native resources and encumber remaining land selections with unresolved claims.

The report also found that the native corporations created by ANCSA have contributed very little to the improvement of native living standards.

The corporations employed only a small percentage of shareholders and most did not pay regular dividends. The corporations themselves, faced with a grab bag of unrealistic and contradictory expectations (promoting the well-being of shareholders, leading the economic development of Alaska, and preserving lands for traditional subsistence ways of life), succeeded only in sheer survival. Strained resources characterized most, with some in danger of collapse. ESG cautiously predicted that "many village corporations and possibly one or more regional corporations may not remain viable" (ibid.:ES–14).

The implications of the status report, that unless Congress extended the stock restrictions or came up with other protections, the natives could lose their land in 1991, were left between the lines. Secretary of Interior Donald Hodel, an ardent critic of extending stock restrictions, allowed the report to remain in draft form and did not use its tentative findings to back Interior's position.

Interior argued that continued stock restrictions would infringe on the rights of individual natives who had counted on selling their stock after 1991. Issuance of new stock to young natives born after 1971 would dilute the value of existing shares. Additionally, the most onerous provision contemplated by Congress, the QTE land transfer, threatened to create racial enclaves of dependency, or the reservations that Congress had so clearly rejected in the passage of ANCSA (U.S. Congress, Senate 1987:116–144). Hodel also expressed concern that the federal government might be held liable if dissenting shareholders, or those who preferred to sell their stock, could not exercise their right to be compensated by the corporation. If Congress gave in to the AFN demands, courts might interpret continued stock restrictions as a taking under the Fifth Amendment, and find the federal government obligated to compensate dissenters (ibid.:139–140).

The assimilationists emphasized individual rather than group rights, whether in the legal-constitutional terms by the Department of Interior or in anti-sovereignty terms by recreational groups such as the Alaska Outdoor Council (U.S. Congress, Senate 1986:471–473). From this perspective, ANCSA was a contract that, even if imperfectly implemented, still stands. No amount of criticism or hindsight can or should change its promise to settle land claims forever.

The assimilationists did not believe that the AFN represented or could act on behalf of individual native shareholders. Congress believed otherwise. Most important to Alaska's three men in Washington was evidence of native will. Absent initiative from Alaska Natives, ANCSA could not be changed.

1991: THE POLICY WINDOW

Because the 1991 amendments concerned Alaska only, the native community had to draw on all its resources to capture the attention of Washington lawmakers. They had to start early, mobilizing the villages, educating the general public, consulting with the congressional delegation. Well before the 1991 phase-out drew near, the regional corporations and the AFN went into action, as described above. While they conducted their leadership retreats, meetings, and conventions, they kept Alaska's congressional delegation constantly informed of their progress (Kitka 1991). Legislative staffers attended the special convention in March 1985 and witnessed the debates over, and finally adoption of, the eight resolutions (Agnew 1991; Chapados 1991). With the eight resolutions as a point of departure, the AFN wrote a legislative proposal to amend ANCSA.

Even as the AFN tried to present a unified front to lawmakers, however, it was clear that the tribal sovereignty advocates and the corporate elite did not see eye to eye. The AVCP and other groups representing villages submitted their own legislative proposal to the AFN convention in March, but the AFN did not formally adopt it. While the AFN intended its eighth resolution on the QTE land transfer to offer maximum flexibility to the corporations, the village groups' proposal removed any legal obstacles to Indian country in Alaska. It recognized the secretary of Interior's authority to create reservations in Alaska, described village lands as Indian country, and affirmed the option of tribal control of native lands, including jurisdiction over fish and game (NARF 1985; AVCP 1985a). Despite the efforts of the tribal sovereignty groups, the AFN did not include the provisions explicitly recognizing tribal sovereignty in the legislation proposed to Congress in 1985.

Two issues threatened to kill the efforts to amend ANCSA. First, if the stock restrictions were to continue indefinitely, with corporations required to hold a shareholder vote to end the restrictions, the dissenting shareholders (i.e., those who voted unsuccessfully for unrestricted, alienable stock) deserve compensation. The Department of Interior held firm in this position, with the native community adamantly opposed. Second, the option to transfer land from the corporations to a village government or other qualified transferee entity worried lawmakers and recreational interests. Would such an option carve up Alaska into 200 sovereign jurisdictions that could regulate such things as hunting and fishing and create their own judicial systems? Mandatory dissenters' rights and the QTE surfaced again and again in the turbulent negotiations among natives, departmental and congressional staffs, and outside interests.

The first bill, introduced in both the House and Senate in early 1986, essentially followed the eight resolutions put forward by the AFN special convention. AFN attorneys and staff drafted it, with input from congressional staff. There were major differences, however, between the House and Senate versions by the end of the 99th Congress. Both extended indefinitely the period of stock restrictions for village corporations, with each corporation retaining the right to terminate the restrictions; allowed the corporations to issue new stock to natives born after 1971; and authorized the corporations to transfer land to QTEs, such as village or IRA governments. The Senate bill included mandatory dissenters' rights, where the House bill left it up to the corporations. All native groups opposed mandatory dissenters' rights, since the obligation to pay off minority shareholders would spell financial ruin for most corporations. The Senate bill also required the regional corporations to hold a shareholder vote to extend the stock restrictions. In the House version, such restrictions would be extended automatically, unless a corporation (regional or village) voted otherwise (*Congressional Record*, House 6 October 1986). Finally, the Senate bill contained a comprehensive disclaimer that closed the door on tribal sovereignty or Indian country in Alaska, while the House disclaimer merely claimed neutrality on sovereignty.

The differences between the House and Senate versions reflect both personal beliefs and institutional characteristics. Neither Senator Frank Murkowski nor Senator Stevens, Republicans from Alaska, favored the QTE; if this option were included, it would need a strongly worded disclaimer designed to discourage the courts from recognizing tribal sovereignty in Alaska. In addition, the Senate Committee on Energy and Natural Resources, in 1986 still under Republican leadership, felt compelled to seek administration support and negotiate with the Department of Interior. As a result, mandatory dissenters' rights and the mandatory vote for regional corporations to extend stock restrictions appeared in the Senate version.

Because the Democrats held a majority in the House and the House Interior Committee staff sympathized with the tribal option, the House bill stayed fairly close to the native community's wishes throughout the 99th Congress (Duchineaux 1991). Alaska's only representative, Don Young, ranking minority member of the House Interior Committee, had no objection to giving the native corporations as much flexibility as possible, even if it meant transferring the land to a village or tribal government. Alaska's senators were less inclined to support the QTE.

While the House bill passed without challenge in late 1986, the Senate version never came to a vote. The AFN tried to convince Murkowski and

Stevens to go with the more favorable House bill. Meanwhile, the ANC, representing tribal interests, spurned negotiation with Alaska's senators and appealed to liberal Democrats. With elections drawing near, and 1986 a pivotal year for the Democrats in the Senate, the ANC found a receptive audience. The Democrats wanted as many seats as possible, including Murkowski's, and quietly passed the bill among themselves, holding it anonymously until the session ran out (*Congressional Record*, Senate 9 October 1986; Agnew 1991; Kitka 1991; Sambo 1991).

When the AFN leaders realized Murkowski and Stevens would not accept the more favorable House bill, they brought the Senate version to the annual AFN convention in October 1986. The delegates voted it down, and that signaled the end of the 1991 amendments for the 99th Congress.

With the new year, Murkowski kept his seat, and the same bills appeared in the 100th Congress, with the same differences between the House and Senate in dissenters' rights and methods for extending stock restrictions. The AFN intensified efforts to negotiate away the mandatory dissenters' rights and the mandatory vote on extending stock restrictions. The ANC, meanwhile, lobbied against the comprehensive disclaimer contained in the Stevens and Murkowski bill. Out of necessity, the AFN and the ANC joined forces and submitted an alternative proposal in 1987, one that included the tribal option, optional dissenters' rights, and automatic stock restrictions (U.S. Congress, Senate 1987:159–222).

Stevens and Murkowski did not move, however, and made it clear that the QTE, or the tribal option, stopped them. By this time, the senators had given up on negotiations with the Department of Interior. However, they did not accommodate the tribal advocates either. The comprehensive disclaimer in the Senate bill was odious to the AFN as well, since the organization relied on village-level support for its legitimacy as a representative organization. In the summer of 1987, the AFN's 1991 committee decided to break the logjam. They would sacrifice the QTE if Stevens and Murkowski would get rid of the disclaimer and mandatory dissenters' rights (Kitka 1991). Delegates at the October convention, after a wrenching debate, voted seventy-five to twenty-five to accept the compromise and drop the tribal option (Morehouse 1988:16). This cleared the way for automatic extension of stock restrictions—continued native control over the corporations—and Congress passed the compromise bill in December.

Alaska's only representative, Don Young, accepted the compromise. He was willing to support the tribal option only if the natives clearly desired it, but was not ready to fight for an unpopular cause. The tribal advocates (the ANC) continued to hope for votes among the Democrats, but they did not find a majority willing to oppose the Alaska delegation on an Alaskan issue.

Once the bill passed both houses, the only opposition came from the administration. The Department of Interior recommended a veto, having opposed the automatic extension of stock restrictions in the first place and, if the natives insisted on the continued protections, advocating mandatory dissenters' rights. Senior Interior officials met with Justice Department officials and persuaded them that the constitutional problems with automatic extension of stock restrictions in the absence of dissenters' rights left Justice with no choice but to recommend a presidential veto.

With Interior and Justice opposed to the bill, the AFN and their congressional supporters approached the White House with caution. Ultimately, Senator Stevens made the case to President Ronald Reagan's chief of staff, Howard Baker. Stevens and Baker had been Senate colleagues, and their relationship turned out to be the crucial step to the finish line. After the president signed the 1991 amendments into law in February 1988, people joked that the only person in the administration who supported the bill was the president himself (Agnew 1991).

The 1991 amendments extended indefinitely native control over the corporations, made dissenters' rights optional, and included automatic Land Bank protections for undeveloped lands. The amendments passed despite strong opposition from the administration and conservative interest groups. Two major factors overcame the opposition. First, the Alaska Natives and the Alaskan congressional delegation agreed to move fast, before other interest groups had a chance to realize the opportunity to acquire choice property from failing native corporations. Second, the Alaska Natives conducted their own review of ANCSA at all levels, from the fish camps to the corporate board rooms, and provided this evidence of native will to their allies in Washington. Their evaluations—in the form of discussions, meetings, resolutions, hearings, reports, and publications—testified to the absolute necessity of keeping land under native control. That the 1991 amendments excluded the QTE tribalization option testified to the fear among non-natives that they suddenly would be faced with exclusive and ever-expanding jurisdictions.

EVALUATION, ACCESS, AND RESOURCES

By performing their own evaluations, minority groups can set the agenda for policy revision. As Carol Weiss points out, evaluation is usually commissioned by the agency responsible for the program, not by the recipient population (1987:59). As a result, the evaluator gears the study to the agency's goals and overlooks the recipients' needs. Evaluations almost always find the policies or programs deficient and recommend reforms. Recommended changes, though, seldom include redefinition of the problem or complete overhauls, but rather tinkering with minor mechanisms. Even modest recommendations such as these can languish in the file cabinet and never make it to a decision agenda. As a whole, the evaluation enterprise becomes part and parcel of a pluralist polity of "satisficing," supporting incremental change, if any.

In the case of ANCSA the recipients had enough resources and institutional devices to conduct their own nontraditional evaluations and combine their review of ANCSA with public relations campaigns, goal setting, and finally lobbying. In other words, the Alaska Natives took the threat of land loss in 1991 and turned it into an all-out agenda for action. They took stock of their needs and concerns and translated them into a decision agenda.

This effort came with a price of exposing and exacerbating intra- and inter-group tensions. The AFN and the regional corporations steered their own information gathering in what can only be characterized as a top-down initiative. The disaffected minority, represented first by the United Tribes of Alaska (UTA) and later the Alaska Native Coalition (ANC), stayed closer to the grassroots. The vote to abandon the QTE option cost the AFN the membership of two important village associations: the Tanana Chiefs Conference and the AVCP. These groups returned, however, and in the long run, the internal dissension had some positive effects, including the restructuring of the AFN leadership. The AFN board of directors now includes village representation.

Three distinct efforts to evaluate ANCSA led to the proposed changes on the decision agenda. First, the AFN unleashed both internal and public discussions, with lawyers and consultants on hand to explain the legal and technical issues to the native population and AFN leaders directing numerous workshops and retreats. Second, the Berger hearings gathered the thoughts of Alaska Natives in the villages, transcribing word-for-word their testimony and summarizing those thoughts in the book *Village Journey*. Third, the Interior Department sponsored a status report on ANCSA, but abandoned the evaluation when the findings supported the AFN position. With the Department of Interior's inflexibility and hard-line individualist ideology, the business of generating evidence fell to the Alaska Natives.

The Alaska Natives had two advantages that minority groups often lack: capital and access. As the largest private land owner in Alaska and major participants in the capitalist economy, the native corporations, particularly the regionals, were in one sense no different than other business lobbies seeking tax advantages and property protections. The corporate leaders were willing to pay large sums to keep their assets. They had a sophisticated lobby that maintained regular contact with Washington lawmakers. Ironically, the same law the tribal sovereignty advocates saw as contributing to the destruction of Alaska Native culture allowed the natives to develop the very resources they needed to keep their land.

The tribal interests presented eloquent arguments in favor of converting village corporation land to tribally held land. They lacked AFN's capital and lobbying experience, but managed to get at least part of their proposal on the decision agenda. Unlike the AFN, they wanted an actual redistribution of property, not simply protections. The property would still be in native hands, but its function would be to allow distinct native subsistence cultures to flourish.

Ultimately, the choice was made by Alaska's senators, Stevens and Murkowski. Neither had favored the land transfer provision and, if the natives wanted the 1991 amendments, they had to accept them without the QTE.

Each logic of evaluation—pluralism, elitism, and assimilation—implies a different distribution of power. In pluralism, power is dispersed among groups, shifting over time. In elitism, power is concentrated at the top. In assimilation, much like classic economic theory, the power lies with each rational individual to make a choice. Not surprisingly, the pluralist assessment of ANCSA won acceptance, since it did not threaten existing property arrangements or the powers of state government in Alaska.

CONCLUSION

Despite the promise of ANCSA and the 1991 amendments, the remoteness of markets, lack of resources, and scarcity of capital mean that private sector development for most areas of rural Alaska is impossible. In health, educational attainment, and income, the Alaska Natives continue to fall behind whites. Reliance on public transfer payments is high. The frequency of alcoholism and suicides has alarmed native leaders (AFN 1989).

It is probably true that recognition of the tribal status of Alaska Native villages would not solve the social and economic problems that exist. Nevertheless, in asserting sovereignty, some villages are trying to regain self-sufficiency and heal social pathologies. With the extension of stock restrictions and protection of undeveloped lands for subsistence, the

Alaska Natives removed the pall of 1991 and have now turned to other pressing concerns.

The case of the 1991 amendments shows the importance of two factors in the conduct and presentation of policy evaluations. First, the evaluations emanate from a political, social, and economic *context*. Context involves not only objective characteristics, such as minority group resources, but perhaps more crucial to the acceptance or rejection of the group's evaluative logic, the degree of coincidence between minority and majority ideology. Second, evaluation emerges as part of a group's *strategy*, either as an instrument or result of strategic choices.

The AFN had, by the 1980s, become accepted as the main representative of the Inuit, Indian, and Aleut peoples in Alaska. Its officers and board members maintained regular contact with federal and state officials, both elected and appointed. Once an umbrella group for the regional native organizations that were mobilizing across the state throughout the 1950s and 1960s, the AFN came to be an umbrella association for the regional corporations created to administer the land and settlement money. The AFN's goal during the 1991 efforts resembled that of other corporate lobbyists: the preservation of property and capital. Thus, the AFN did not constitute a threat to the existing order but instead acted as any rational economic actor would have done under similar circumstances.

In such a context, AFN chose a mixture of strategies, beginning with an outside strategy of public meetings, workshops, and media outreach in an effort to build support among the membership and prepare non-native Alaskans for the demands that would follow. Once the organization had the attention of lawmakers, however, it switched to an inside strategy of lobbying.[11] In fact, a major accomplishment of the initial public efforts was to convince congressional leaders that the AFN truly had a native majority crafting the AFN positions, easing the transition to an inside strategy.

The tribal interests, such as the UTA and its successor, the ANC, rejected the business-oriented focus of AFN and presented their demands as social concerns. Theirs was seen as a separatist agenda, however. Not surprisingly, they were confined to an outside strategy, never quite succeeding as insiders.

In short, minority interest groups that enjoy some form of patronage (e.g., among public or private elites), present a preservationist rather than redistributive agenda, and use inside strategies are more likely to have their policy evaluations accepted than those who lack patrons, present a redistributive or otherwise radical agenda, and use outside strategies. This does not negate the important role of the tribal interests, however. To answer the second question posed in the early pages of this chapter, disunity *can* have positive effects in forwarding a minority group agenda if the mainstream or more established subgroup sees potential harm in excluding factions. The tribal interests forced the AFN to include, if not argue vehemently for, the tribal option. If the AFN had openly spurned the tribalists, it would have alienated a good portion of its own membership and hurt its legitimacy in Washington. Furthermore, the tribal option added a third area to the policy space, making AFN's pluralist position seem a middle ground between the extremes of elitism and assimilation.

The third question, the constraints a decision agenda holds for culturally distinct worldviews, has less to do with resources or strategy than with resources and ideology. The Berger hearing transcripts provide valuable insight into what Alaska Natives think of the laws made for them in contrast to their own village practices. Yet the hearings had little impact on policy outcome. *Village Journey*, along with piles of thick ethnographic studies of Alaska Native subsistence cultures, gathers dust as the federal and state governments now prepare hunting and fishing regulations. The fear that the tribal option would lead to enhanced native hunting and fishing rights virtually eliminated that option, since sports and recreation interests remain powerful constituencies in Alaska. The fight over natural resources is connected with belief systems: the Alaska Natives value flexibility, but they seldom see this value reflected in legislation. Instead, laws like ANCSA have transformed aboriginal *rights* into corporate *privilege*. Under a veil of pluralism, the 1991 amendments continue the trend.

NOTES

1. Public Law 100–241, February 3, 1988 (101 Stat. 1788).
2. Public Law 96–487, December 2, 1980 (94 Stat. 2430).
3. 21 U.S. (8 Wheat) 534 (1823).
4. 30 U.S. (5 Pet.) 1 (1831).
5. 31 U.S. (6 Pet.) 515 (1832).
6. *Native Village of Stevens v. Alaska Management & Planning*, 757 p. 2d 32 (Alaska 1988). For a critical discussion of the case, see Kisken (1989).
7. *Native Village of Venetie v. State of Alaska*, 918 F. 2d 797 (1990); *Native Village of Noatak v. Hoffman*, 896 F. 2d 1157 (1990). The Supreme Court reversed the latter decision on grounds other than tribal sovereignty on June 24, 1991. Writing for the majority, Justice Anthony Scalia explicitly refused to consider whether Alaska Native villages qualify as tribes. See 1991 WL 107382.
8. ANCSA revoked all reservations in Alaska except Metlakatla. Metlakatla was established by an 1891 act of Congress, after the missionary William Duncan and a group of Tsimshian Indians from British Columbia obtained permission from President Cleve-

land to move to Alaska's Annette Islands because of a dispute with the Canadian government (Case 1984:16, note 26).

9. The Arctic Slope Native Association, the only regional association voting against ANCSA, objected to the methods by which land and money were allocated (Arctic Slope Native Association 1984).

10. The federal government has since taken over management of fish and game on federal lands, after an Alaskan Supreme Court decision found the state law unconstitutional.

11. For a thorough discussion of inside versus outside strategies see Chapter 6, "Pathways to Influence in American Politics" (Walker 1991).

III

UNITED STATES—STATE
PERSPECTIVE

7

Issue Selection by State Legislative Black Caucuses in the South

Cheryl M. Miller

THE EMERGENCE AND SIGNIFICANCE OF STATE LEGISLATIVE BLACK CAUCUSES

Blacks are serving in state legislatures in unprecedented numbers since the "one person, one vote" judicial decisions of the 1960s and the single-member districting a majority of state legislatures began to adopt in the 1970s (Bullock 1987; Lawson 1985; Thompson 1982). The number of black state legislators increased from 169 to 423 (of 7,466 state seats) from 1970 to 1990 (JCPS 1990:10). Their access to state legislative policy agendas places black legislators in a position to exercise considerable influence in the policy process. One vehicle black state legislators now utilize to maximize their policy influence is legislative black caucuses. Through collective demands and bloc voting, some state legislative black caucuses have become an important factor in some legislative outcomes. Twenty-five of the forty-two states with elected black legislators have such organizations. Nine of the eleven southern states, where 43 percent of black legislators serve, have legislative black caucuses, most dating back to the 1970s (Miller 1990:340).

There is scant research on the processes by which the policy goals of black legislators reach state legislative agendas. As Figure 1 depicts, there are now at least two routes of access many black state legislators have to legislative policy agendas: as individual legislators, and via legislative black caucuses. This latter route is being used by a number of caucuses in advancing legislative policy initiatives desired by or beneficial to blacks. In this chapter we focus on the agenda-setting role of state legislative black caucuses, using Roger Cobb and Charles Elder's definition of institutional agenda status. Success in getting "items explicitly up for active and serious consideration of authoritative [legislative] decision makers" (1983:85) is the minimal role in agenda setting we might expect of a state legislative black caucus (see Figure 1).

The Congressional Black Caucus (CBC), formed in 1969, is the prototype for this type of policy influence by black legislators. Unlike their more visible national counterpart, state legislative black caucuses have not been a focus of scholarly research. There has been little systematic research to frame or test the assumption that state legislative black caucuses attempt and may have some impact on legislative outcomes that affect minorities. Most of the existing research consists of a few state-specific dissertations (Bragg 1979; Colston 1972) or uses aggregated black legislators, not the caucus, as the unit of analysis (Harmel et al. 1983).

In this research we explore two questions regarding the policy role of state legislative black caucuses. First, we examine the types of issues they select and advance, as well as the commonalities of issue areas across caucuses. Second, we assess the import of some situational variables on issue selection.

The insights this research provides are important for several reasons. Given the devolution trend begun under former President Richard Nixon and fine-tuned under Ronald Reagan, the state level is increasingly where the hard policy decisions will be deliberated and made for a host of issues like AIDS, homelessness, education, and economic development. Further,

Figure 1
Two Routes of Access of Black State Legislators to Legislative Policy Agendas

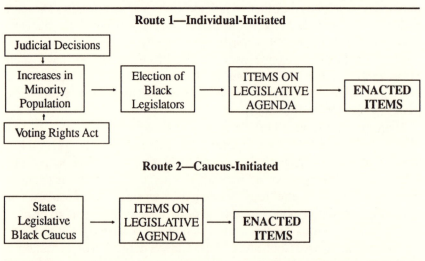

because of recent and chronic revenue shortfalls in numerous states, policy decisions are increasingly being made in a state budget deficit environment. State legislative black caucuses, because of their access to legislative policy agendas, may be in a unique position to advance minority interests in the choices state legislatures make in allocating shrinking resources. As Neal Pierce has observed, "just being 'inside the house' creates an opportunity to influence decisions" (1991:33).

DATA AND METHODS

The caucus is the unit and object of analysis. Southern states were chosen for the research focus because of the prevalence of legislative black caucuses in the South. Black representation approaches or exceeds parity with black population densities in the southern states (JCPS 1990:21).[1] Further, many of the southern states share similar political attributes: a strong tradition of Democratic party dominance in the legislature; recent resurgence of the Republican party; only black Democrats serving in state legislative chambers; dramatic increase in black representation due to creation of single-member districts; and a sizeable black population so that minority policy issues are likely to surface (Black and Black 1987; Bullock 1987). While southern state legislative black caucuses may not be typical of all legislative black caucuses, at the very least, they are representative of an emerging force in getting minority policy issues on legislative agendas in numerous states.

We examine which legislative initiatives several southern state caucuses selected and advanced in one recent legislative session.[2] While it would be desirable to conduct a systematic over-time content analysis of all southern state legislative black caucus agendas, where such agendas are part of a written public record, it would be a vast undertaking. Instead, we obtained information on the legislative policy initiatives of seven southern state legislative black caucuses during the 1987 or 1989 legislative sessions using multiple data collection methods. We utilized chamber- and caucus-compiled information on caucus activities, reviewed committee hearings and roll call votes, and read media accounts.[3] The research states and year of caucus formation are: Arkansas (1979), Florida (1982), Georgia (1967), Maryland (1970), Mississippi (1980), North Carolina (1983), and South Carolina (1975). Table 1 summarizes relevant contextual features of the seven states.

Additionally, we conducted structured in-depth interviews with past and current legislative black caucus leadership in three of the seven states (Georgia, Maryland, and North Carolina).[4] (See Appendix 1.) This re-

Table 1
Black Legislative Representation in Seven Southern States, 1987

State	% Black Voting Age Population	No. in State Legislature	% of State Legislature	Year Caucus Was Formed
Arkansas	12	6	4%	1979
Florida	13	11	7%	1982
Georgia	31	30	13%	1967
Maryland	24	27	14%	1970
Mississippi	33	22	13%	1980
North Carolina	21	17	10%	1983
South Carolina	26	21	12%	1975

Source: Joint Center for Political and Economic Studies, 1990:11–12.

search design had the virtues of sufficient and diverse cases and a time horizon including several data points. The state caucuses chosen for in-depth analysis included: (1) the southern states having the longest (Georgia) and the shortest (North Carolina) experience with a caucus, and (2) two states having about the same length of experience with a caucus (Georgia and Maryland). Interviews were conducted with the first caucus chairperson, the current chairperson (1991 legislative session), and the 1987 legislative session chairpersons. In cases where the initial caucus chairperson was not available for an interview (e.g., by virtue of a move to another state, death) interviews were obtained with the earliest former chairperson possible and/or with a member of the initial caucus still serving in the state legislature.[5] The perceptions of this leadership elite provided a rich source of comparative data on similarities and dissimilarities in caucus issue selection.

THE RANGE AND TYPE OF ISSUES ADVANCED

Two expectations about issue selection were that caucuses might advance a limited number of legislative initiatives in any one legislative session to maximize effectiveness and would choose issues having a clear or targeted benefit to minorities (Miller 1990). Both expectations were confirmed. Data on the issues advanced by southern state legislative black caucuses during two recent (1987 and 1989) legislative sessions reveal a limited repertoire of initiatives which can be categorized into issue areas that focus on minority concerns.

The most obvious and expected commonality among the legislative initiatives listed in Table 2 is their dominant minority-interest focus. The targeted, though not exclusive, beneficiaries of these bills were blacks.

Most of the initiatives have this cast, although the case could be made that several target and would benefit a larger constituency than blacks (e.g., economic development for North Carolina women, employer job tax credits for poor and rural county residents in South Carolina, prohibition of the death penalty for white disadvantaged youth in North Carolina who commit felonies punishable by the death penalty).

Table 2 also reveals a marked similarity in the types of legislative initiatives advanced by the caucuses. Almost all of the enacted and failed legislative initiatives of the seven caucuses can be grouped under five issue areas: (1) minority economic development, (2) increasing the number of black appointed and elected officials, (3) enhancing minority state colleges and universities, (4) judicial system reforms, and (5) provision of human services. In addition to these five categories, we label a sixth category of other legislative initiatives symbolic, to distinguish their essential difference from the kinds of substantive policy initiatives which characterize those items in the first five issue areas. Two issue areas are listed in this category: advancement of a Martin Luther King, Jr., state holiday and anti-apartheid bills.

We note two typologies that attempt to describe the policy impact of black representation. One typology (Button and Scher 1984) compares symbolic and material benefits. A second categorization scheme (Bullock and MacManus 1981) contrasts symbolic versus programmatic representation. The term *substantive* can be substituted for the material and programmatic categories of these two typologies. Substantive impacts refer to new or different policies or laws that benefit blacks in particular (though not necessarily exclusively) and affect the "relative distribution of goods and services to the minority community" (ibid.:366). On the other hand, symbolic impacts "include the psychological, attitudinal, and educational benefits of having blacks in elected office" (Button and Scher 1984:204), are "psychologically liberating" (Lawson 1985:268), but do not guarantee substantive representation (Bullock and MacManus 1981:358).

Although there is not much empirical work to guide the framing of our assumptions, we might expect a state legislative black caucus to focus on substantive rather than symbolic (nonprogrammatic) policy initiatives because of the enhanced bargaining leverage such a focus would afford. We would expect a caucus to use much of its political capital pursuing substantive policy goals having programmatic impact (Pitkin 1967).

The results in Table 2 appear to support this hypothesis. Using a symbolic versus substantive impact conceptual framework, it is apparent that the caucuses' legislative initiatives[6] largely had a substantive focus.

Table 2

Legislative Black Caucus Initiatives of Seven Southern States (1987 or 1989 Legislative Session)[1]

Issue Areas and Their Legislative Initiatives	State and Session	
	1987	1989
I. Items Having a Dominant Substantive Policy Impact		
1. Minority Economic Development		
Minority and women business enterprise bills for three cities[2]	NC	
Department of Transportation 10% set-aside program[3]		NC
Minority economic development funding package		NC
Increased funding for the Maryland Small Business Financing Authority (to increase minority vendors)	MD	
Amend the procurement code to include the services of black professionals		SC
Remove the exemption of the Highway Department from the state's 10% set-aside program		SC
15% minority set-aside law as part of a lottery bill	FL	
$100,000 appropriation for the Federation of Southern Cooperatives (works with poor farmers)	GA	.
10% economic incentives set-aside law[4]	AR	
20% set-aside of annual commodity budgets[4]	MS	
Black land loss bill (provided for sibling sale for tax property sales); Arkansas has highest rate of black land loss[4]	AR	
Employer job tax credits increased (to $1,000 for poor and rural counties)	SC	
2. Increasing the Number of Black Elected and Appointed Officials		
Appointment of blacks to university and community college boards	NC	NC
Superior Court judges election bill to draw 10 minority judicial districts	NC	
Abolish run-off primary[4]	NC	
Establish a 40% plurality as sufficient to avoid a run-off election		NC
Appointments (all firsts) to the State Highway Commission; State Racing Commission; Public Service Commission; circuit and chancery judgeship, Jefferson County	AR	
Ward election system for Little Rock[4]	AR	
Appointment to the State Lottery Commission	FL	
3. Enhancing Minority State Colleges and Universities		
$3 million additional appropriations	NC	
$10 million for capital improvements	NC	
$5 million construction grant (for Morgan State)	MD	
$5 million appropriation (to Morehouse Medical School)	GA	
4. Judicial System Reforms		
Prohibit the death penalty for youths 17 and under[4]	NC	
Bill to allow race of jurors for blacks on trial to be reflective of their percentage in the population		SC

Table 2 (continued)

Issue Areas and Their Legislative Initiatives	State and Session	
	1987	**1989**
5. Provision of Human Services		
Sickle cell newborn screening testing law (the test is coverable by insurance)	AR	
$213 million to indigent health care	FL	
Raise income eligibility for qualifying low-income women and children for Medicaid services	FL	
Expansion of Medicaid services to decrease infant mortality	MS	
Various child health care funding bills	MS	
Child Abuse and Neglect Prevention Act[5]	GA	
Increased prenatal care funding ($450,000)	GA	
100% funding of the AFDC Standard of Need[4]	GA	
II. Items Having a Dominant Symbolic or Educational Policy Impact		
1. Martin Luther King Jr. Holiday		
Creation of a paid holiday	NC	
Creation of a paid state holiday	MS	
Extended the King holiday for another year		FL
Creation of a King holiday[4]	GA	
2. Anti-Apartheid Efforts		
Local Anti-Apartheid Requirements[6]	NC	
South Africa Divestment[7]		NC
South African Divestiture[8]	AR	
South African Divestment[4]	FL	
Reduction in South Africa investment from $320 million to $20 million	FL	
Divestment of all pension funds from institutions doing business in South Africa[4]		GA

[1] A nonexhaustive listing which includes only high-priority caucus items. Also, the table omits local bill initiatives which were caucus-supported but not caucus priorities. States include: Arkansas, Florida, Georgia, Maryland, Mississippi, North Carolina, and South Carolina.

[2] These bills allowed Charlotte, Durham, and Winston-Salem to reject low bids when there is not sufficient participation by minorities and women.

[3] Of projected state highway spending of $9 billion.

[4] Bill was not enacted that session.

[5] Was enacted as a constitutional amendment which 77% of voters approved. Funds will come from a marriage license and divorce fee surcharge.

[6] To allow local governments, if they have an anti-apartheid law, to reject low bids for public contracts if the bidder supports a racist government.

[7] Require the state treasurer to divest of state-owned stock ($20 million) in two companies that did not endorse the Sullivan principles.

[8] Law required state to divest over a four-year period the pension funds invested in South Africa or companies doing business with South Africa.

Most of the initiatives depicted in Table 2 have a dominant substantive policy focus, although a case can be made for a number of the initiatives, like the anti-apartheid legislative items (categorized as symbolic even though reallocation of large sums of money are involved) and appointments to boards and commissions items (categorized as substantive), having both a substantive and symbolic impact. Rufus Browning, Dale Marshall, and David Tabb (1984:157) note the use of appointments to boards and commissions by elected officials to "give at least symbolic representation to groups," but state that such appointments in many cases present significant "opportunity to influence" programs. We concur that such appointments may eventually alter the substantive policies of these governing bodies as well as yield attitudinal benefits.

Table 2's static look at only one or two points in time does not reveal how many of these issue areas have consistently been on the individual agendas of several caucuses. Not only has minority economic development been a focus of caucus initiatives in all seven of the states, but it has been a persistent focus in a number of the states. For example, the Maryland legislative black caucus got a Small Business Development and Financing Administration enacted in 1983 to help minority entrepreneurs secure funds. The following legislative session, a Loan Guarantee Fund was created when the caucus learned that part of the problem was that minority applicants were not able to obtain bank loans. Next session, the caucus got a Surety Guarantee Fund enacted because even after minorities secured loans they could not get the bonding necessary to perform the work. Finally, in 1987, as shown in Table 2, the Maryland caucus added to the law by increasing the pool of money allocated. The same pattern can be recounted in North Carolina; from 1985 through 1991 the North Carolina caucus initiated various minority economic development bills.

Three of the other issue areas reveal the same consistency among the seven state caucuses as that manifested in the minority economic development issue area. Most of the caucuses promoted bills relating to human services provision. Three of the seven state caucuses advanced initiatives in the areas of increasing the number of black appointed and elected officials and enhancing minority state colleges and universities.

Despite the numerical dominance of substantive policy initiatives, symbolic policy goals were a clear focus of caucus efforts in these states. Caucus attention to legislative initiatives having a symbolic dimension may be analogous to CBC advocacy over the last twenty years of what Congressman Charles Rangel has called "conscience" issues (Ruffins 1990). There is indeed a similarity of the symbolic-type issues of Table 2 with some of the CBC-advanced initiatives having a conscience dimension (e.g., recurrent national Martin Luther King, Jr., national holiday bills [finally enacted in 1983] and the 1986 Anti-Apartheid Act imposing economic sanctions) (ibid.).

Clearly, the number of issues with a compelling ideological or conscience dimension which state legislative black caucuses can coalesce behind is limited. Conscience may, however, guide the selection of state caucus initiatives like the King holiday and anti-apartheid sanctions. In referring to Florida's enactment of a King state holiday in 1987, then state senator Carrie Meeks (D-Miami) noted that it "would never have happened if we weren't there" (Holly 1989:1D). Similarly, the North Carolina caucus fought a protracted battle over four legislative sessions before a King holiday bill was enacted in 1987.

ISSUE AREA CONSISTENCY

Interview data from the first and most recent legislative black caucus chairpersons in three states (Georgia, Maryland, and North Carolina) supplement and further support the data of Table 2. All the chairpersons interviewed expressed a similar view of their caucus's role. A kind of intuitive guidance seems to have shaped issue selection in the early years of these state caucuses and continues to do so presently, though less so. This leadership elite sees these caucuses as dually representing all the state's blacks, not just those blacks residing in member districts. They function as a self-selected "reference public" (Lipsky 1968) in translating and activating the demands of a relatively powerless group to the legislative agenda. Further, these caucuses appear to operate proactively and not just in the reactive vein of focusing on blocking legislative agenda items. They seek out policy issues that are of clear concern and benefit to most blacks, like minority economic development and provision of human services. Consistent with this role, throughout their existence, both the Maryland and North Carolina caucuses have held open meetings across the state to solicit the concerns of their states' blacks.

Earlier we noted the continuity in focus of some of the caucus legislative initiatives. One reason for this continuity is pragmatic. Typically, the bulk of initiatives caucuses advance tend to be old items. This is because the success rate of first-time caucus-initiated bills is low. In most cases, bills have to be "softened up" over time for eventual enactment.

Illustratively, former representative Benjamin Brown, who served as chairperson of the Georgia legislative black caucus from its founding in 1968 until 1977, cited affordable housing as an ongoing goal of the Georgia caucus. It took the caucus eight years to get legislation enacted establishing the Georgia Residential Financing Agency. Similarly, the North Carolina legislative black caucus needed four legislative sessions to get the 40 percent Runoff Primary Abolishment bills enacted. Incrementalism prevailed. Abolishing the run-off primary had been a legislative effort of the caucus since 1983. In 1987 the run-off primary bill did not even get out of committee and members acknowledged that the most they could hope for was to build more support for the bill so that eventual enactment would be possible. Indeed, in the 1989 discussions about the advisability of seeking a run-off primary law, the caucus sought a lesser victory. In 1989 a bill to establish 40 percent as the threshold to avoid a runoff primary was enacted.

As is obvious from Table 2, even when new initiatives evolve or arise, the issue areas still show durability as foci of interest. There are a finite number of issue areas of caucus interest. Observations of two Maryland caucus members demonstrate this point. The 1991 Maryland caucus chairperson, delegate Christine Jones, explained the consistency in issue areas succinctly in her assertion that the "issues will remain the same as long as there is a Maryland General Assembly. . . . We are working for the benefit of black people." However, emphases among the various issue areas do and have changed. According to Maryland state senator Larry Young, the early caucus's "mission was to project the black agenda in terms of human resources and civil rights, not so much in economic development." However, in the 1980s the Maryland legislative black caucus focused on getting enacted several landmark minority development set-aside laws.

The five issue areas listed under the substantive policy impact of Table 2 are clearly not inclusive of all the issues that might be targeted by caucuses as having a clear and beneficial interest for blacks. In that regard, an issue area conspicuously absent in Table 2 is that of initiatives relating to improving elementary and secondary education. While most of the caucus chairpersons cited this issue area as one that the caucuses have focused or should focus on, in 1987 such legislative items were not part of the policy goals of the caucuses listed in Table 2.

An external constraint is surfacing which may make the number of issues caucuses take on in the future even more limited and predictable— that of national and state budget deficits. Former four-term Georgia legislative black caucus chairperson Benjamin Brown observed that the "issues that black legislators are addressing are bigger" now and the responsibility of the state is greater as the federal government has retrenched, thus "imposing a greater duty on the legislature to know where the money ought to go and that it gets to where it should go." Current (1991) North Carolina legislative caucus chairperson James Richardson voiced the same sentiment in articulating that the present caucus "goal is to hold things steady, . . . where blacks won't slip back in economic development and medical care."

ASSESSING CRITICAL VARIABLES IN ISSUE SELECTION

Despite the commonality of issues revealed in Table 2, it was noted repeatedly by caucus chairpersons that a legislative black caucus is not a monolithic machine always of one mind or will in discerning what benefits minorities or which initiatives to advance. In earlier research (Miller 1990), we laid out some propositions about possible factors of state legislative black caucus agenda-setting success. We conceptualized two important sets of variables: situational attributes (e.g., caucus size, cohesion, seniority of members) which act as enabling resources in caucus effectiveness, and political skills (e.g., vote trading, procedural use of the rules) caucuses use to advance their policy goals.

In this research we ask, what factors affect the type of issues and legislative initiatives state legislative black caucuses take on? Beyond noting the tendency of these caucuses to advocate legislative initiatives having substantive policy impact, initiatives which primarily fall within the issue domains of minority economic development, increasing the number of black-appointed and elected officials, and the other categories of Table 2, we sought evidence of common factors that may affect issue selection. Based on the insights gained from our interview data, we again note the importance of situational attributes—depicted in Figure 2, factors like caucus size and cohesion, internal leadership, chamber leadership positions, and majority party status. All of the caucus chairpersons interviewed cited several of these factors as affecting issue selection.

For example, both the Maryland and North Carolina legislative black caucuses have varied in the number and type of issues they took on over the 1980s. Caucus willingness to promote legislative initiatives that would be difficult to enact varied with the strength and quality of caucus leadership. Each caucus tended to emulate the chair—if the chair was weak so was the caucus agenda that legislative session. A case in point is how recurrent internal leadership turf struggles between Baltimore City and Prince Georges County members have prevented the Maryland legislative black caucus from uniting behind many issues besides minority economic development.

Figure 2
Factors Affecting Issue Selection

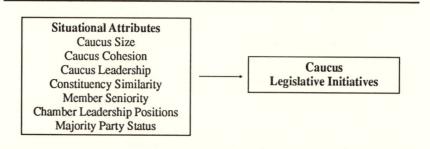

More and more, regional or constituency differences, as well as personal factors, can mitigate issue unity. Without exception, the current caucus chairpersons in Maryland, North Carolina, and Georgia noted that consensus in issue selection is more problematic than it used to be. Besides weak caucus leadership, they cited factors like differences in types of constituencies represented by black legislators and member personal ambition. Even with single-member districting, urban and suburban/rural constituency differences among black legislators in the three states can make issue selection difficult. Consensus building is impeded when the needs of different constituencies cloud the determination of which of the issues that have a clear and tangible benefit for blacks the caucus should coalesce around.

Issues can cut different ways for legislators representing black constituencies from Columbus (suburban/rural constituency) versus Atlanta (urban constituency) in Georgia, or Baltimore (low-income black constituency) versus Prince Georges County (middle-class black constituency) in Maryland. Baltimore blacks need economic development programs, whereas Prince Georges County blacks may have more need of public services and amenities like transportation and community swimming pools.

We can illustrate with examples the importance to issue selection of two of the other situational attributes in Figure 2. First, the importance of leadership positions, especially committee chairmanships, in both the choice and outcome of legislative initiatives cannot be underestimated. According to delegate Curtis Young, 1989–1991 chairperson of the Maryland caucus, "one of the major weaknesses of the caucus is that we have not done well in retaining leadership positions." On the other hand, in its most recent legislative sessions, the North Carolina caucus chose issues based on and benefiting from the "power of the chair." Caucus-enacted initiatives (e.g., the King holiday, 40 percent threshold runoff primary, Superior Court Judges judicial districts) were invariably referred to friendly ports. However, it is more difficult to attain committee chairmanships in Maryland than in North Carolina. There is a smaller pool of chairmanships in Maryland—each member of the legislature can serve on only one standing committee. Thus, in 1991 only one member of the Maryland caucus holds a committee chairmanship, compared to ten of nineteen North Carolina caucus members being appointed by chamber leadership to various strategic chairmanships.

Second, a caucus's relationship to the majority legislative party (as well as to the governor) can affect how ambitious its issue agenda is. The Georgia legislative black caucus, as advocates and a part of former governor Jimmy Carter's progressive coalition during his 1970–1974 gubernatorial tenure, had extraordinary success in moving items it placed on the legislative agenda. This was due to the caucus moving from being a marginal vote to an important nineteen-member voting bloc of the progressive coalition. Another illustration is found in current North Carolina legislative politics. With the resurgence of the Republican party in the North Carolina General Assembly and a sometimes liberal-conservative schism within the Democratic ranks, the North Carolina caucus engages in *quid pro quo* with white legislative Democrats for many of its legislative initiatives in return for its solid bloc vote on some Democratic bills.

However, possession of committee chairmanships and other leadership positions by caucus members can be a double-edged sword because of the divided loyalty that will likely arise. As blacks serve in their state legislatures longer, they harbor the same ambition and have the same opportunity to advance to positions of chamber leadership. This dilemma was observed at the CBC level when Representative William Gray, in his new role of House budget chair, voted against the CBC budget (a caucus practice begun in 1981 which cut military spending to increase social program spending) (Kenworthy 1989:A23). According to Florida representative Jim Burke, fitting into the leadership and serving a black agenda can sometimes conflict. In 1986 when Representative Burke learned he was being considered for president pro tempore, he stated he "began to think about what I was doing and how I was doing it" (Holly 1989:7D). The 1991 North Carolina legislative black caucus lost one of its most effective advancers of caucus initiatives with the election of Representative Daniel Blue, a two-term previous caucus chairperson, to Speaker of the House. Speaker Blue could not take on the same advocacy of caucus legislative initiatives as he could before his election.

CONCLUSION

It is beyond the scope of this chapter to make a systematic comparison of the policy priorities of all state legislative black caucuses with those of other state caucuses to ascertain the general relevance of a substantive versus symbolic framework of analysis. But, Table 2's comparison of the common legislative initiatives of seven state caucuses reveals that the legislative initiatives of many of these caucuses had a dominant substantive policy impact. From the capsule view provided by Table 2, it appears that these selective caucuses placed substantive policy items on their legislative agendas relating to: fostering minority economic development, increasing the number of black elected and appointed officials, enhancing the minority colleges and universities in their states, promoting judicial reforms, and providing human services.

In the two legislative sessions we examined, we found the seven state legislative black caucuses primarily advanced policies having a beneficial impact for blacks (e.g., minority economic development, enhancing historically black colleges and universities). Further, part of their agenda in a number of the states consisted of legislative initiatives having a clear symbolic (attitudinal or educational benefit) dimension. One of the most apparent findings of this research is that there are limits to the number and type of issues caucuses take on in any one session and constraints that circumscribe which issues are advanced. In the latter regard, we highlighted some situational attributes that may set the context for issue selection and enactment success. Finally, we noted the difficulty some caucuses increasingly have in forging a consensus on which issues to take on due to factors like urban-rural constituency cleavages and member ascendancy to leadership positions.

These research findings are probably most relevant to legislative black caucuses in southern states that have similar political attributes, but also offer some generalizability. What is instructive from both our static snapshot (Table 2) and our over-time lens (caucus chairperson interviews) of caucus issue selection that may be more generally relevant to the policy role of state legislative black caucuses? The research findings that the initiatives caucuses advance fall in a limited number of common issue areas and may be constrained by a number of situational variables should be further investigated with longitudinal data and in other states.

APPENDIX 1

Caucus Interviews

State	Name	Title
Georgia	Mr. Benjamin Brown	First Caucus Chairperson, Chairperson 1968 to 1977
Georgia	Rep. Michael Thurmond	1991 Caucus Chairperson
Maryland	Sen. Larry Young	Caucus member, 1975 to the present
Maryland	Delegate Curtis Anderson	1989 Caucus Chair
Maryland	Delegate Christine Jones	1991 Caucus Chair
North Carolina	Speaker Daniel Blue	1987 Caucus Chair
North Carolina	Rep. H. M. Michaux	1989 Caucus Chair
North Carolina	Sen. James Richardson	1991 Caucus Chair
North Carolina	Sen. William Martin	Caucus member, 1983 to the present

NOTES

1. Only three nonsouthern states (Illinois, Michigan, and New York) have state legislatures composed of more than 10 percent black legislators. Eight of the southern state legislatures have percentages ranging from 10 percent to 16 percent black (JCPS 1990:21).

2. This is true for all seven states of this analysis but one. The exception is North Carolina, where we present data on two legislative sessions.

3. For example, the South Carolina legislative black caucus has been publishing *The Forum*, a summary of its legislative goals and victories, for a number of years. We used the usual sources to supplement the on-site data, such as the Library of Congress for local media accounts of caucus activities over the relevant legislative sessions.

4. We utilized written and follow-up phone requests for the interviews. The interviews were taped. As a supplementary source of data, and to gain insights into caucus dynamics, the author sat in on all meetings of the North Carolina legislative black caucus over the 1987 legislative session.

5. The author acknowledges and thanks the American Political Science Association (APSA) for its financial support of this research. The travel expenses necessary for the caucus chairperson interviews were funded by an APSA Small Grant Program award.

6. This research addresses only the legislative agenda focus of caucus activities. Other foci of caucus activities during legislative sessions (e.g., casework/intervention upon constituency request, the planning and execution of caucus fundraisers) were not examined.

8

The Industrial Areas Foundation and the Mexican-American Community in Texas: The Politics of Issue Mobilization

Benjamin Marquez

Neighborhood organizations, their membership, and their ability to create change at the local level have long concerned political scientists. The potential for minority political organizations to achieve lasting social change through the public sphere is an important issue as they pressure city government, enter biracial coalitions, or capture important local political offices (Eisinger 1980, Browning et al. 1984, Preston 1987:chs 7–11; Browning et al. 1990). This chapter examines the political agenda and activities of the Industrial Areas Foundation (IAF) in Mexican-American barrios in Texas, the current locus of Alinsky-style organizing. Representing communities throughout Texas, the IAF has revitalized Saul Alinsky's organizing principles and activist style to gain concessions on issues ranging from street paving to utility rate hikes and property taxes.

The two major questions addressed in this chapter concern the Alinsky style of organizing and whether or not that program can empower minorities to create lasting social and economic change. First, we ask whether the Industrial Areas Foundation network has been able to articulate the needs of the poor and translate them into a viable public policy agenda. In other words, has the IAF brought a set of policy proposals to the formal decision-making stage, received active consideration by public officials, and succeeded in receiving concessions from those public officials? Second, we ask whether or not any of the political successes they have enjoyed can eventually lead to changes in the economic problems facing the Mexican-American community such as poverty and unemployment.

The analytical approach to neighborhood mobilization which has dominated U.S. political science has been the group theory of politics, or pluralism. According to the pluralist school, individuals are independent decision makers who are free to participate in local politics whenever they judge it in their interests to do so. Group membership is overlapping and follows no rigid class pattern, and organizations usually dissipate once the issues that brought the group together are resolved. Even traditionally excluded groups like the poor or racial minorities who are willing to organize, invest their resources in the political process, and are prepared to compromise can have a decisive impact on local policy. Since social inequalities are said to be dispersed and not cumulative, poverty should not be an insurmountable obstacle since readily available political resources such as the vote, intelligence, and commitment can be utilized successfully by insurgent groups.

Political events, most notably the racial conflicts of the 1960s, not only called into question the major tenets of pluralist theory, but spawned a series of radical critiques of pluralism's interpretation of social conflict and political change. The general thrust of these critiques is that pluralist theory takes the capitalist political economy for granted and ignores vast inequalities in power and income in the United States. The elitist school of community power argues that a closed circle of elites have a far-reaching ability to constrain community mobilization efforts. Their social network, access to resources, and allies in decision-making centers give them an advantage rarely matched by neighborhood groups. Furthermore, the reputed power of local elites acts to demoralize the poor, thereby making the initiation of urban insurgency less likely. Neo-Marxist approaches to community decision making expand the critique of pluralism by arguing that the political and economic order is a power relationship in itself, one that works against the initiation of political demands which call for a redistribution of power and wealth. Because of the city's dependence on privately generated wealth, local authorities are predisposed to cooperate with upper-class interests and resist those who challenge the existing order.

For radical urban analysts concerned with minority political power, the relevant task is not only to critique the "apologetic" nature of U.S. pluralism (Kesselman 1983), but to understand the extent to which urban political organizations can increase the political participation of the poor as well as improve their lives. Recent studies of grassroots organizing from this perspective have argued that not only are community organizations growing in strength, but that they hold the potential to democratize local politics. Some authors see community organizations as the primary instruments through which political struggles with the state are waged and the class interests of poor neighborhoods are articulated (Delgado 1986:213). Given this hopeful outlook, the critical question is whether or not that participation can lead to real changes in local economic decision making (Boyte and Evans 1984).

The most far-reaching assertion concerning the power of urban political movements to turn political gains into economic change has been made by Manuel Castells. He argues that urban social movements hold the potential to radically change local and, ultimately, national life. Based on his crossnational study of urban political movements, he found two common trends among urban political groups. First, these insurgent movements challenged local business investment decisions and land use plans which promoted the notion of a city as a place for profit, and where services and space were distributed according to income level. Second, they sought to replace hierarchical political decision making with neighborhood self-management. For him, these groups were reacting to economic and political trends, and proposed an alternative to the interests and values of the dominant classes (1983:318–320). What makes his work unique in urban studies is his insistence that these goals constitute an imperative, a demand that political and economic democracy be implemented if the needs of the poor are to be resolved. He argues that anything less than democratic control of economic decision making would constitute reformism, a mere cosmetic change in a system that needs radical restructuring (ibid.:299).

This chapter demonstrates that, in the relatively short period of time the IAF has been active in Texas, it has successfully introduced a number of political initiatives on the public policy agenda. Since its first organization was established in 1974, the IAF network has confronted local power structures throughout the state and established a reputation as a formidable and aggressive player in local and state politics (Reitzes and Reitzes 1987:119). The network has also scored a number of impressive public policy victories in the areas of public works, education, and water service delivery. However, while it appears that the IAF is slowly altering the political character of the state, it will be argued that their potential to radically alter the economic problems that plague the Mexican-American community is problematic. Not only are the problems facing poor Mexican-Americans tied to national and international economic trends, but Alinsky's (1971) theory of community organizing is based on a conservative political philosophy designed to achieve piecemeal reform. Although Alinsky and his followers advance a populist vision of politics and economic deprivation in the United States, they fail to formulate an explicit political strategy which would counteract economic processes and market-driven decisions in economics.

The IAF's efforts represent a new chapter in the history of political organizing in the Mexican-American community and a departure from the cultural nationalism of the 1960s (Gomez-Quiñones 1978; Barrera 1979, 1985; Muñoz 1989). The IAF network is composed of eleven organizations in eight different cities in Texas including Houston, Fort Worth, San Antonio, El Paso, Austin, and communities in the Rio Grande Valley. Although the network has organized a wide range of neighborhoods throughout the state, the group's membership is largely Mexican-American, the bulk of the poor and powerless in Texas. With their statewide network, organizational skills, and record of success, the IAF represents an important new form of political activism in the Mexican-American community in a state that has a long history of racial conflict (Montejano 1987).

Utilizing the organizing principles of Alinsky (1971), the Industrial Areas Foundation has mobilized the poor and their limited resources in a renewed fight for social justice in Texas. They have brought with them all the earmarks of traditional Alinsky organizations: detailed research on community concerns, the development of umbrella organizations, the involvement of local churches, and the use of full-time professional organizers (Reitzes and Reitzes 1987:238–239). Alinsky-style groups inspire the poor to become involved in politics by organizing around issues that directly affect their lives, issues that the residents themselves have identified as important. A large part of an organizer's job is taken up in interviews with people in neighborhoods to find out who the potential leaders are, what concerns the community, and what will motivate them to act (Boyte 1990). The pattern of political action is to identify a target, a concretely defined embodiment of the causes of a neighborhood problem, and then attack that target with all the resources at the community's disposal (McKnight and Kretzmann 1984). To gain a response from public and private officials, the IAF makes ample use of the harsh confrontational style of politics that gained Saul Alinsky notoriety in the 1950s and 1960s. The acidic denunciations of public or corporate officials who oppose them also serve to involve their members emotionally in the group and to place their opposition in a defensive position (Levine 1973).

Has the Texas IAF network successfully initiated a policy agenda for poor Mexican-Americans? If the minority community is to create successful strategies for social change, it is important to understand how their issues can be translated into formal consideration by public officials (Polsby 1984; Nelson 1984). If the media attention they have received in recent years is a valid indicator, they have clearly articulated the social needs of Mexican-Americans in Texas. However, as Roger Cobb and Charles Elder (1972:85–86) have noted, the "systemic" agenda of legitimate social issues is distinct from the formal agenda, issues which are being given active and serious consideration by authoritative decision makers.

Cobb, Jennie Keith-Ross, and Marc Ross have developed a model through which one can understand the agenda-building process and through which the IAF's political platform and record of achievements can be assessed. They argue that there are four stages which shape all issue careers: initiation, specification, expansion, and entrance. Initiation is where grievances are articulated; specification is where grievances are translated into specific demands; expansion is where widespread support is rallied in order to attract the attention of decision makers; and finally, entrance is where there is movement to the formal agenda, where serious consideration of the issue takes place (1976:127–130).

The IAF's philosophy is one which accepts the challenge of moving their concerns through these stages. Indeed, they claim to prepare their members for a lifetime of political participation. A crucial aspect of IAF politics is the process by which the poor are urged to think about their problems and identify specific solutions to those problems and act upon them. IAF activists see their organizations as training grounds through which democratic principles are learned and practiced. One leader observed that the organization has a commitment to political literacy and that each organization in the IAF network was like a "mini-university" where people learn to participate in the policy-making process (Cortes 1988). Organizers see one of the network's main functions as helping people become part of public life by becoming directly involved in community decision making (Valle 1987). One IAF organizer observed that his organization provided a vehicle "where people learn about public debate and participation . . . politics in its highest form. We agitate and teach people how to act in their interests. Where else does that happen? It doesn't happen in the universities. It doesn't happen in the churches. I don't know where else it occurs. People love it" (Holler 1988).

Although Alinsky recognized the tendency for a political and economic elite to usurp power in U.S. communities, he believed it was within the power of grassroots insurgency to counterbalance their structural advantages. He held a deep faith in political pluralism and the need to protect a multigroup, competitive political system. In other words, established interests are entrenched and powerful, but with the proper organizing efforts, their power could be curbed, and poor people's lives could be transformed. In a classic pluralistic fashion, Alinsky defined power as the ability to act, the successful participation in local, citywide, or national decision making (Reitzes and Reitzes 1987:41). Alinsky-style groups in Texas endorse this approach as they seek to manipulate the political system through use of intelligence, persuasion, confrontation, and the vote. The relevant skill is learning how to hold public officials accountable, how to negotiate.

The IAF's strategy of involving the poor in the political process begins with a consciousness-raising process, one by which individuals are taught to think about their problems and act upon them. A central element of the IAF's organizational strategy is to raise people's expectations about themselves, their families, and their communities (Fisher 1984:149). Through the process of consciousness raising, individuals broaden their concept of the possible and cast off any self-imposed restraints (Obregon 1987). As Maria Luisa Vasquez of The Metropolitan Organization (TMO) in Houston noted, "you sort of relate power to what politicians do to the people, to what the rich do to the poor. I now know darned well that I'd better act on my self interest, politicians and corporations act on theirs all the time" (Boyer 1985). Furthermore, they learn to see themselves as part of a wider community. They are encouraged to look beyond their narrow economic interests and embrace community values such as the well-being of their neighbors and friends, their traditions, and their feelings of dignity and worth (Boyte and Evans 1984:94). "We have been united in one voice," notes one activist. "And when I speak on behalf of the organization. And it's not for me that I speak, but for all the poor people" (Obregon 1987).

Organizers spend a great deal of time speaking with residents of poor neighborhoods before they begin asking individuals to attend meetings or to volunteer their time. Once information about community conditions and resident concerns is collected, then a group is organized around the issues that neighborhood residents have identified. The focus on participation and the need for citizens to become involved in local affairs is part of the IAF's appeal. They try to politically re-educate the people they work with so that they not only see the possibility for social change, but see the necessity for them to become actively involved in the process. One activist recalled that it was the style of persuasion used by IAF activists that involved him in his local organization: "[When it was pointed out] . . . what was happening in the country as far as the family, the condition of American values, what we could do to maintain those values that were being attacked, that was sort of the spark" (Reed 1986). Saul Alinsky's broad and sweeping vision of social change was designed to create a society where people's potentials would be realized, where they could "live in dignity, security, happiness, and peace" (Alinsky 1969:15). The Texas IAF's rhetoric adopts the same tone of alarm and moral condemnation. In a recent statement of their political agenda they argued that

The situation that the IAF Network organizations find today in Texas is one of economic decline that is eating away at the social fabric of our communities. The quality of life is deteriorating for families throughout the state as unemployment grows, school drop out rates soar, neighborhoods deteriorate for lack of public investment, medical care and health resources move beyond the reach of more and more people. Our agenda calls for investment in Texas; in human capital, in social capital, and in technological capabilities. (IAF 1988)

Once Alinsky-style groups have motivated their members to understand their common problems, the next step is to advance to Cobb, Keith-Ross, and Ross's final stages of agenda setting and attract the attention of decision makers and move their demands to the formal decision-making agenda. This is by no means a simple process, but the underlying premise of the IAF's political strategy is that the U.S. political system is malleable enough to accommodate the demands of grassroots groups. The record reveals that they have done quite well in the governmental sphere. With the skills of their professional organizers and a core of dedicated activists, the IAF network has been able to influence local public policy through a combination of unconventional political tactics and an accurate mapping of neighborhood and local power patterns. In San Antonio, Communities Organized for Public Service (COPS) is the oldest IAF organization with the longest record of success. It has won millions of dollars in capital improvement monies, housing, new jobs, and other material benefits for the barrios of San Antonio. Between 1974 and 1981 San Antonio received $178.7 million in federal Community Development Block Grants, where $86 million went to COPS districts and 91 percent of the money was spent on projects favored by the group (Reitzes and Reitzes 1987:123).

The first joint action of the Texas IAF network demonstrated their political clout. In 1984, they acted to pressure the Texas governor to call a special session of the legislature to equalize the distribution of funds for education in the state. In 1984 the legislature passed an appropriations bill which stated that 70 percent of the total state appropriation to education will be distributed equally to all districts. As Donald and Dietrich Reitzes (1987:125) note, their skills and influence were formidable:

COPS and Texas Interfaith leaders spend hundreds of hours in meetings with the governor, lieutenant governor, and key members of the House and Senate. After winning the battle for a special session, Texas Interfaith had thirty days, the maximum legal length of a special session, to "educate the legislators about the issue and its impact on the community." Delegations of Texas Interfaith organizations converged on Austin for rallies and to lobby representatives. Careful planning and coordination brought more than a thousand people to a mass rally to show popular support for the bill and generate favorable public opinion. Later, the rally broke up into small groups to lobby hometown lawmakers. During the period of crucial deliberations, key legislators were visited four or five times a day by Texas Interfaith delegations.

Similar successes have been recorded in other issue areas. In El Paso, the Inter-Religious Sponsoring Organization (EPISO) was instrumental in securing the passage of nine bond issues in El Paso in 1987 which brought $93 million worth of capital improvements to the city, much of which would be spent in Mexican-American areas of the city (EPISO 1987). In 1988, EPISO successfully fought for the creation of the Lower Valley Water District to provide water and sewer service to the growing number of *colonias* (unincorporated subdivisions) outside of El Paso, where an estimated 28,000 Mexican-Americans live without running water and about 53,000 have no sewer service (Applebome 1988; Cook 1988). Activists from the Texas IAF network of organizations spearheaded a drive to obtain state funding to extend water and sewer services throughout Texas. In June 1989, this effort resulted in the passage of the "*colonias* bill," which provided $30 million in general appropriations and cleared the way for bond sales to more than 2,000 Mexican-Americans, and forced the Environmental Protection Agency to cancel its plan to allow private firms to dispose of toxic waste by burning it in ships off the Gulf of Mexico (Acuña 1988:436). While other IAF organizations cannot claim the same degree of success, they too have won concessions from local government and corporations on issues as diverse as insurance premiums, utility rate increases, roads, and property taxes.

More established groups like EPISO, COPS, and Valley Interfaith have attracted the attention of the media and forced local politicians to make them part of the regular decision-making process. IAF groups have also sought to elect public officials sympathetic to their issue agenda. The network has been able to regularly mobilize hundreds and, on occasion, thousands of people for public meetings and voter mobilization drives. Since 1977, in three elections in the five districts served by COPS in San Antonio, thirteen of fifteen candidates most in accord with the group's positions have won election. Henry Cisneros, in his first election to the mayor's office, although not formally endorsed by the organization, benefited from the mobilization of the Latino vote (Lind 1984). In 1984, Valley

Interfaith claimed to have registered 25,000 new voters for that year's presidential election (ibid.). That same year, approximately 21,000 Mexican-Americans were registered to vote through a registration drive conducted by EPISO. The drive produced the largest number of voters registered in the history of El Paso and increased the Mexican-American registration by over 4 percent (Navarro 1986:8). EPISO's fight for the extension of water to the outlying areas of El Paso was only one part of a larger struggle for empowerment of the Mexican-American community, a struggle that the IAF network has taken to the Texas state legislature. The statewide network has sponsored rallies in Austin that have attracted as many as 3,000 people to lobby the legislature on their social service agenda which included education, indigent health care, and aid to families with dependent children (*The Texas Observer*, "Levantando" 1987).

Following Alinsky's dictum that public officials respond to political strength rather than moral appeals, the Texas IAF has won praise from some and grudging respect from others. TMO in Houston has had a pact with mayor Kathy Whitmire committing her to meet with the group on a monthly basis to review progress on their issue agenda (Reitzes and Reitzes 1987:127). In San Antonio, where COPS has established a long record of working both with and against mayor Henry Cisneros, he has always acknowledged their power and influence. In 1988, he stated: "I can say unequivocally, COPS has fundamentally altered the moral tone and the political and physical face of San Antonio. It has also confirmed the judgment of the U.S. Catholic bishops' pastoral letter Economic Justice for All—that one way to overcome poverty is to empower the poor to participate more fully in decisions that affect their lives."

THE LIMITS OF PRESSURE GROUP REFORM

As specified by Cobb, Keith-Ross, and Ross (1976), the Texas IAF network has effectively articulated problems in several Mexican-American communities in Texas, translated them into specific grievances, and brought a number of policy initiatives to the formal decision-making stage. While they have successfully ushered through a number of important public policy initiatives, at this point it is important to ask to what extent these policy initiatives can lead to success in the area of economic development and a redistribution of resources.

Although Cobb, Keith-Ross, and Ross (1976:130–131) try to predict how the characteristics of a group's issue agenda affect its eventual success on the formal policy-making agenda, they do not distinguish between the policy initiatives the IAF has won thus far (public works, education, and water delivery) and the more global issues that concern them such as unemployment and poverty (see Polsby 1984:165–166). There is a growing literature which questions the ability of insurgent organizations to institute populist or redistributive politics through conventional means (Peterson 1981; Swanstrom 1985). These authors argue that the forces shaping the conditions under which low-income minority people live are not under the control of local governments, even governments run by minority regimes. They note the change in the U.S. economy from manufacturing and distribution activities to administration, information, and services has increased the number of problems minorities face and made their resolution prohibitively difficult without a nationally coordinated political and economic program (Browning et al. 1990:226–227; Wilson 1987).

The preceding argument speaks to the problems involved in political organizing and coalition building, but the more relevant critique contained in this literature asserts that it is the free market itself that victimizes minorities and isolates the poor (Logan and Molotch 1987). If insurgent politics is to be ultimately successful in counteracting poverty and powerlessness, a specific program designed to counteract market-driven decisions must be formulated. One charge leveled against Alinsky-style groups is that they are conservative in nature because they do not advocate a restructuring of the economy through political means (Levine 1973). Although Saul Alinsky has been recognized as an organizational genius, his political theorizing has been interpreted as one that leads to compromise and limited social reform. His philosophy of organizing has been criticized as a variation of pluralism that does not prescribe methods by which economic structures that dominate the poor and perpetuate their status can be transformed (Fisher 1984; McKnight and Kretzmann 1984).

At first glance, this criticism seems unfounded. The difficulty of overcoming adverse economic trends and structures presents the single most difficult problem insurgent groups face, and the IAF's political pronouncements are highly critical of the economic status quo. As one member of Valley Interfaith stated: "I want to see enough jobs for everybody that wants to work. I want jobs to be in the [Rio Grande] Valley, not welfare. . . . I want people on assistance to regain their dignity" (Lerma 1988). The lack of a generally accepted position on the political economy by the IAF network of groups is troubling since activists agree on the issues and their severity. One activist summarized the concern of the Texas IAF network when he argued that the United States was becoming "a two tiered society, a lower class and an upper class. We have families where the husband and wife don't see each other. They are working more and more and getting less and less" (Korcsmar 1988).

Social movement could pose a threat to the existing class order by working to restructure the social relations of production by challenging the right of free enterprise to set wages as well as make autonomous production and investment decisions (Wright 1985:ch. 1). However, in the case of the IAF, the biting critique of social institutions implied in its rhetoric does not reflect a radical vision of a future society. Indeed, an elimination or restructuring of the free enterprise system is explicitly rejected by the group. Alinsky himself was a virulent anti-socialist and shunned political ideologies that mapped out specific goals or had clearly articulated theories of economic processes—a central concern if anything other than reform is to be sought. Constructing elaborate theories about the workings of industrial capitalism and the inequalities it generates is not part of the IAF's consciousness-raising process.

The IAF's reformist stance toward the modern industrial state is one reason Alinsky-style groups have worked well with religious institutions. In Texas, it is the Roman Catholic Church that provides a set of moral values as well as spiritual and political guidance to the IAF network (IAF 1978). Activists cite their commitment to Christian principles as one of the major reasons they participate in the IAF network of organizations: "For me it is almost a ministry. . . . We do a lot of scriptural readings, our work is centered on the gospel" (Petry 1988). Some borrow from liberation theology in their analysis of poverty and injustice, but the connection to a more materialist interpretation of economic oppression is not made. Occasionally activists defined the problem in class terms. One organizer asserted: "If you are underprivileged because someone wants to make a profit, you are being oppressed" (Rodriquez 1988). Nevertheless, such views are not widely articulated among Texas IAF activists.

Formal links between local groups and churches are an essential aspect of the Alinsky form of organizing since they provide community organizations with experienced leaders as well as other resources, such as money and office space (Reitzes and Reitzes 1987:52). But the acceptance of these resources can act as a constraint on political activity. As Lawrence Mosqueda (1986:ch. 4) has argued, the historical role of the Catholic Church in the Mexican-American community has been to control or restrain any radical political activity. Isidro Ortiz (1984), in a study of the Alinsky-style group United Neighborhood Organization (UNO), found that not only were the resources of the Catholic Church essential for the survival of the East Los Angeles group, but that the church exerted considerable control over the group's activities. The degree to which the church would support the activities of UNO depended on the political orientation of local bishops as well as the outcome of bureaucratic struggles within the Catholic hierarchy. Even the strong links Alinsky himself established with the Catholic Church were broken because of these disputes. The IAF national headquarters itself was moved from Chicago to New York because of a conflict over goals and tactics between the organizers and a newly installed, conservative Catholic administration in Chicago (Finks 1984).

The question of the church's restrictions on the radical potential of the Texas IAF is academic. The IAF's goals are construed within a tradition of social conservatism and its demands vis-a-vis the question of private property and the market are limited. The first assumption made by the Alinsky school is not that the poor are victims of a class hierarchy or economic imperatives. Rather they assert that people can be motivated by their immediate self-interest and it is the job of the organizer to identify those interests and use them to develop political agendas (Alinsky 1969:13). Alinsky saw neighborhoods as units of "collective consumption" and building effective political groups was, in effect, the building of consumer-oriented interest groups defined by geography (McKnight and Kretzmann 1984:15). Ernesto Cortes, lead organizer for the IAF network, pursues the same line of reasoning when he asks: "What are most of us interested in? Our everyday lives and our families and the schools that our kids go to and the quality of those schools and how much money we have and our real estate and our property" (1986:15). Organizing efforts in the Mexican-American community by IAF organizers begin with this premise, and thousands of hours of one-on-one interviews with residents of barrios in Texas precede any effort to bring individuals into active participation in an Alinsky-style group. While the specific issues found in Texas barrios and poor neighborhoods may vary, the general themes are constant. IAF organizers find that people identify issues such as drainage, utility rates, traffic problems, and other concerns that blight their daily lives as issues that concern them the most. Following Alinsky's admonition to avoid theoretical analysis or debates, IAF organizers do not attempt to make causal links to economic processes that lack immediate importance to their followers or coalition partners (Sekul 1983:176).

Levine (1973) has argued that Alinsky-style organizations get their radical reputation from their confrontational style rather than the content of their political agenda. That is, they demand access to decision-making arenas, vilify public officials who disagree with them, and identify with the plight of the poor all while seeking limited goals. For example, IAF activist Father Armand Matthew notes that "the ministry of the church is to liberate in the name of Jesus Christ." Likewise, the Reverend Virgilio Elizonso appeared to accept the charge that his political philosophy was socialist in nature by stating: "I'd consider it an honor if someone called me [a Marxist] because that would mean I'm doing my job" (Obregon 1987). Nevertheless, other sponsors of the IAF are closer to the mark when they emphasize the limited nature of their goals. Bishop John McCarthy, explaining the support the Galveston-Houston Roman Catholic Archdiocese has given to their local IAF organization, noted that "there is nothing more conservative, nothing more American than these types of organizations" (del Olmo 1983). By conservative, the bishop was arguing that their organization was not questioning the basic social and economic basis of society, but rather was seeking to become an active participant in the decision-making process and to eventually redirect its public policy priorities. Ernesto Cortes, director of the Texas IAF network, observed that "being a radical in the American tradition is about making that framework work" (1988).

Making the system work does not involve questioning its foundations. Edward Chambers, national director of the IAF, has eliminated references to the IAF being "radical" or to "radicalism" of any kind in its program. The network appeals to church or family values and the need for citizens to defend their beliefs actively through participation in local community organizations. Their appeal to traditional values is a strategy designed to broaden the base of community support and allay the fear of middle-class or conservative residents. The IAF clearly supports the free enterprise system, and today the IAF organizations are not fighting for community control but for a broader participation in decision making and an expansion and improvement of city services (Reitzes and Reitzes 1987:115).

Framing political objectives in terms of people's immediate needs limits the universe of the possible. The first question IAF activists ask themselves before deciding to concentrate on a social problem is whether or not it can be changed through the political process. Defining winnable issues is done by making a distinction between what are called "issues or problems." Issues are those problems which can be corrected through conventional pressure group politics. Problems are those structures or processes that are beyond the immediate influence of individual political groups. As one activist put it, "world hunger is a problem, not an issue" (Ceasar 1988). While these terms are open to various interpretations, the IAF defines problems as social trends or economic processes that cannot be resolved through pressure group politics while issues are those concerns which can be resolved through government action. Although Alinsky's legacy is one of forcing local institutions to respond to the needs and concerns of the poor, the processes and assumptions of a free market economy were never brought into question (Boyte and Evans 1984:86). In the end, politics and economics are distinct. As one IAF activist remarked: "You fight issues that are winnable. You have to let some things go. I know that it's hard" (Petry 1988).

DISCUSSION

In the fall of 1988 the IAF network in Texas initiated a campaign to register as many voters as possible in low-income areas for the upcoming presidential election. The campaign was called "sign up and take charge," and eight of the eleven organizations that are part of the network mobilized over 1,950 activists to canvass Mexican-American barrios and get their constituents to vote on election day. The theme was popular sovereignty. The network wanted to strengthen local organizations in order to force the federal government to give a higher priority to such issues as education, health care, and employment. The network was also preparing its members to gain experience so that they could develop leaders who would become involved in politics at the national level. This organizing drive was but one in a series of campaigns that the network has sponsored over the years to gain control of the decision-making process in the Southwest. Thus, Castells's first claim that neighborhood organizations represent a move toward democratization and can successfully acquire a larger say in local policy making is correct. Their efforts are motivated by a recognition that powerful forces opposed them, that government had always been biased toward monied interests, and that politics had been corrupted by money and unaccountable power.

Still, there is a tension in the IAF's analysis of political economy. IAF activists recognize the wide range of economic problems facing the Mexican-American community, yet they do not argue that they are rooted in the imperatives of the free market. Indeed, very little time is spent building theories of politics and the economy. Saul Alinsky rejected ideological schemes because, for him, theoretical understanding implied a belief in basic and immutable truths (Alinsky 1969:xii–xv). Alinsky was action oriented and believed that it was immediate needs, not an appeal to abstract values, that would motivate people to act (Alinsky 1972:72). Furthermore, Alinsky believed his organizers should avoid the dangers of theory and have no more than a blurred vision of a better world. It should be up to the communities they organize to define their own future (Finks 1984:255). To the extent that the IAF network remains true to Alinsky, theory building will not become a central part of their agenda.

The lack of concern with theory is not unique to Alinsky-style organizations. Mark Kann (1983:371) argues that the new urban movements in the United States as yet have no theoretical solutions to concrete problems they face. He characterizes contemporary populist movements as "pioneers in ambivalence" who oppose corporate capitalism but in turn support "human scale" accumulation and ownership, exchange value, and market relations. However, drawing on ambiguous human or community values leaves too much unsaid and many urban organizations may carry conservative or counter-progressive baggage. As Robert Fisher notes, "it is not always clear whose traditions, whose hopes, whose community the new populism supports. Whose traditions are supported for example, when new populist organizations refuse to take a stand on busing, school integration, or abortion?" (1984:140–141). If these problems are ever to be worked out, urban neighborhood organizations must eventually develop long-range goals which address imbalances in a class society, whether they are fighting for a stop sign or for eviction blockage. Otherwise, group victories that win concessions from local government or corporations may deflect more radical possibilities by proving that the existing system "works" by being responsive to poor and working people and, therefore, is in no need of fundamental change (ibid.:162).

The economic dominance of business in any community is a structural feature of the local political economy that the IAF has not adequately addressed. As John McKnight and John Kretzmann (1984:17) have observed, the most difficult challenge to community building is to devise ways to insert local concerns into the equations by which businesses make decisions. In San Antonio, COPS found itself battling economic trends by attempting to pressure local businesses into paying higher wages. COPS fought the local Economic Development Foundation and its campaign to attract business to San Antonio by promoting the city's low wage scales and unorganized labor force. They asked that businesses coming into the city pay a "decent wage" of $15,000 a year for a family to support itself (Boyte 1984:151–152). However admirable this political crusade was, the enormity of the economic problems poor Mexican-Americans face may lie beyond such political pressure. Their economic vulnerability was dramatized in 1983 when a freezing storm put 20,000 farm workers out of work in the Rio Grande Valley, an IAF stronghold. Robert Marel (1989:57) summarized the impact of the storm:

It is estimated that more than 7,000 jobs have been lost for the next several years, and that 3,000 to 4,000 jobs have been permanently lost because the new, smaller groves will require less manual labor.

Prior to the Big Freeze the Valley's unemployment rates were among the highest in the United States, but after the Freeze unemployment soared even higher. The McAllen-Edenburg Pharr MSA site of the majority of citrus groves, registered the highest unemployment rate (19%) of any area in the United States in 1984. Cameron County was only a few rankings behind Hidalgo County.

Valley Interfaith lobbied the Reagan Administration for a $66.7 million public works project to provide jobs in the hardest hit areas, but despite the crisis atmosphere and their efforts to sway the president, their request was denied (Lind 1984).

The political victories and public recognition achieved by the IAF have galvanized the network in Mexican-American barrios throughout Texas. Yet there are limits to social change through IAF-sponsored tactics and political maneuvering. Carl Boggs, a political activist who has worked with groups like the Texas IAF, observes that the main failing of insurgent neighborhood groups is that they fail to spell out the class content and political form of the challenge they pose to corporate structures. There is no critical or transformative approach to power relations or domination, and neither the workings of the free market nor the legitimacy of existing institutions is questioned. He further argues that the aggressive new populist critique of the free market's excesses never questions the logic of accumulation itself (1983:359).

By confining political activity to legitimate institutions, the new populism is forced to define what is possible strictly in conventional normative terms. This observation is a critical one since Boggs asserts that, without a concrete plan to challenge material interests embedded in capitalist property relations, they are likely to fail in their efforts to permanently transform the lives of the poor. This theme is echoed by Henry Flores (1989), who found that, in San Antonio where the IAF has experienced its most spectacular successes, the relationship between business and government has always been an unequal one. In this activist city, where grassroots organizing had yielded millions of dollars in projects for Mexican-American neighborhoods, private interests continue to exercise a free hand when making investment and production decisions.

CONCLUSION

The record reveals that the IAF has articulated the needs of the poor and translated them into a successful public policy agenda. Following the pattern outlined by Cobb, Keith-Ross, and Ross (1976), IAF-affiliated organizations have brought a series of crucial problems to the formal decision-making stage of government and can claim credit for policy changes in a wide range of issue areas. Public works, property taxes, and education are areas in which the IAF network has had a profound influence. Although the network has focused on smaller, more manageable issues, it has won many political victories on behalf of the Mexican-American community and improved the lives of thousands of people in Texas. Thus, the ability of the IAF to expand the participation of the poor in the democratic process is real. The IAF network has fought its way into the policy-making agenda following the traditional pluralist criteria of organization, resource mobilization, and coalition building.

While the IAF has experienced a degree of success in the governmental field, can these reforms lead to changes in the larger economic problems that Mexican-Americans face? On this count there is reason to doubt that it can. First, one must take into account the extraordinary effort the poor must exert when participating in the policy process in the first place. The constant uphill political battles the IAF has fought on behalf of poor Mexican-Americans have mired them in years of conflict and compromise. Even when local IAF affiliate groups have established themselves as a force to contend with in local politics, they have not been accepted as part of the local political establishment. For example, El Paso mayor Jonathan Rogers did not acknowledge the role that EPISO played in bringing water to the *colonias* and publicly stated that "in my opinion, they were not a factor at all" (Cook 1988).

Even in IAF strongholds, local politicians have successfully rebuffed the network's demands. San Antonio mayor Henry Cisneros fought COPS over the issue of a domed stadium which would be paid for with an increase in the sales tax. Cisneros took the position that the sports stadium would promote economic growth in the city, while COPS felt that the poor would be paying for the project while other needs such as housing and education were neglected (Hagerty 1987). The debate reached such an acrimonious level that Cisneros openly declared he was ending his relationship with the group because of the "personal abuse" they heaped on him when fighting the proposal (Martinez 1987). That break from their former ally cost COPS much of their political capital when the mayor eventually prevailed and the referendum on the domed stadium won in the 1989 referendum. With the backing of the business community, whose extensive media campaign promoted the initiative, Cisneros was able to hand the IAF a major defeat. Ironically, it was the Mexican-American precincts, heavily canvassed by COPS, that carried the vote for the mayor (Flores 1989).

There is also reason to believe that lobbying local governmental officials and business elites may yield palpable reforms, but long-term structural change may lie beyond the grasp of neighborhood insurgency. Issues such as educational reform will pay long-term economic benefits to the Mexican-American community, but the issues addressed by the IAF have not confronted the fundamental economic disadvantages minorities must confront on a day-to-day basis. As the radical school of community power suggests, the economic order itself is a power relationship, one that works against the redistribution of wealth and power. Indeed, the depressed economic system along the Texas-Mexico border continues to generate new economic hardships faster than the IAF has been able to generate solutions for them.

A case in point is the issue of water service delivery. The campaign that EPISO initiated to bring water to El Paso's *colonias* was accomplished by an entire decade of laborious effort, a period in which their problems grew exponentially. An estimated 185,000 poor Mexican-Americans live in *colonias* from California to the lower Rio Grande Valley of Texas (Applebome 1988). Poverty, substandard housing, and a lack of water are manifestations of economic processes along the U.S.-Mexico border which generate low incomes, a labor market glut, and high unemployment (Briggs 1984:ch. 7). By the late 1970s, the *colonias* in El Paso were growing at a ten-year rate of 200 percent, exceeding the rate of such subdivisions across the border in Juarez (Maraniss 1987). These settlements were so unregulated that when an engineering firm was hired by the state in 1987 to assess water needs, six weeks were needed to find and list the 435 *colonias* in three counties (Morris 1989). Although the new water and sewer services will dramatically improve the health and well-being of the *colonias'* residents, poverty and the underlying processes that create it have continued unabated. Even the redistributive effects of the water plan are minimal. The ten-year battle created a water district which would have to fund between $60 and $70 million in water and sewer pipe construction, as well as legal and environmental requirements in one of the most property-poor districts in Texas. And once construction is completed, each family will be charged an average of $1,500 for a first-time hookup (Rocha 1989).

The link between such issues as water service delivery and the task of influencing the market in matters such as jobs, wages, training programs, and investment has not been explored by the new Alinsky organizations. IAF activists and liberal public officials claimed that extension of water and sewer services to the *colonias* would help residents "pull themselves out of the cycle of poverty," but it is not clear what steps would have to be taken in order for that change to occur (Applebome 1988; Morris 1989). In fact, the reforms initiated by the IAF network have resulted in some negative consequences for their low-income constituents. The El Paso County government had to adopt strict new subdivision rules that govern sewage and water supply systems, paved roads, curbs, and gutters in order to be eligible for a portion of the $100 million in help state legislatures earmarked to aid the *colonias*. These regulations, designed to ensure sanitary conditions in the *colonias* and protect residents from unscrupulous developers, will result in driving the price of land up and thereby crowding the poor out of another source of low-cost housing. As Maureen Hilton, a lawyer for the county, commented, "it's really a choice between two evils. Are you going to have a clean environment and not have people dying of hepatitis, or are you going to stop giving housing to the poor? You can't win either way" (Bezick 1990).

Freeing people from the daily burden of securing clean water will allow them to focus their energy on self-improvement, but the economic constraints that pushed them to live in the substandard unincorporated areas continue unabated. For all their strident rhetoric, the Texas IAF network has yet to directly confront the question of private property and a free market economy and how its functioning relates to the problem of poverty. If the political and economic system directs the IAF from one issue to another without confronting its source, Saul Alinsky's strategy of community mobilization methods may be inadequate to counteract national and international trends that are creating unemployment and a declining standard of living in the United States. The network's faith in political pluralism is strong, but it is not evident what the limits of interest group politics may be or how one may distinguish between solvable "issues" and unsolvable "problems."

In sum, the IAF's success in the world of pressure group politics has not translated into the ability to alter their constituents' structural disadvantages. What has been revealed in this chapter is that the successful initiation of an issue agenda can be accomplished without threatening existing hierarchies of wealth and power. Pluralism's prescriptions for agenda setting and social change poorly reflect the problematic nature of politics among the poor and dispossessed. Likewise, Castells's (1983) claim that insurgent organizations represent a force that will eventually transform local politics takes few of these barriers into account. A more likely interpretation of the IAF record is one which reveals the limits of urban political change. The network will continue to organize in communities throughout the state and it is likely that they will experience further successes in the public arena. However, the widespread changes anticipated by scholars and activists alike will be difficult to achieve. The barriers to fundamental social change are firmly entrenched and the resources the poor are able to mobilize are meager in the face of the market's ability to make investment and production decisions that have far-reaching implications for the Mexican-American community. In the end, the activities of the IAF in Texas may lead to a more pluralistic public order, but it will be one "whose future is stamped by the logic, rules, and legally protected power of capitalism" (Plotkin 1983:157).

Saul Alinsky himself offered no solution to these questions, yet implicitly recognized that real change in the lives of the poor required far more than increased political democratization. As he wrote: "The Back of the Yards Council at the zenith of its power could not deal with its most pressing problem of its time, the issue of widespread unemployment, until our whole economy boomed as a result of world developments" (Alinsky 1969:225). Luther Jones, an El Paso County executive, who has worked extensively with EPISO on the issue of water for the *colonias*, has noted the same dilemma facing IAF activists and their reform style of politics: "There are immense problems along the border that El Paso didn't cause and can't control. We can get these people water, but we're not going to solve poverty" (Applebome 1988).

9

State of New York Minority Internship Program: Avenue to Gaining Access in the Public Policy Arena

Carl E. Meacham

The enactment of the 1965 Voting Rights Act symbolized an important benchmark in the struggle of racial minorities in the United States to gain equal access to the policy-making agenda. No longer confronted with discriminatory state voter registration laws and procedures, they registered to vote in large numbers, and elected to office blacks and Hispanics, particularly in southern states where they had been generally denied the ballot and representation for almost a century. Over 6,000 members of racial minority groups held elected offices in 1988, compared to less than 500 before 1965 (Williams 1982; Stanley and Niemi 1990). During this same period, the racial makeup of state legislatures, for example, went from a few in eastern and midwestern states to 400 blacks and 123 Hispanics throughout the country (Stanley and Niemi 1990:369). Scores of minorities became mayors; hundreds were elected to city councils and school boards.

Their entrance into electoral politics, however, was only an important initial step. This achieved, M. Margaret Conway suggests, a representation of their political views; for example, legislators vote "in accordance with the views of the majority in the represented district" (1991:179). While this type of representation satisfies the represented demand to have their views heard in the legislative arena, it does not necessarily lead to a consideration of their long-term interests. This can only be accomplished with the adoption and implementation of statutes aimed at translating representation into policy outcomes beneficial to them. But, if the statutes are not appropriately implemented by public executives (that is, providing services and channeling benefits to the representatives' constituents), representation remains, at best, symbolic. It is this avenue of the public policy process, *implementation*, to which racial minorities have traditionally experienced the most difficulty in gaining access. In this regard, two barriers are important to point out: statutes protecting the employment "rights" of civil servants, and an absence of a large pool of qualified minority applicants seeking careers in the public service.

Numerous solutions have been proffered to overcome these barriers. Some have been met with resistance, such as ignoring seniority rights in laying off workers, while others, such as providing training programs for minority employees seeking promotions, have been supported. All are designed to ensure a continuous minority presence in the "permanent government," making certain minority citizens' long-term interests are recognized by public officials. This concern has been a prime motivation behind persistent efforts by minority state legislators to expand the pool of minority applicants seeking careers in the public service. This chapter focuses on one of those initiatives: the Minority Public Policy Internship Program (MPPIP), created by the New York state legislature at the urging of African- and Hispanic-American legislators in 1987.

In this chapter, I argue that programs like the MPPIP are excellent vehicles to facilitate minority access to all phases of the agenda-building process. Although the program was initiated in New York State, the circumstances surrounding its creation were not peculiar to New York: minorities in every state have limited access to the systemic and institutional agendas. Lessons learned from the New York experience can be transferred to other, similarly populated states; how the program is implemented necessarily varies depending on the level of political commitment and resources. An important task, nevertheless, is to identify a conceptual framework which allows the New York model to be considered from a broader public policy perspective.

A conceptual framework which takes into account the role of race in political participation and agenda building is the most appropriate. Such a framework allows for an analysis of the extent to which notions about race, prevalent in the general society, have either impeded or facilitated minority participation in every part of the political system over time. As racial barriers to electoral politics have been lowered, resulting in increased minority representation in the legislative arena, similar changes have occurred in the bureaucracy. The ability of minorities to influence the development of both the systemic and institutional agenda has been enhanced. The creation and implementation of the MPPIP was directly related to declining majority resistance to minority political participation. Discontinued after three years of operation, the program's initiation and implementation, nonetheless, provide sufficient experience from which to draw relevant conclusions about the impact this effort has on or has had on racial minorities gaining access to all phases of the public policy agenda-building process.

A CONCEPTUAL FRAMEWORK FOR EXAMINING MINORITY ACCESS TO THE PUBLIC POLICY ARENA

A number of comprehensive theoretical frameworks have been advanced to guide the investigation of participation in the U.S. political system. However, most fail to take into account the issue of race and politics, and disregard the dynamics of U.S. racial public policy and the extent to which this phenomenon impacts on political participation in a pluralistic society. David Easton's (1965, 1971) pioneering works, for example, on political analysis "raised, at least, peripherally, problems of agenda-building" in the political system (Cobb and Elder 1983:18). But, his emphasis on the interplay and interrelations of various systems incorrectly assumes that all groups of citizens are potential participants regardless of race. Implicit in Easton's scheme is the importance of the group's relative political power status in the community and how that group competes with others for political benefits. Easton's *general systems approach* is appropriate to guide investigations in which race is not considered a factor. It is not applicable in this examination because it fails to take into account the dynamics of race and politics in the U.S. political system, and by inference, also ignores the participants' race as a factor in the agenda-building process.

By considering racism as a factor, other approaches have been advanced to overcome the inherent constraints of the system's approach. Marguerite Barnett (1976:7), for example, asserts that "(t)he theory of institutional racism presents the most popular analysis of racial public policy failure and the low political payoffs received by blacks for political participation." Briefly described by Edward Greenberg, Neal Milner, and David Olson (1974:14) as "those practices built into the ongoing process of institutions that, perhaps through no intent of the people involved, serve to exclude or disadvantage members of minority racial or cultural groups," the approach, on closer examination, while not as constraining as Easton's model, is inadequate in placing the issue of race and politics in the appropriate perspective.

According to Barnett (1976:6), the model is not useful in explaining the race/politics dilemma because "it fails to articulate, explain, and analyze the complex linkages between historical patterns of racism and discrimination and present public policies." Primarily descriptive, it fails to take into account the changing level of racism over time, and the subsequent impact on the degree of accessibility of racial minorities to the agenda-building process. For example, during Reconstruction, and more recently during the 1960s, blacks gained limited access to the systemic agenda in spite of racism. Finally, the institutional racism model does not provide an appropriate framework useful for analyzing the impact minority public managers have on altering the racist behavior of some white public managers over time. In other words, the model assumes that racism is ingrained in the society and its institutions; because of this, substantive change will not occur. A convincing argument is made by Barnett for dismissing this model as inappropriate for examining minority political participation in the context of the U.S. political system. Other conceptual frameworks, like the *ethnic group model*, also are of limited value in reconciling this theoretical dilemma.

Milton Morris (1975:10), for example, has questioned correctly whether "the black experience" can be treated "as part of the ethnic group experience in the United States." To apply this model the assumption must be made, *a priori*, that racial minorities have been permitted to follow the same path toward acquiring political acceptability as immigrants from eastern and southern Europe. Similar to Easton's general systems model, the ethnic group model ignores race as a factor in political participation, and, therefore, is useless in any investigation focusing on the issue of race and politics. Other less popular models, although far from flawless, may offer a way out of this theoretical quagmire.

Approaches advanced by Morris (1975), Jewell Prestage (1968), and Hanes Walton (1972) are useful because they take into account the issue of race and politics in the broader context of participation in the U.S. political system. Morris (1975:42), for example, suggests some use the *comparative approach* because it identifies and clarifies "the pattern of subordinate-superordinate relations which characterizes black-white relations in the society and the basic thrust of black political activities in relationship to this status ordering," and "it suggests an underlying consistency and sense of direction to black political activities." Further,

> although it recognizes and emphasizes important differences between the present conditions of life for black Americans and Africans in South Africa, the study attempts to emphasize the fundamental similarity in status of non-white populations in these societies as well as virtually all other societies of similar racial composition. Third, a brief comparison of the struggle in both societies to achieve fundamental change in pattern of race relations permits us to identify some of these characteristics of the societies that facilitate or obstruct change. (Ibid.:42)

Moreover, Morris maintains the approach is useful to some because

not only can it substantially increase awareness of the scope and complexity of race relations and racial conflict, but by elevating the level at which these issues are examined it can considerably enhance our understanding of the impact of race on politics. (Ibid.:26)

While the comparative approach has obvious strengths because it takes into account the subordinate-superordinate relationship between blacks and whites, and considers race an important variable, it is primarily descriptive and disregards the changing political relationship between the two groups over time. This latter factor cannot be ignored, since the struggle by blacks to become involved in the political mainstream has resulted in marginal economic and political gains, as well as acceptance by whites that their political demands are legitimate, and thus deserve to be considered in the formulation of public policy.

A conceptual framework, then, which takes into account race as well as the evolving and changing political relationship between blacks and whites is the most appropriate to use in the mini-case study highlighted in this chapter. The *developmental approach* fits more accurately than other models. Intended for examining black participation in electoral and nonelectoral processes, the model also can be used in analyzing increasing black access to the policy-making agenda in the bureaucracy. The discussion below illuminates this conclusion.

Prestage recognized its utility in studying black politics in 1968 and Walton expanded on its efficacy in his book *Black Politics: A Theoretical and Structural Analysis* (1972). In essence, the developmental approach identifies and clarifies the evolutionary changes in the white population's racial attitudes, and the extent to which the changes impact on black political participation. Walton asserts, "Conceptual frameworks that used electoral participation to inquire into black politics have rendered partial, incomplete, and inadequate analysis" (1972:10). He further maintains that "the nature of segregation and the manner in which it differs not only in different localities but within a locality have caused black people to employ political activities, methods, and devices that would advance their policy preferences" (ibid.:11). This has entailed civil disobedience, coalition building with whites, and bloc voting. These activities support his conclusion that "*black politics is a function of the particular brand of segregation found in different environments in which blacks find themselves*" (ibid.). Activities, methods, and devices used to gain access to the agenda and obtain policy objectives depend on the existing intensity of segregation and racism.

Walton has identified four stages in the development of black political participation as blacks have sought to take advantage of evolutionary positive changes in their relationship with whites: (1) nonparticipation, (2) limited participation, (3) moderate participation, and (4) full participation. One stage does not necessarily precede or preclude another because participation depends on the extent to which segregation, *de facto* or *de jure,* is enforced by political and economic decision makers. In sum, exclusion, presumably by custom and law, of blacks from the political system is categorized as nonparticipation; limited participation is characterized by inclusion of a few; moderate participation occurs when more than 50 percent of blacks eligible to vote enter the political arena, and as a result secure the consideration of their items on the political agenda while at the same time witnessing the inclusion of blacks in public executive positions; and full participation denotes the complete mobilization of blacks "in acting upon the political process to translate their choices into public policy" (ibid.:15). In this final stage, blacks gain unobstructed access to all phases of the policy-making agenda.

The significant utility of the developmental approach is twofold: (1) segregation is considered the dominant variable in the model, and (2) implicit in the model is the extent to which segregation has been used to limit black participation in the political system. Walton does not argue that segregation is synonymous with racism, but this does not appear to be an inappropriate inference to draw based on Walton's analysis. To restate the obvious: as racism declines in a particular geographic region, racial minorities increase participation in all areas and phases of the system, and reap benefits proportionate to the level of involvement. They benefit by gaining increased access to the policy-making agenda: they may be appointed to public executive positions where they implement policies often related to the legitimate interests of racial minorities. When these interests are recognized for the first time, and, more importantly, acted upon, many may conclude that progress has occurred between blacks and whites in the political system. In other words, segregation or racism has declined.

While the developmental approach best describes and explains the extent to which racial minorities enter the political mainstream by first securing the vote, getting elected to office, and acquiring positions in the public service, its pitfalls should not be overlooked. They underscore the phenomenological difficulties of grappling with the issue of race and politics in the pluralistic U.S. political system. In using this conceptual approach, the most blatant pitfall cannot be easily overcome because the twin factors of race and racism pervade any analysis of racial minority participation in any phase of the political system. Institutional racism is not explained or accounted for in this model. Its overt presence or latency appears to be a permanent fixture of the political system, making it practically impossible for blacks to achieve full political participation. All avenues are not closed, but entry is restricted and limited because the majority population must accede to requests, pressure, and so on, from minorities to gain access to the avenues; the majority has shown only a sporadic willingness to allow unlimited entry and access to *all* avenues. Nonetheless, despite its pitfalls, the developmental approach best explains the extent to which racial minorities enter the political system and gain access to additional avenues of the public policy agenda over time.

The developmental approach set out above presents a conceptual framework for assessing minority participation in all phases of the political system. Initially advanced to explain changes in the electoral and nonelectoral processes, like lobbying, but since minority participation in all phases of the political system is driven by the intensity of majority resistance, this approach best explains the process by which minorities gain access to additional avenues of the public policy agenda.

Prior to highlighting the MPPIP as an example of another brief yet positive step in black political development, it is useful to place its establishment in a broad political-historical context. Its initiation relates to the evolutionary and gradual elimination of racial barriers to black political participation throughout the political system, especially in the bureaucracy.

OVERVIEW OF AGENDA BUILDING AND IMPORTANCE OF MINORITY PUBLIC MANAGERS IN THIS PROCESS

Unquestionably, opportunities have been provided for newly elected minority lawmakers, along with appointed minority officials, to influence the setting of the systemic and institutional agendas. For the first time in this century, political leaders have begun to address seriously policy preferences of their minority constituents—improved fire and police protection, greater spending on social service programs, and so on (Campbell and Feagin 1975; Keech 1968; Karnig and Welch 1980). All too often, however, the implementation of these programs by the bureaucracies has been deliberately obstructed or ignored for a variety of reasons including lack of personnel, duplication of effort, inadequate funding, bureaucratic inertia, and opposition from powerful interest groups. Few political leaders, for example, have dared to tamper with protective merit and seniority-related statutes as a means of exerting pressure on public executives to implement policies relevant to long-term minority interests. To pursue such a course of action would put in danger the implementation of more desired policies. Contributing to this dilemma is public employee union opposition to revising statutes designed to protect seniority rights they consider sacrosanct (Wurf 1974).

Together with the historical exclusion of minorities from the public service through custom as well as statute, the protective legislation under-scores the enormity of existing barriers preventing minorities from gaining access to all stages of the political system. Success in electoral politics and securing important appointed positions have not guaranteed minorities equal access to the agenda-building process in all governmental institu-tions, especially in the bureaucracy. Denied access to the agenda-building process in the bureaucracy means the anticipated significant shift in the balance of political power in the long run, combined with electoral successes, cannot occur unless concerted strategies are initiated to change the racial makeup of the public management corps, or at least their perceived racial attitudes. Anecdotal evidence, as well as a number of studies, for example, shows that white bureaucrats' views on race are largely negative (Wynia 1974). Considering the difficulties of changing attitudes, the easier concerted strategy to pursue is to "desegregate" the public service with capable, professional minorities who share similar policy concerns as minority officeholders, and who can be relied upon to use their influence to retain items of interest to minorities on their agenda. They have the ability to be pivotal actors in contributing to the significant role bureaucracies play in translating policy preferences into action when they are items on the institutional agenda.

In the development and implementation of public policies, it is well known that public executives play crucial roles, from recognizing issues to placing items on the agendas in the executive and legislative branches. Their expertise, experience, and knowledge are exploited, and used to guide the behavior of political leaders. Legislatures delegate significant powers to them and, through the use of discretionary authority, they make public policy by deciding the appropriate courses of action to take. Their influence is further enhanced by their alliances and close association with powerful interest groups and key legislative staff in policy development and implementation (Selznick 1949; Lineberry 1977).

Minority public managers, a small but growing cadre, have only re-cently been included in these "iron triangles" or "sub-governments." As majority resistance to minority participation in all stages of the political system declines, this cadre is bound to increase accordingly. Because key legislative staff and interest groups play significant roles in issue recognition, agenda building, and blocking changes in existing public policies, minority public managers have no choice except to seek to cultivate their associations with them. However, even as majority resistance to minority participation in electoral politics and the public service declines, other participants in the agenda-building process, although outside of government, may undermine the effectiveness of both minority elected officials and by extension, minority public managers. This spoiling role is played all too frequently by the mass media.

Scholars and government officials alike often portray the media "as powerful agenda setters" (Kingdon 1984:61). They publicize issues, making policy makers aware of what citizens consider important. They may also persuade policy makers to place issues on their agendas. A television story on a community concern, for example, can lead to the quick consideration of the issue by policy makers. Whether in Washington or Waterloo, the power of the media on agenda building is enormous. To wit, it is not surprising that minority organizations or erstwhile minority leaders attempt to use the media to publicize their causes. But issues of concern to minority communities, such as street crimes or muggings, only receive intensive media attention when violence results; community action to prevent crime and bring the problem to policy makers are often ignored.

That big city newspapers, national television networks, and local media employ few journalists sensitive to minority concerns or minorities enhances the public perception that minorities only create problems and have little interest in putting forward solutions (Jones 1991). This perception seems to confirm the generalization that "blacks are external to the American ideological system and not effectively integrated into the political system" (Barnett 1976:13), and are not interested in contributing to the improvement of society. In reality, the reverse is the case.

Minorities have taken advantage of federal statutes, enacted as a result of protests and declining majority resistance to minority participation in electoral politics, to open other avenues for their constituents to influence the makeup of the policy-making agenda. While the election of minorities facilitates the inclusion of items on the systemic agenda, their slow progress in gaining access to bureaucratic jobs, and even slower progress in obtaining public management positions, make it difficult for them to include and sustain items of interest on the institutional agenda.

According to a number of studies, minority gains in electoral politics, although not extremely dramatic since 1965, suggest that elected minority officials have had an impact on the policy output of government. Minorities have increased their access to the public policy agenda in general, and have sparked the enactment of programs beneficial to their constituents. For example, "Several studies of black mayors in both southern and non-southern jurisdictions suggest that their election has had an effect on the policy outputs of city government" (Conway 1991:183). Moreover, "(o)ne study has shown that representation of blacks increases the employment of blacks in the state bureaucracy" (ibid.). Employment in state bureaucracies is related to the increasing number of black legislators who help to set the legislative agendas as committee chairs. In New York State, for example, the number of minority legislators and standing committee chairs increased during the 1980s to thirty (Stanley and Niemi 1990) and four (all in the assembly), respectively. There are 211 legislators, thirty-eight standing committees in the assembly, and thirty-two in the senate. Since committee chairs are appointed by the assembly speaker and senate majority leader, it is difficult to determine whether region, race, seniority or expertise, and so on, is the dominant factor in their decision-making process. The only common denominator is membership in the majority party.

Between 1981 and 1985, the percentage of minority public managers in the state bureaucracy increased from 9 percent to 11 percent (New York State Department of Civil Service 1987). Overall employment of blacks and Hispanics also increased. It is difficult to infer that the increase in minority employment in the bureaucracy was a response to increased minority representation in the legislature. But pressure for minority hiring increased as minorities gained more representation in the legislature and power at the polls. The rationale for this pressure was uncomplicated.

First, minority lawmakers in New York, similar to their counterparts in other states, realized that without allies in the bureaucracy, their ability to influence the makeup of the institutional agenda would be negligible. Second, unless they could prove to their constituents they could influence the outcome of redistributive policies, they confronted difficult reelection campaigns. Finally, although they had sufficient power to influence legislative decision making by having their items included on the legislative agenda, this feat alone could quickly become meaningless. That is, unless action was taken on the items, first by their becoming statutes, and second, by being implemented in the bureaucracy, their representation would be symbolic. Access to agenda setting and *the implementation process* in the bureaucracy can overcome this symbolism.

The importance, then, of opening a new avenue to agenda building in the bureaucracy is pivotal to minorities who, while successful in electoral politics and credible members of the state legislatures, have not experienced public policy successes equal to electoral successes because of the absence of allies in the public service, mainly capable, professional minorities who share their policy interests. As a result, their constituents are denied services and benefits due them because at the implementation stage of the policy-making system, key bureaucratic actors generally ignore them for a variety of reasons.[1] A change in the complexion first, and later in the psychology of the public service will help to remedy much of the neglect that is based on race or color. So-called affirmative action programs enacted during the 1970s and 1980s had little impact on altering the complexion of New York State's bureaucracy, especially in the public executives corps. Considering the decisive roles these managers play in policy making and agenda setting, they can obstruct the implementation of policies with which they disagree on administrative, moral, or racial grounds. The long-term objective, then, of minority legislators is to change the complexion and psychology of the public managers corps in order to have in place potential allies capable of influencing the outcome of items on the institutional agenda on a permanent basis. Various approaches already have been attempted to accomplish this twofold, interrelated objective, and marginal success has been realized.

In the wake of the 1960s civil rights movement, minorities, especially blacks, began to pressure political leaders to eliminate all barriers obstructing full minority political participation. Various affirmative action programs were initiated: recruitment programs began at historically black institutions of higher learning; minorities in lower-level civil service jobs were encouraged to compete for policy-making positions; and others were encouraged to attend professional schools of public administration and policy (Hunt 1974). Minority public executives would act as surrogates, along with minority politicians, for deprived groups in the United States. And equally as important, they would help these groups to "[crystallize] their objectives into clear proposals . . . [in order to] claim agenda status" (Cobb and Elder 1983:13). Through these officials, minority influence would be enhanced, issues pertinent to minorities would become part of the agenda, and the political system would be responsive to their concerns.

Indeed, minorities gained access to the policy-making agenda in the state bureaucracies, but minority legislators throughout the country remained dissatisfied with the pace of change. Their criticism was directed at recruitment methods designed to attract minorities into entry level, upwardly mobile positions. They also argued that while some of the approaches were positive, many were ineffective because they did not take into account apprehensions many potential recruits had about public service.[2] For example, a number of minorities continue to view public servants as adversaries based on unpleasant experiences with street-level bureaucrats (Ermer and Strange 1972). Minority legislators and public executives also maintain that in any organized concerted effort to recruit talented prospective minority public managers, the program has to deal with minority perceptions about the negative aspects of the bureaucracy.

In sum, the MPPIP was one example of a vehicle: (1) created to enhance minority access to the agenda-building process by expanding the pool of qualified minorities seeking public service careers, (2) aimed at addressing and dealing with the apprehensions about the bureaucracy of talented minority students interested in pursuing these careers, and (3) designed to supplement existing affirmative action programs established to increase minority representation in state government (Nolan 1987b). Additionally, the program was set up to create a permanent cadre of minority civil servants to assist the legislators in agenda setting, and to ensure continuous attention to issues of concern appearing on the institutional agenda.

THE NEW YORK STATE MINORITY PUBLIC POLICY INTERNSHIP PROGRAM (MPPIP)

The Program's Creation

The MPPIP's creation represented a successful group effort by minority legislators to broaden and demonstrate their commitment to the long-term interests of their constituents. As members of the legislature, they had seemed content to accept their share of legislative pork, called "member items," distributed by legislative leaders annually. While a few constituents benefit directly from these "items," budget crises and shifting political priorities make a long-term impact on the political system problematic. Except in local areas where white flight to the suburbs has resulted in predominantly minority districts, shifts in the political balance of power have not occurred. No minority legislator, for example, represents a district with a white majority population. All minority legislators are perceived as representatives of minorities and their parochial interests, such as securing money to support black or Hispanic cultural programs. Although blacks and Hispanics are committee chairs in the Democratically controlled assembly and a black is a deputy speaker, they do not appear aggressive in obtaining widespread support in the legislature for broader agenda items.[3] An annual black and Hispanic caucus cultural program appears to be one of the few times minority legislators collectively publicize "their agenda."[4] Unfortunately, this event is perceived as a convenient excuse for "partying" in the state capital, in spite of the quality of programs presented and the opportunity for minority citizens to become acquainted with state government leaders and the policy-making environment. High-ranking minority public servants are also "paraded" as evidence that minorities participate in agenda setting. Their presence is designed to show by example that minorities have achieved responsible governmental positions, and conversely to show the few persons of color who occupy important policy-making positions in the bureaucracy or have access to the agenda-setting process.

By showing simultaneously the presence of minorities in high-level positions, and their small number, one intended objective of the caucus's activities is to encourage minorities to pursue careers in the public service. This particular strategy led to a cooperative effort by well-placed minority staff in the legislature and bureaucracy to assist the caucus in securing this objective.

During the mid-1980s, Elaine Frazier, a legislative budget analyst with the Assembly Ways and Means Committee, Arthur Walton, a deputy commissioner of education, and Normal McConney, chief of staff, assembly deputy in Majority Speaker Arthur Eve's office, began to discuss ways to expand the pool of minority public managers and accelerate the inclusion of minorities into administrative and management positions in the state bureaucracy.[5] In 1986, they developed a proposal designed to create a special public policy internship program for minority students in the legislature and in executive agencies. Although several intern programs existed in the state and were available to minority students, their participation in them was limited for a variety of reasons, primarily because many perceived them as programs for white students.[6] Instead of addressing the reasons for their absence in established programs, they opted to push for the initiation of the special program. Their intention was not to undermine minority recruitment in established programs. Rather, like the minority legislators, they wanted to emphasize the absence of minorities in the public service and provide a program aimed at addressing what they perceived as the special needs of minority students in contemplating careers in the public service.

During the 1987 legislative session, they succeeded in convincing two minority legislators, Assemblymen Arthur Eve and Angelo Del Toro, to sponsor legislation to create the Minority Public Policy Internship Program (MPPIP). After approval of the legislation and an initial appropriation of $200,000, the State Education Department's (SED) Division of Post-secondary Equity and Access Programs was given the responsibility for implementing the program.[7]

The Program's Establishment: Recruitment, Assignments, and Training

The division devised a recruitment scheme to attract a pool of students from which twenty to thirty junior- and senior-level students would be selected as participants. Applicants were required to have "C" or better grade point averages and recommendations from staff or faculty on their respective campuses. Selections would be made by division staff in Albany. Contacts were made on the various State University of New York (SUNY) college and university campuses to facilitate this process. State agencies were notified of the program and asked to accept students. They also were asked to participate in an orientation program for the interns and designate mentors/supervisors for those assigned to their agencies. An arrangement was made with the Rockefeller College of Public Policy and Affairs at SUNY Albany to offer two public policy courses to the interns and provide intensive academic support services, including special writing classes, and individual academic advisement. In conjunction with this arrangement, two minority political scientists developed public policy courses, incorporating minority citizens' concerns.

The recruitment and agency assignment processes of the implementation phase were similar to those used in other internship programs. The MPPIP diverged from its counterparts in other ways. First, agency supervisors were asked, in addition to assigning and overseeing their tasks, to help them in the bureaucratic socialization process. Second, since many of the applicants were expected not to have been enrolled in public policy courses emphasizing minority public policy issues, the offerings would enhance the interns' participation, and demonstrate the necessity for minority involvement, in all phases of the policy-making process. Third, academic support services were provided to assist in sharpening their writing and research skills. Finally, restricting the program to minority students, while ostensibly an endorsement of segregation, was considered necessary to underscore the failure of traditional internship programs to attract minority students, and to provide, as part of the experimental nature of the program, an opportunity to address the special problems and negative perceptions minorities have about public service. While the MPPIP would not and could not completely eliminate these views, it would help to show that minority involvement at every stage of the policy-making process, where they could have an impact on agenda setting, would place them in appropriate positions to help develop strategies to ease adversarial relationships. Minority legislators, although not directly involved in shaping the components of the program, endorsed them. To them, a successful internship program promised a great deal more than the participants' individual accomplishments.

The Minority Legislators' Expectations of the Interns: Before and After

The legislators viewed the MPPIP as an effective means for expanding and accelerating minority participation and influence in agenda building by ensuring the continuity of minority input in all stages of the policy development process.[8] While their future presence in the bureaucracy would not guarantee greater attention to their communities' problems, particularly those related to civil rights, housing, and welfare, their participation would guarantee they would not be ignored. In the bureaucracy they were thought of as future allies of minority legislators, concerned with the formation and implementation of public policies beneficial to their communities. It was inconceivable, given the marginal involvement of minorities in New York State's political system, that minority public managers would disassociate themselves in the long run from problems plaguing their communities. Even if they were accommodationists or integrationists, they could not escape or avoid the reality of the minority communities' needs and the predicament they confronted as minority managers in a segregated society. Adam Herbert places their dilemma in perspective, suggesting that minority public managers often ask themselves two significant questions: "(1) What responsibility do (we) have to minority peoples? and (2) What role should (we) attempt to play in making governments more responsive to the need of all people?" (1974:560) When and how they respond to these questions would determine the extent of their effectiveness as public managers. But until there was a substantial change in the balance of power in the political system, they could not escape this dual responsibility. The MPPIP provided a unique opportunity for the next generation of minority public managers to ponder these questions and how best to deal with them. Beyond a consideration of these weighty questions, the legislators, as pragmatists, understood any internship program has pitfalls.

Obviously, interns do not have access to existing decision makers, relevant information, pressure groups, or the media. They cannot determine "the types of issue conflict that receive the attention and action of governmental decision makers" (Cobb and Elder 1983:13). Because they lack official standing in any government institution or pressure group, they cannot create issues or mobilize the community into demanding a redress of grievances. As "outsiders," even if their opinions are valid and relevant, they are usually not taken seriously by public managers. More than a few policy makers participating in the program viewed the interns as distractions, tolerated them, and considered the program as part of another affirmative action experiment. Their familiarity with the agenda-building process thus could have been diminished, and the expectation by minority legislators of their future usefulness in implementing public policies could have been dashed. Equally as important, the internship experience could act as disincentive for some participants to pursue public service careers, if their supervisors were inattentive to them or delegated them tasks irrelevant to the decision-making process. Nonetheless, there were positive aspects of such a program, which will be manifested in the long run.

In the broader area of agenda building, the long-run impact of the internship program was significant. Placed in various state agencies, even as observers, the interns were in unique positions to enhance the ability of racial minorities to influence the decision-making process and serve as future participants in the process. As prospective "gatekeepers" in all levels of government and interest groups, they were exposed to the process of political development, especially "the institutional and structural factors that affect agenda-building" (Cobb and Elder 1983:82). For example, learning what separated an issue from a demand was crucial; and ascertaining how an issue was created, and the public managers' role in this process, broadened their understanding of policy development. As future representatives and even surrogates of their communities, they will be able to assist legislators in translating legitimate demands into issues, an important first step in agenda building.

For minority legislators, prospective sympathetic public executives, on the other hand, will likely make themselves available as resource persons and informal advisers in the policy development process. This will entail increased substantive contact with minority communities, which because of the segregationist nature of the political system, are unaware generally of how policies are developed. As the interns work with and observe public managers, and learn from their experiences, they place themselves in unique positions to assist later in the complex process of translating demands into identifiable legitimate policy alternatives. This ability can be exploited by minority legislators looking for other effective means to generate ideas and support and to sharpen the definition of issues.

In sum, MPPIP participants who opted to pursue other careers will become valuable resource persons in minority communities. Conversely, in the public service, their potential role in policy development will complement and supplement the activities of minority legislators. This combination offers the most far-reaching possibility for participation in agenda building throughout the political system, and enhances the ability of minorities to cause a shift in the balance of political power in the long run.

Impact on Changing Majority Opposition to Participation

The involvement of minorities initially as observers and later as participants in the bureaucratic agenda-building process enhances their sense of efficacy and legitimacy in the political system and in the broader community. The outsider status will not change simply because of the outstanding performance of a few minority public managers nor will their dual personality which Herbert alludes to undergo a radical transformation. Their acceptance as decision makers by the majority population will further diminish segregation and majority resistance to minority participation, and facilitate the inclusion of minority long-term interests at every stage of the policy-making and implementation processes. Arguably this is an overly optimistic view of the long-range outcome of programs like the MPPIP, but it is not an unrealistic expectation, if the minority experience in blunting majority resistance in the electoral arena in some areas can serve as a precedent (Cole 1977).

SUCCESS AND DEMISE OF MPPIP

Given the long-term objectives of the program as envisaged by minority legislators and public servants, it was far from successful, but not a failure. It may be continued. From the perspective of individual participants, the program was a success. In the short term, at least, their individual accomplishments are worth noting.

During its three years of operation, over two hundred minority students applied for participation; seventy-seven were accepted and assigned to several executive agencies, the Assembly Ways and Means Committee, the Lieutenant Governor's Office, and the Governor's Office of Employee Relations.[9] Most were African-Americans, and the rest, a sprinkling of Hispanics, Asian Americans, and Native Americans. They were almost equally divided between juniors and seniors; most were females. New York State independent and public universities and colleges were well represented. While the vast majority of the interns were liberal arts students, a few majored in electrical engineering, biology, and physics. Several were uncertain about pursuing careers in the public service, but some decided, after the conclusion of their experiences, to reconsider their career goals and seriously think about becoming public managers. During each of the three years the program was in operation, minority student interest in participation substantially increased. If this nascent interest is exploited by existing internship programs, the long-term goals of minority legislators and public managers will be accomplished.[10] None of them include the special components of the MPPIP, but expanded minority participation may result in the inclusion of some of MPPIP's features, such as providing academic support services. In sum, a tacit goal of MPPIP initiators may also be realized: further segregation of existing internship programs resulting in the creation of a larger pool of capable minorities seeking careers in the public service.

Accurate information on the whereabouts of each of the seventy-seven "graduates" was not available when this chapter was written in late 1991. Based, however, on correspondence, formal surveys conducted by the New York State Department of Education (SED), and anecdotal data from the Academic Advisement Office of SUNY Albany's Rockefeller College of Public Policy and Affairs, some interesting feedback had been obtained.[11] Two were accepted in 1989 into the highly successful SUNY Stony Brook's Public Policy Summer Institute for Minority Students. After completion of the program, both received full scholarships to finance advanced study in public policy or public administration; one attended Princeton University; another, Columbia University. One was accepted into the extremely competitive New York City Urban Fellows Program for prospective public managers in 1990. Three served as New York State Assembly interns. Several entered law school. At least a score entered graduate schools of public administration and social welfare.

A few students entered the public service after graduating from undergraduate school. Two went to work for the New York State Assembly Ways and Means Committee; another became a staff person in the New York State Office of Mental Retardation. Most of the interns from the first MPPIP class in 1988 pursued advanced degrees in public administration or policy. One student in the final class in the spring of 1990 obtained a position with a public interest group in New York City, and another was appointed the coordinator of Native American affairs at a SUNY four-year college in 1991.

Although the individual accomplishments of the former interns were impressive, they failed to convince Governor Mario Cuomo that the MPPIP was nothing more than an expensive piece of "pork." He eliminated the program from his 1989 and 1990 executive budgets, only to have it restored by the legislature at the urging of minority legislators. Perhaps restored as much for symbolism as for a demonstration of legislative independence, the continuation of the MPPIP represented a political victory for minority legislators.

However, the MPPIP became a victim of New York State's fiscal crisis in late 1990. Governor Cuomo successfully eliminated it from the state's 1990–1991 budget. Minority legislators and their supporters refused to use valuable political capital to save a program which won or could have won them few votes. They were distressed over the impact other cuts had on more important programs—unemployment benefits, Medicare, and so on—and directed their energies toward an even more important concern— preventing even deeper cuts. Reviving the MPPIP was not a key part of their new agenda.

DISCUSSION AND CONCLUSION

In operation only three years and producing a mere seventy-seven graduates, the MPPIP's long-term impact on the agenda-building process will be marginal even if all of the participants become public managers. While the number of minorities who become public managers is but one important factor in determining the extent to which minorities can impact on policy making, it is a significant barometer. By radically changing the complexion of the public managers corps, white executives might be less inclined to use their influence to eliminate institutional agenda items in the legislature or agencies, and choose instead to engage in negotiations and compromises to reach decisions. The mere presence of minority public managers in arenas previously closed to them might make white executives sensitive to the demands of the underrepresented. The death of the MPPIP will probably make this possibility far less likely.

The positive impact of the MPPIP on minorities gaining another avenue to agenda building, and thus to the public policy-making process, is difficult to assess. On the positive side, several of the seventy-seven graduates are now in positions to encourage others to seek careers in the public service. Other internship programs exist in New York, and they all aggressively pursue minority students.[12] Moreover, no one knows yet to what extent the seventy-seven graduates favorably impressed their mentors/supervisors, encouraging them to advocate the establishment of agency programs to "beef up" minority recruitment.

Granted, absent empirical evidence, the assessments presented above are primarily speculative. In ten to twenty years, if and when the seventy-seven graduates or some of them enter the public service (some already have), data can be collected regarding their impact, or that of those they have influenced, on agenda building. In the meantime, underrepresented minorities in New York State may gain access to the systemic and institutional agendas through other avenues: existing internship programs; graduate schools of public administration, policy, and affairs; affirmative action programs; and the electoral process, perhaps the most effective avenue available for minorities to have an impact on agenda building and gain access to all stages of the policy-making process.

However, elections in and of themselves, according to Roger Cobb and Charles Elder, "are still rather blunt instruments for influencing the governmental agenda" (1983:181). Officeholders may be successful in getting items on the systemic agenda, but not on the institutional agenda. This process involves a great deal more assistance from interest groups, public executives, and the media. Minority officeholders are constrained even more so than white officeholders because they have to deal with racial politics. If they are successful in getting items on the systemic agenda, usually support from white allies is required for them to elevate the items to proposals and statutes, and then to have them implemented. An additional group of well-placed allies, public managers, in the agencies would enhance their ability to secure benefits for their constituents and provide minorities a permanent role in the decision-making process, even if at some point these same allies assume other interests not considered exclusively minority interests. Minority legislators in New York State expected the MPPIP to play a leading role in establishing this permanency in the policy-making system.

The significance of programs like the MPPIP, therefore, is in their capability to produce public managers in the long run who can act as brokers for minority legislators "to see an idea through the maze of institutional processes necessary for its adoption as policy" (Cobb and Elder 1983:187). Obtaining and maintaining an additional avenue to agenda setting in the public service helps to neutralize the changing makeup and fluid influence of electoral political alliances, facilitates the inclusion of items on the governmental agenda, and mitigates even a powerful governor's role in controlling bureaucratic agenda setting, especially as he or she loses popular support and finally leaves office. If minorities are successful in expanding the pool of qualified professionals seeking careers in the public service, they do not have to depend solely on the "good graces" of political leaders to guarantee their access to agenda setting. As public managers, they are positioned to help shape the systemic and institutional agendas. By achieving this status, the minority legislators' goal of shifting the governmental balance of power is more assured than waiting for political leaders elected with their support to make changes allowing the shift to occur. This is the essence of redistributive policy making. As the process continues, the fluid changes in the U.S. political system become more evident as reflected in diminished majority resistance to minorities voting, resulting in minority electoral successes. In the long run, these successes translate into gaining and maintaining access to the systemic agenda first, and the institutional agenda later.

NOTES

1. Key public managers are influenced by a number of factors at the implementation stage, including their interpretation of the statutes and their individual biases. Charles S. Bullock III and Charles M. Lamb in *Implementation of Civil Rights Policy* (Monterey, CA: Brooks/Cole Publishing Company, 1984) suggest that some civil rights legislation has not been implemented because of the reluctance of some public executives to obey the law.

2. In my experiences as a coordinator of internships and instructor in the MPPIP, black and Hispanic students have voiced negative comments about the public service. Their experiences and/or those of family members had been unfavorable or perceived to have been unfavorable.

3. A number of black journalists in the New York City area have been very critical of minority legislators in that they have been very content to go along with the white leadership and not make waves.

4. Unfortunately, this event is reported in the press as a "festive" celebration because of the perceived emphasis on socializing. Some of the local (Albany, the state capital) press people do not report the event at all. The caucus was organized in 1971 to provide a forum for minority legislators to publicize common interests.

5. I had conversations with both Frazier and McConney about the origins of the MPPIP. McConney was especially helpful in explaining what transpired from the inception of the idea to its translation into a statute.

6. A host of internship programs existed in the state in the early 1990s. I was familiar with the Washington, DC, Semester Program, New York State Assembly Program, New York State Senate Internship Program, and Albany Semester Program. These programs usually placed about 200 students yearly; less than 10 percent tended to be Hispanic and black, although Asian-American students have steadily increased their participation.

7. Initially, the New York State Education Department's Division of Post-secondary Equity and Access Programs exclusively administered the program, but during the last two years of MPPIP's operations SUNY Albany became increasingly involved in its implementation. I should add here that I was involved in the implementation scheme, and was aware of the progress of the program. I maintained a great deal of contact with relevant SED personnel.

8. A small, experimental program, the MPPIP promised to be a vehicle that could be expanded and influence other minority students, contemplating careers in the public service but not interested in participating in an internship program.

9. As one of the professors in the program, I had access to information about intern assignments, and the gender, ethnic, and so on, makeup of the interns.

10. The internship programs mentioned in Note 6 appear to have stepped up their efforts to recruit minority students.

11. The statement speaks for itself. I have written recommendations for several graduates, and have received correspondence from them about their activities.

12. Evidence exists indicating these programs are actively pursuing minority students, with varying degrees of success.

10

Mobilization in Crisis: Setting an Agenda for Minority Health Through Socially Transformative Action

Francesca Schmid Thomas

Since the mid-1960s, there have been few successful efforts on the part of minority populations to attain either public or institutional[1] attention to the injustices they perceive to be operating in this society (McClain 1990:267). This theme is currently being played out around the AIDS epidemic insofar as the populations which are increasingly affected by the epidemic, namely racial minorities, have been largely unsuccessful in their efforts to mobilize to reduce risk and affect political decision making (Quimby and Friedman 1989:403). Although this lack of success for these populations can be variously attributed, limited resources and the effective manner in which monies have been allotted clearly lie at the center of their difficulties (ibid.:412).

This chapter presents the case study of a crosscultural, crossracial coalition which is seemingly attempting to reverse this pattern.[2] Cultural Communities United in Health and Wellness (CCUHW) is a nascent organization which appears to be creating alternatives and pushing forward a new agenda for minority health in Arizona. Without conforming to the archetypical models of mobilization, this volunteer coalition nonetheless seems to be progressing through the stages of agenda setting as put forth by Roger Cobb, Jennie Keith-Ross, and Marc Ross (1976). By contextualizing the coalition in the agenda-setting literature, then, CCUHW can be portrayed as a potential site for addressing the injustices facing minority populations in the area of health services.

Simultaneously, this chapter questions the legitimacy of traditional agenda-setting models for wholly describing political struggles minority populations undertake. Specifically, the agenda which CCUHW is trying to set incorporates issues which clearly lie outside the limited confines of institutional redress, and its actions are directed toward more than merely attaining governmental attention. The reality of the coalition's struggle thus highlights the inadequacy of traditional agenda-setting models, and further destabilizes the notion of pluralist politics upon which these models rest. An introduction of the literature on New Social Movements (NSM) seems to provide a means for expanding these models by incorporating broader notions of contestable issues. The NSM literature establishes a lens for focusing on this group's efforts to engender socially transformative action, or action which "redefines the grammar forms of life" (Gamson 1989:353) and creates a "space of action" for excluded groups within the existing structure of society (Offe 1985:828). Thus it is hoped that the analysis of CCUHW provided herein engenders a discussion on both the potential for agenda-setting mobilization within minority populations and the alternative assumptions which necessarily accompany any complete understanding of these minority struggles.

METHODOLOGY

This study is based on observations and interviews I conducted during an eighteen-month period between the winter of 1989 and the spring of 1991. I attended the monthly meetings of the coalition, as well as participated in some of its functions and assisted some of its co-chairs in the secretarial and administrative work of the coalition. These observations provided a basis for understanding the internal structure of the organization, and established my relationship with the coalition members.

In addition, I conducted two series of open-ended interviews. The first round focused on the inception of CCUHW, its history, and its membership. The second set of interviews revolved around uncovering the goals of the organization as perceived by its members, and the means by which those goals were to be realized. Twenty-three interviews were conducted in total.

Literature on the topic, namely that of agenda setting and NSM, was researched between the first and second rounds of interviews. This strategy enabled me to collect some initial data without the pressure of a theory-driven model, while still allowing for the latter interviews and observations to uncover the possibility of an agenda-setting process and/or socially transformative action. Thus, the research strategies employed were qualitative in nature, while the process of analysis combined inductive and deductive methods. I believe the mixed methods of my inquiry have proven those to be most adapted to this topic. While I may have sacrificed methodological purity in the eyes of some critics, I contend that the gain has been a more authentic portrayal of this coalition.

CCUHW: THE ORGANIZATION

CCUHW comprises a select group of Hispanic, African-American, and Native American health professionals. These individuals voluntarily come together on a monthly basis to discuss problems related to their work as minority health providers, and obstacles faced by their client populations, namely lower-income minorities. Their motivations for collective action thus stem from both a desire for support and networking possibilities, and from their commitment to change the status of minority health in Arizona.

The members of the coalition speak of the impetus for organization along two lines. First, and similar to John Kingdon's notion of a "gradual accumulation of knowledge" (1984:18), these professionals began to realize the blatant lack of health services and insensitivity in service delivery for the populations they served. Members described this realization as an initial individual perception which was reinforced through their professional encounters in the field. Specifically, what informants observed in the field was reiterated by their colleagues in other communities, with whom they associated for cultural sensitivity training and county project report meetings (Appendix 2, Interview E). This process of association both contributed to a collective recognition of minority health problems and provided the relational foundation upon which the coalition would ultimately be built.

Second, the HIV crisis seems to have played a pivotal role in the formation of this organization. The effects of AIDS on minority populations, and the lack of sufficient societal attention and sensitivity to these effects, were repeatedly indicated as the common issues which served to galvanize CCUHW. In fact, several of the informants maintained that the HIV crisis, due to the immediacy and magnitude of the problems it encompasses, engendered mobilization among previously divided peoples. One member noted: "[AIDS] brought different communities together because it is such a costly problem. It is so deadly. It is so ugly, so emotional. . . . Not like housing [in which] no big effort is made (Appendix 2, Interview K). Thus, AIDS seems to have been the trigger event and health problem that initially motivated this group of professionals to organize. The importance of the HIV epidemic in this mobilization becomes further elucidated in considering the coalition's history.

February 1989 is the earliest date to which the roots of this coalition may be traced. That date marks the creation of a panel on AIDS by the

Phoenix Indian Medical Center Health Education Department. The members of this panel quickly realized there was a lack of information, organization, and connectedness among the Native American populations on the issue of AIDS; and they decided to expand the panel to include members of other minority populations (Appendix 2, Interview F). Initially the meetings were held at the Indian Health Center, and twelve tribes and the Hispanic populations were represented. According to the informants, the coalition was conceived as also including representatives of the African-American and Asian-American communities from the outset; however, only Hispanic and Native Americans composed this first prototype of CCUHW (Appendix 2, Interview E).

By August 1989, another group of minority health workers was forming to discuss the issue of AIDS. At that time, a meeting was facilitated by the Greater Phoenix Affordable Health Care Foundation (GPAHCF). As a result of research GPAHCF had undertaken (with funding from the Flinn Foundation), it had become apparent that there was a lack of communication and coordination among all the cultural communities in Phoenix with regard to health services. The purpose of the August 29 meeting was to help bridge the seeming gaps among the various health workers in the field of AIDS, especially with regard to services available for minority populations (Appendix 2, Interview G).

If one looks at the sign-in sheets for these two working groups, it is evident that there was little if any overlap of membership attendance. However, by September 12, 1989, the first agenda item for the meeting facilitated by GPAHCF was "Why two groups?" It seems clear that two particular events helped alert these two groups of each other's existence, and brought them together to form what is now CCUHW: they were the Arizona Governor's Task Force on AIDS, and the coordination of an event in Guadalupe to commemorate "Minority AIDS Awareness Day."

The Governor's Task Force on AIDS originally had only a few official minority representatives. According to the former chairperson, the task force primarily relied on "resource people" from the various cultural and racial communities for input on issues specifically related to the minority populations (Appendix 2, Interview D). These resource people comprised individuals on a mailing list of every group that was involved in AIDS work. In addition, "every single person who had ever been considered or nominated or nominated themselves got on [the] mailing list" (ibid.). Evidently, this remained the modus operandi for the task force for the initial months during which it convened, for it was not until an actual document was being drafted that the issue of minority participation was raised. Specifically, in putting together the interim report the lack of minority input became apparent. Special meetings were held; and after several vociferous confrontations, a new task force committee was formed, the Minority Issues Committee.

The Minority Issues Committee was composed mainly of resource people. Two task force members were nominated as committee chairs; another minority was recruited and appointed by the governor to sit on the task force. The Minority Issues Committee did not limit its work to the planned task force meetings; these committee members would meet on their own in order to confer on the proposals they ultimately wanted to make (Appendix 2, Interviews D, A). According to the informants, these outside meetings helped to expand and solidify the organization that had already begun to take root (Appendix 2, Interview E). In essence, a working relationship began to be forged among people who had previously limited their encounters to coincidence and periodic project report meetings at the Maricopa Health Department (ibid.).

While the task force was meeting, another event which would serve to further consolidate CCUHW was underway. The expanded Indian Medical Center panel on AIDS had decided early in its formation to focus on "Minority AIDS Awareness Day" as its first big project. As the day for the event drew nearer, this coalition began expanding even further, incorporating for the first time members of the African-American community. Among the participants were the three people who originally served as the co-chairs for CCUHW. Until this point, no plan had existed to continue the coalition which had emanated from the task force. The event at Guadalupe seems to have been, then, the final unifying force in a series of events which culminated in the founding of CCUHW.

As an organization, CCUHW seems to conform more closely to a collectivist-democratic model than to traditional bureaucratic organizations.[3] Specifically, its rules and roles are neither codified nor written; it functions by consensus of the group. There are three agreed-upon co-chairs of CCUHW (one each from the Native American, African-American, and Hispanic communities) among whom responsibility for the meetings rotates. These chairpersons basically function as secretaries and moderators for the group, although their exact roles are undefined. They are in charge of sending out the monthly flyers, organizing an agenda for a particular meeting, and conducting the meetings.

In maintaining that the meetings are conducted by the co-chairs, it is important to note the overall informality of these events and the difficulty in discovering the operating rules. Specifically, meetings rarely begin on time; people are often fraternizing prior to, during, and following the meetings; once the chairperson has begun the meeting, she or he may allow conversations to take their own course, thus essentially giving up control; while some attempt is made to "stick to the agenda," members often interject with related concerns and opinions. This generally contributes to the length of the meetings, and to the fact that the agenda is rarely covered. However, one member noted that this informalism helps alleviate some of the bureaucratic tension which serves to undermine other organizations, and may actually contribute to the cohesiveness of this group (Appendix 2, Interview H).

The lack of codification is also apparent with regard to membership. There are no clear written criteria for inclusion in CCUHW. Yet, certain qualifications seem to emerge from an analysis of the membership. Clearly, identification with a minority community appears to demarcate membership. From its inception, CCUHW was intended to comprise "American Indian, Asian/Pacific, Black and Latino communities."[4] Also, the position of health professional serves to delineate CCUHW members. While this characteristic did not emerge in the interviews as a requirement for inclusion, it does reflect the current composition of the group. Finally, concentration on AIDS work seems to constitute an unwritten measure of inclusion. According to the most recent membership list, every member of CCUHW is either directly working on the HIV issue, or takes work on AIDS to be an integral part of his or her program.

Given this background, it should not be surprising that the CCUHW members consider the HIV virus one of the preeminent health problems of their clients, and that most of their work to date has centered on the disease and its social ramifications. The most recent statistics for the state of Arizona indicate that of the 1989 HIV cases 1 percent were Native American, 9 percent were Hispanic, and 4 percent were African-American (Mofford 1989:49). While these numbers may not appear high, one member rephrased the situation as follows:

> I think it's a big risk that we're going to lose . . . a significant number of our young. . . . We're a small population of ethnic people. When you have a hundred youth die that are college educated, I mean that's going to make an impact on these generations. (Appendix 2, Interview A)

In this light, the effects of HIV on minority populations become far more ominous, with the potential for vast devastation. Thus, the immediacy of the HIV virus, coupled with the funding that is currently available for HIV programs, has led the coalition to focus its attention on this aspect of health (Appendix 2, Interviews K, Q).

Despite the amount of attention given to the HIV virus, the members of CCUHW do not envision the organization as one solely dedicated to the problems of AIDS; rather they see its mission as pooling together the scarce resources for the benefit of their communities' overall health (Appendix 2, Interviews C, H, Q). However, the AIDS epidemic has provided this group of minorities with a "policy window" (Kingdon 1984:174) through which to address other issues of minority health. Specifically, HIV has illuminated and emphasized already existing problems in the health arena for minority peoples. The lack of minority representation in the field of health, of adequate and sensitive services for ethnic populations, of community input regarding minority problems, and the issue of skewed resource allotment have all been forced to the forefront of governmental attention due to the crisis which HIV presents. In the state of Arizona, this attention resulted in the creation of a separate task force committee for minority issues, the members of which ultimately authored a complete chapter of the task force report specifically dedicated to issues of minority health. It appears that CCUHW hopes to capitalize on this attention by pushing alternatives for minority health onto a system which has recently felt the burdens of mounting problems in the face of crisis; CCUHW is trying to set a new agenda for minority health.

CCUHW: SETTING AN AGENDA FOR MINORITY HEALTH

An agenda, according to Cobb and Charles Elder, is "a general set of political controversies that will be viewed at any point in time as falling within the range of legitimate concerns meriting the attention of the polity" (1972:14). Kingdon distinguishes between two types of agendas: the governmental agenda and the decision agenda. The former represents "the list of subjects to which people in and around government are paying serious attention," while the latter denotes "the list of items that is being decided upon" (1984:174). Cobb, Keith-Ross, and Ross (1976) speak of the public and formal agendas in much the same terms respectively. Barbara Nelson, however, presents a categorization involving three agenda types. Specifically, while retaining the category of formal agenda, she subdivides the notion of governmental or public agenda into two concepts.[5] The "popular agenda" is described as designating issue awareness on the part of the mass public (1984:20). The "professional agenda" describes awareness "among those members of the public informed about a given issue who may promote a particular expert view of a problem" (ibid.). Her concept of "professional agenda" most closely approximates the phenomenon of this study. Yet, the broader terms of public and formal agenda better serve the purpose of the analysis, both in terms of their clarity and in illustrating the larger process of agenda setting. Thus, borrowing from Cobb and his associates, the terms *public agenda* and *formal agenda* are used exclusively for the remainder of this chapter.

Setting an agenda, then, entails moving an issue from the public agenda to the formal agenda. Nelson describes the process as one whereby "public officials learn about new problems, decide to give them personal attention, and mobilize their organizations to respond to them" (1984:25). Kingdon speaks of agenda setting as the culmination of a series of processes involving problems, policies, and politics (1984:17), locating the critical locus of initiative with elected officials and policy elites. Finally, Cobb, Keith-Ross, and Ross conceive of agenda setting as the translation of a public demand into an item "vying for serious consideration of public officials" (1976:126).

They go on to describe three different agenda-setting processes: outside initiative, mobilization, and inside initiative (ibid.:127). I was initially led to question the legitimacy of adopting only one of these models as a complete account of what CCUHW is undertaking. Specifically, the outside initiative is intended to account for processes by which issues are advanced from nongovernmental groups (ibid.). Since CCUHW is a voluntary organization of health professionals, it would seem that this model should be the most valuable in illuminating the phenomenon of CCUHW. However, while the members of CCUHW do not officially represent the organizations for which they work, many of them have direct access to government in their jobs, and some have served in governmental positions. This, combined with the fact that the organization is so small and seeks to address issues for which even the most affected do not seek redress (i.e., they are not supported by mass mobilization), led to further consideration of the inside initiative model. This model describes issues arising in the governmental sphere but not expanding to the mass public (ibid.:128). It would seem that this model can also contribute to an understanding of the processes of CCUHW, and I contend the data support this view as well. The foundation for this point will be shown by turning to the specific stages of agenda setting associated with each of these models.

The first stage in both the models is the initiation phase. In the outside initiative model, this stage is marked by an extragovernmental group articulating a general grievance. This is precisely how informants described their impetus to coalesce into CCUHW.

We were talking about minority issues and they were going, "Well, this happened in the black community," "This happened in the Hispanic community," and when it came down to it, across the board we were all affected the same way. So it was the whole thing of getting us together and realizing that we were in this whole thing together and that we were going to have to work together. (Appendix 2, Interview A)

We were underrepresented [in decision making] and we were disproportionately affected by the AIDS virus. So that was the original reason for us coming together. (Appendix 2, Interview C)

The three ethnic communities had come together and they saw they had been given the royal shaft. (Appendix 2, Interview L)

Thus, the beginnings of CCUHW seem to conform to the outside initiative model of agenda setting.

The initiation phase in the inside initiative model similarly entails the articulation of a general grievance, but it must be made from "a group or agency within government, or a group with close ties to governmental leaders" (Cobb et al. 1976:135). Two of the comments quoted above were made by individuals who, at the time of their realizations, were working on the Arizona Governor's Task Force on AIDS. In addition, any of the members who work for Native American agencies work in the government, as do all county and state health workers. Furthermore, one of the seed organizations for CCUHW was begun within Indian Health Services as a result of the employees realizing their lack of information and organization regarding the HIV virus. In this sense, CCUHW also appears to fit definitions under the inside initiative model.

Specification marks the second step of this agenda-setting process, and it too is similarly defined for both models posited here. Specification entails the translation of the general grievance into specific demands (ibid.:128). Though CCUHW is composed of a multitude of varied people, and hence theoretically more akin to an outside group, as a coalition it is more aptly described by the depiction of an inside initiative group, namely one which is privileged and more homogeneous (ibid.:135). All the members are employed health professionals, and as one woman put it, "We all see ourselves as minorities" (Appendix 2, Interview H). Hence, despite the diversity which is typical of outside groups, CCUHW members have adopted an identity which allows them to function more in keeping with the homogeneous groups associated with the inside initiative.

There are two examples which seem to demonstrate CCUHW's attainment of this phase of agenda setting. One is the publication of the Minority Issues section of the Governor's Task Force on AIDS Report. As was mentioned, in this document there are several specific recommendations to the governor on behalf of the minority populations which participated in its writing. Also, the members' descriptions of the coalition goals, including addressing the problems of AIDS (Appendix 2, Interviews H, M, O, Q, S), cultural insensitivity (Appendix 2, Interviews V, W), lack of insurance and access to adequate services due to economic status (Appendix 2, Interviews H, I, M, N, S, V), and fund reallocation (Appendix 2, Interviews C, J, Q), show how the broad grievance of insufficient attention to minority health is being translated into specific demands. It is true that their comments do not reflect any official mission statement. However, the overlapping consent on several topics illustrates the type of issue convergence this author interprets specification to mean.

Expansion denotes the third stage of the agenda-setting process. For the outside initiative model, it constitutes creating sufficient pressure to attract the attention of decision makers. This is typically done by engaging new groups in the population, or linking the specific issue with other pre-existing ones (Cobb et al. 1976:128). It does not appear that CCUHW has engaged in either of these tactics; yet the coalition has been able to gain the attention of decision makers. Specifically, the members of CCUHW have chosen to maintain control over the issues, and have been reluctant even to expand the membership criteria (practically, if not theoretically). In so doing, the organization has still gained some status among government decision makers. For instance, the assistant director of disease prevention attended the February 14, 1991, meeting to discuss the Ryan White Comprehensive AIDS Resource Emergency (C.A.R.E.) Act, and the input of CCUHW was being requested. While this may not be tantamount to directly addressing the legislators, it is certainly a step toward expansion. And the coalition took this step within the confines of the inside initiative model; namely, it kept control of the issues and adopted selective group pressure to attract governmental attention.

The final stage of the agenda-setting process in both models is entrance, or the point at which the issue achieves position on the formal agenda (ibid.:136). CCUHW has not been able to move its issues to this point, although the members are still waiting on a gubernatorial response to their task force recommendations. It is important to note that at the final stage of the agenda-setting process in both these models an alternative institutional response is possible. Specifically, even if an issue is raised to the attention of policy makers, it may never be addressed. When this is the case, it can be said that a nondecision-making situation exists (Bachrach and Baratz 1963:952). Simply stated, those who are in power, or who control resources, can obstruct reform simply by doing nothing (Frohock 1979:83). The effect of nondecision is to relegate those with less power to positions in which the disequilibrium is perpetuated. The reader should note, then, that while it may be shown that CCUHW seems to be moving through the above-described stages of agenda setting, the members' low-status power positions threaten the potential of their efforts to effect real change.

This, then, is how the data seem to portray the movement of CCUHW through the stages of agenda setting. It is equally interesting that the members themselves see their endeavors as an effort to "set the agenda." Specifically, many of the interviewees felt that CCUHW provided the means to influence legislators to distribute services and program funding more equitably. Lobbying was often cited as a major organizational goal to achieve this end. According to these members, lobbying would entail identifying key people in decision-making positions (Appendix 2, Interview I), and holding minority politicians accountable to their constituents (Appendix 2, Interview N). One member noted, "Our main purpose is to get health care concerns addressed at the state level" (Appendix 2, Interview U). The interviewees maintained that lobbying should ultimately result in the coalition having influence in the legislature (ibid.), providing input to the Department of Health Services and the governor's office (Appendix 2, Interview R), and generally "having some say-so in positions that are underrepresented by the ethnicities . . . in health things" (Appendix 2, Interview L). Fundamentally, they describe CCUHW as an organization to "represent minority interests in social welfare and health promotion" (Appendix 2, Interview J).

None of these individuals specifically cited the means by which lobbying could or would occur. However, several of the recommendations under the Minority Issues section of the Governor's Task Force on AIDS Report seem to speak to this issue. For instance, the document calls for the appointment of a "standing Minority Community Panel," the creation of "an Office of Minority Health and Social Services," and the increased allocation of funding to minority community-based organizations (50–51). All of these recommendations appear directed toward providing alternatives in the minority health policy area.

CCUHW members also spoke of alternatives with regard to policy formulation. Notably, several people mentioned that CCUHW should work toward affirming the value and rights of minority populations.

For too long . . . [we have] made judgment calls. . . . That's got to stop. (Appendix 2, Interview L)

[CCUHW should] enable minorities to take their problems into their own hands, to make changes from that amongst themselves. (Appendix 2, Interview O)

[We need to be] telling people to demand the services they deserve . . . closing in that gap between patient and doctor. (Appendix 2, Interview H)

In addition to these proposals involving the client populations, CCUHW was described in terms of advocating for the minority professionals. In particular, two people mentioned that CCUHW is intended to pressure existing agencies "to hire minority outreach" (Appendix 2, Interview J), and to "let the larger community [know] that there were [*sic*] people [representative of the communities in question] who were specifically trained to deal with the issues and speak to health" (Appendix 2, Interview Q). One individual described this function as being the "community conscience" (Appendix 2, Interview J), namely to ensure that services on paper are actually being provided, and that they are being rendered in a culturally sensitive and knowledgeable manner.

These latter goals allude to the shortcomings of complete reliance on the agenda-setting models to account for minority mobilization. Specifically, while the issues CCUHW is seeking to address may be partially realized through institutional redress, it appears that a distinct facet of the coalition's intent is social change. CCUHW seems to be striving for more than simply compelling decision makers to adopt and act on their issues of importance; the coalition is seeking to redefine "grammar forms of life" (Gamson 1989:353) and establish a "space of action" for their group within the existing structure of society (Offe 1985:828). In addition, the organization is seeking to redistribute resources within the field of health services. By viewing the data through the lens of the NSM literature, it becomes clear that the coalition's agenda-setting efforts reach far beyond the confines of governmental solutions. Several examples will help illustrate this point.

AGENDA SETTING THROUGH SOCIAL TRANSFORMATION

The agenda-setting models posited herein are reliant on the notion of pluralism, namely, that diverse peoples in this society have the potential for equal access to and influence on the decision-making process. To the extent that complete racial, political, social, and economic integration does not exist in our society, these models fall short of describing the reality for minorities in policy struggles. For the populations whose members are not effectively integrated into the political system, setting an agenda is insufficient to ensure the changes that are necessary; policy alone cannot solve the injustices they face. Greater change, change that transforms the nature of the playing field on which these struggles take place, is needed to allow for the effective participation of minority populations. It is precisely this type of change, socially transformative action, which CCUHW appears to be undertaking simultaneously with its agenda-setting process. Namely, the coalition seems dedicated to change with regard to both identity legitimation and resource mobilization, both of which lie outside the confines of institutional redress.

First, CCUHW seems to be attempting to foster socially transformative action regarding identity legitimation. Specifically, the literature describes identity-oriented mobilizations as focusing on the redefinition of social identities, and the establishment of a space of action for those newly defined groups (see Cohen 1985:708). Given the organizational goals which were elaborated in the interviews, CCUHW can be seen as both an attempt to redefine the parameters of "minority," and legitimate a space of action within our society for that group.

In particular, CCUHW seems dedicated to creating a new definition of *minority* in the state of Arizona. For instance, several of the interviewees mentioned the need for the white population to recognize and respond to the needs and capabilities of minorities.

> [We need to] educate existing agencies to providing services that are culturally sensitive, and pressuring [them] to hire minority outreach. (Appendix 2, Interview J)

> There are certain things we can only do for ourselves. [We can] educate ourselves, [and] know what we're saying. (Appendix 2, Interview L)

This author contends that a legitimation of minority populations is implicit in these comments. Specifically, in calling for more active and appropriate responses to these populations in matters of health, it appears the coalition members are fundamentally asserting the social identities of minority peoples. Namely, they are defining the people in their identity groups as participating citizens with the same right to expect adequate and appropriate services as the rest of the citizenship. As one CCUHW member put it, "You are talking about people that are Americans. We are Americans, we are part of this society. . . . Minority is not that this is the society and they are the minorities; and we are tired of that situation" (Appendix 2, Interview E). This definition, although inherent in the Fourteenth Amendment and the Civil Rights Act of 1964, is clearly not the one operating in this society, which systematically discriminates against and allows for lowered standards of living for its minority members. Hence, the goals of CCUHW may be seen as attempting to transform the identity of minority peoples in Arizona.

CCUHW is also trying to redefine "minority" insofar as it is trying to put forth an image of unified action among various minority groups in the state. While "minorities" have been traditionally divided in terms of their competition for service funding, this coalition is now establishing a united front, and demanding that it be given a voice and a space of action. The coalition seems directed toward ensuring that those in power are made to be sensitive to their issues, and further that those who are sensitive by virtue of their racial status are allowed into structures where they have previously been absent. In the words of the members themselves, CCUHW will pressure existing agencies into hiring and serving minority peoples (Appendix 2, Interview J), and carve out spaces of action by ensuring that "a few dark faces [are] in a few select places where they have an influence on policy" (Appendix 2, Interview K). Thus, CCUHW seems directed toward challenging the current definitions of "minority," especially regarding the legitimacy of their voices in the area of health care.

Second, CCUHW appears to be attempting socially transformative action through the mobilization of resources (Oberschall 1973; Touraine 1985), or what members termed as a conscious effort to pool their scarce resources (Appendix 2, Interviews B, C, F, K, M, Q, S). This pooling of resources should not be mistakenly interpreted as merely petitioning and enticing governmental powers for funding. Rather, the members of CCUHW recognized the underrepresentation and inadequacy of services to their identity groups, and have made a conscious effort to collect and organize the resources at their disposal (including money, labor, and time) to address the injustices they perceived. The coalition subsequently chose to address these perceived discrepancies through both governmental redress and public education. However, those actions were separate from the initial impetus to harness resources. Thus, while CCUHW may be setting an agenda to garner resources for its perceived clients, it is also engaging in socially transformative action insofar as its members are uniting resources which have heretofore been successfully divided. As one member noted, "The government sets us up to bicker over funds" (Appendix 2,

Interview H). If this type of resource mobilization were to occur on a large scale, it seems fair to say that the face of U.S. politics would be drastically altered.

Resource mobilization is also taking place in the sense that CCUHW is attempting to transfer resources from one arena, namely the established service-providing organizations, to another. Unlike in the past, the coalition members are no longer willing to support and endorse other organizations' projects; they are formulating proposals of their own to ensure sensitivity to and an addressing of the relevant cultural issues. In this real sense, CCUHW is challenging the established service-providing agencies for the monies they have traditionally expected. These efforts will ultimately either lead to a change in the way our society is distributing its resources, or it will merely foster "stealing" on the part of the established agencies to attain "minority" professionals, thus justifying their application for the funds (Appendix 2, Interview V). For now, attempts are being made to ensure the former.

Thus, CCUHW appears to be striving for social changes to ultimately enable the health alternatives which it proposes to reach decision-making ears, and have an effect on the peoples for whom they are intended. In the absence of this struggle for socially transformative action, it is questionable whether their agenda-setting efforts could ever reach fruition. For without equal access and an equal voice, the ideas of CCUHW and other minority groups are likely to remain silent in a system which has only partially integrated the totality of its constituents.

CONCLUSION

For close to three decades, it has appeared that minority populations in this country have been unable to attain adequate redress for the injustices they perceive to be operating in this society. Recently, discussion of this failure has focused on the uniqueness of minority struggles in the public arena. Specifically, contemporary works have suggested that minorities must employ nontraditional means[6] in their attempts to set policy (Korsmo 1990; Marquez 1990), given their exclusion from traditional accesses to decision makers. I maintain that CCUHW represents an example of this type of nontraditional protest, and that this study suggests modifications to the established models of agenda setting in their application to minority struggles.

The paramount issue which emerges from this study is the limitation of agenda-setting models in accounting for minority struggles in a nonpluralistic society. The political arena, like the entirety of this society, by no means represents an "equal playing field." Access to centers of power is neither evenly distributed nor equally attainable. Any model, therefore, which seeks to describe sociopolitical activity must necessarily incorporate and account for this disequilibrium of power. Insofar as traditional agenda-setting models fail to reflect the reality of this disequilibrium of power, they fall short of adequately describing the true nature of minority struggles in the political sphere.

I do not intend to suggest that agenda-setting models are completely void of value for understanding the processes by which issues are brought to the attention of decision makers. On the contrary, this study has shown the usefulness of the models in tracing the strategies of a nascent organization attempting to influence health policies. However, the models are neither sufficient to describe the totality of the activity involved in the process, nor can they account for the expanse of goals to which the process of agenda setting must be directed for minority populations. Only by introducing literature on NSMs can the agenda-setting models begin to reflect the actuality of these nontraditional protests. Namely, it is only when agenda setting is interpreted as encompassing the actual creation of a space for action, an entree to power, that it speaks to the mobilization undertaken by CCUHW and other minority groups.

Finally, the study of CCUHW indicates that the sites for minority struggles for justice may lie outside the traditional boundaries of political action. CCUHW is not a lobby group, a political action committee (PAC), or any kind of governmental entity. One would not see the coalition represented at congressional hearings; one could not find them picketing on their representatives' steps. Yet this organization is clearly attempting to influence the formal health agenda, and there is some reason to believe that its strategies may succeed. There seems to be some potential, then, for the existence of these nontraditional struggles in other nontraditional sites which have yet to be explored. These sites may very well represent the core of minority protest in a society which discriminately allots access to power, and only legitimizes the voices of those in power. To the extent that this is true, the actual range of minority struggles for justice has just begun to be discovered; CCUHW represents only one of possibly many sites where minority peoples are currently mobilizing to have their voices heard and legitimized on policy issues.

APPENDIX 2

Interviews with Author

By the interviewees' request, names have been omitted from this documentation.

First Round Interviews

A (March 14, 1990).
B (March 28, 1990).
C (March 28, 1990).
D (April 6, 1990).
E (April 9, 1990).
F (April 10, 1990).
G (May 7, 1990).

Second Round Interviews

H (January 20, 1991).
I (January 20, 1991).
J (January 23, 1991).
K (January 23, 1991).
L (January 24, 1991).
M (January 24, 1991).
N (January 25, 1991).
O (January 25, 1991).
P (January 25, 1991).
Q (January 28, 1991).
R (January 28, 1991).
S (January 29, 1991).
T (January 29, 1991).
U (January 31, 1991).
V (February 1, 1991).
W (February 13, 1991).

NOTES

1. Borrowing from Cobb et al. (1976:126), I distinguish between public and institutional attention in the following manner: Attaining public attention entails elevating issues to a high level of public interest and visibility; institutional attention is garnered when decision makers accept an issue for serious consideration.

2. This research was supported by a National Science Foundation Grants Law and Social Sciences Program (SES–8908456).

3. There is a substantial body of literature on organizational structure, constituting a topic worthy of its own consideration. Without going into too much detail, one should simply note that traditional bureaucratic models put forth definitions regarding authority structures, labor divisions, recruitment, and management strategies which do not accurately pertain to CCUHW (see Vroom and Jago 1988; Tosi 1984; Meyer and Rowan 1977; and Haas and Drabek 1973). Recently, a new body of literature on alternative organiza-

tions has emerged, which defines organizations more closely approximating CCUHW. Using an article by Rothschild-Whitt (1979), which concisely contrasts bureaucratic and collectivist organizations on eight dimensions, this author has categorized CCUHW as a democratic-collectivist organizational type.

4. This quote was taken from a draft mission statement which was never discussed or adopted. The statement was formated based on a project proposal by the People of Color Advisory Committee on AIDS in San Francisco.

5. Although Nelson does speak of the concept of formal agendas, she refers to these issues which are being considered by governmental by the terms *governmental agenda* and *public agenda* (1984:21). In order to simplify the terminology, this author chose not to use Nelson's original terms, employing the term formal agenda instead.

6. Nontraditional is used here in the sense that Aldon Morris has elaborated: "A dominated group is defined as one that is excluded from one or more of the decision-making processes that determine the quantity and quality of social, economic, and political rewards that groups receive from a society. Because of this exclusion, dominated groups at different times attempt to change their situation of powerlessness by engaging in non-traditional and usually non-legitimized struggles with power holders" (1984:282).

IV

CONCLUSION

11

Racial Minorities and Agenda Setting: Is There Access and Influence?

Paula D. McClain

An entire generation of political science research on interest groups (pluralism) identified competition between groups as the source of policy initiatives. Public policy researchers have renamed this particular line of reasoning the agenda-setting process. Agenda setting has been termed the predecision stage of the public policy process. The policy agenda-setting phase has been described as probably the most important stage in the public policy process, for if an issue fails to reach the institutional or governmental agenda, clearly no action will be forthcoming. Additionally, the initial definition of a problem occurs in this phase, and that definition will often determine the direction in which policy solutions will be formulated. The chapters in this book have addressed a variety of policy issues from several perspectives. The extant literature on agenda setting is limited and these chapters build on that narrow theoretical foundation. Minority influence on the policy process has been discussed internationally, at the national (domestic) level, and at the state level.

Remember, several questions were initially framed to organize the chapters in this book on racial minorities and the policy agenda-setting process: What role do minority citizens play in policy agenda setting? Do minority citizens have access to the policy process? If so, to what extent are they able to influence public policy? If not, what are the barriers? As these chapters demonstrate, the results are mixed on these questions. Recognizing that these chapters represent a very small slice of the agenda-setting activities of various minority groups, the weight of the evidence in this book seems to fall on the side of minimal influence of racial minority groups on the policy agenda-setting process. The reasons for the lack of access and influence can be broadly categorized as the structure of the process itself, as well as the nature of the U.S. pluralist system (Korsmo, Marquez, Solop, Henry, Meacham, and Thomas), a lack of group cohesion (Studlar), and the idea behind a policy problem (McClain).

Several of these chapters have joined in the continuing debate over the utility of current agenda-setting paradigms, which are essentially pluralist in foundation, for examining and understanding racial minority group views, inputs, and perceptions of the process. Both Benjamin Marquez and Frederic Solop conclude that Latino and African-American pressure groups have limited influence on the policy process in the long term. Marquez's analysis of the Industrial Areas Foundation (IAF) suggests that the organization was successful in articulating the needs of the poor Mexican-American population and successfully placed issues on the policy agenda. However, IAF failed in bringing about a change in the economic conditions of Mexican-Americans in Texas. Marquez concludes that community organizing and pressure group activity bring about small, piecemeal changes, but will never overcome the barriers to fundamental social change. Solop, examining the anti-apartheid movement in the United States, reaches a similar judgment in arguing that African-Americans were unable to prevent the repeal of sanctions against South Africa, and when the sanctions were removed, little was heard from the anti-apartheid movement. The structure of the U.S. political system prohibits sustained influence by African-Americans.

Fae Korsmo, studying several Alaska Native organizations, continues the debate on the utility of prevailing agenda-setting paradigms by arguing that those minority interest groups that have been able to exert some influence on the agenda-setting and policy process are those that enjoy some form of patronage among the elite decision makers. Therefore, in order to continue the patronage relationship and enjoy the benefits, minority interest groups adopt a strategy that avoids redistributive issues. Yet the patronage relationship, while confining for the minority group, may provide some opportunities for the group to advance some of its issues. Thomas weighs in with the observation that the pluralist playing field is not level for minorities; thus, the current agenda-setting models are incomplete. She argues that an appropriate model for examining minority group influence must abandon the traditional pluralism that is firmly embedded in the extant agenda-setting models. She proposes the social transformation model as a way of encompassing minority organizations that develop strategies to level the uneven playing field. Her study of Cultural Communities United in Health and Wellness is illustrative of her social transformation model.

Another aspect of the pluralist nature of the agenda-setting process is the importance of the development of the public "idea" in defining public policy issues. As I argue, many public policy issues are already defined by the time they are raised to the agenda. Moreover, the particular definition of a problem determines the direction of the policy responses that are developed during other stages of the policy process.

While not joining directly in the debate over pluralist paradigms of the agenda-setting process but related to the pluralist process, Charles Henry argues that the perception of whether or not policy proposals are viewed as "innovative" may be crucial to the success of policies that directly benefit minority communities. Henry shows that the full employment bills were innovative, but the obstacles preventing the implementation of the acts—the debate over responsibility and the substitution of technical innovation for political innovation—made the acts appear not to be innovative.

The second factor preventing access is political organization. Donley Studlar demonstrates that while racial discrimination has decreased in Britain, racial indifference still exists. Thus, it is extremely difficult to place nonwhite concerns on the public agenda. Moreover, the lack of nonwhite cohesion exacerbates an already difficult access problem, particularly since the British government has exploited this lack of cohesion among the various races, for example, Afro-British, African, Afro-Caribbean, and East Indian, to its advantage. Thus, nonwhites have limited capacity to influence the political agenda in Britain and must rely on liberal white allies, both inside and outside of government, to set the political agenda on race-related issues. Although Studlar's analysis is of Britain, there are clearly parallels that could be drawn with the situation of U.S. racial minorities. Organizational factors, as Cheryl Miller demonstrates, may account for some of the few successes minority groups have achieved in placing items on the agenda.

The agenda-setting successes are few, and in some instances only partial successes. Although narrowly focusing on legislative black caucuses, Miller perceives a high degree of cohesion among the state black caucuses and identifies clear agenda-setting successes, but nevertheless recognizes several situational variables that constrain legislative black caucuses in their choice of issues to pursue. These constraint variables are: (1) regional differences within the caucuses; (2) ability of the legislative black caucus to gain leadership positions within the legislative body; and (3) the caucuses' relationship with the majority party. These constraints pushed legislative black caucuses to focus their policy agendas on substantive rather than symbolic issues.

Paula McClain argues that a third barrier to successful agenda setting is the way in which, through public discourse, issues are defined—defined in ways that bare little resemblance to the true nature and structure of the problem. The manner in which an issue is defined determines the direction and form the policy prescriptions will take. Moreover, once the "idea" behind an issue takes hold, it becomes extremely difficult to redirect the public discourse in a way that allows for the problem to be more accurately reconceptualized, thus generating policies that will actually begin to solve the problem. The difficulty of problem reconceptualization is magnified when race is a factor in the equation.

Carl Meacham's analysis of the New York State Minority Internship Program found that while the internship program was successful in bringing a limited number of racial minorities into the public service, the graduates of this program will have marginal effects on the agenda-setting process. He speculates that the mere presence of minority public administrators will heighten sensitivity to minority agendas. Thus, he concludes that the significance of the internship program to the agenda-setting process is in the potential to produce more minority public administrators. Unfortunately, the internship program fell victim to state budget cuts; thus the limited potential for opening access to minority administrators has been curtailed.

Yet, this particular perspective of the importance of minority public administrators to the agenda-setting process may have some validity. Some would contend that various public administrators have more influence than elected officials over the policy arenas that directly affect the lives of minority groups. For example, if one is concerned about the relationship between the police department and minority communities, the appointment of a minority police chief may yield faster and more permanent structural changes than the election of a minority city council person or even mayor. Moreover, increases in minority employment may come more quickly if a minority person is hired as director of personnel, city manager, or agency head (McClain and Karnig 1988:5).

Whether holding elective or administrative office, minorities within government may be extremely important as agenda-setting agents. This conjecture, of course, needs further exploration because elective and appointed officials clearly operate within a set of constraints that may limit their ability to influence the agenda-setting process. Nevertheless, it is a line of argument that deserves further research.

The essays in this book have addressed an important, yet much underestimated and understudied, aspect of the policy process—agenda setting. The argument could be made that of all of the stages in the policy process, agenda setting is the most important. For, if issues are not recognized as significant and identified by public decision makers for public action, no governmental action will occur. Given its importance, the broader question of minority group influence on the agenda-setting process requires serious study. This book is a step in that direction. Obviously, influence and access to this crucial predecision stage would have considerable influence on the direction of policy solutions for issues of concern to minority communities.

Bibliography

Acuña, Rodolfo. 1988. *Occupied America: A History of Chicanos*. New York: Harper and Row.

Africa Fund, The. 1986. "Divestment Actions on South Africa by U.S. Colleges and Universities." Unpublished article distributed by The Africa Fund.

Agnew, Rick. 1991. Interview with Fae Korsmo. 16 August.

Alaska Federation of Natives. 1969. "Position with Respect to Native Land Claims Issue." In *Curry-Weissbrodt Papers*. Fairbanks, AK: Rasmuson Library, University of Alaska–Fairbanks.

———. 1983. "ICC-Alaska Native Review Commission." *Alaska Native News*, April.

———. 1984. "1991: The Challenge Must be Met." *Special Supplement to the Tundra Times*, 24 September.

———. 1985. "1991 Resolutions." *Alaska Native News*, June.

———. 1989. *The AFN Report on the Status of Alaska Natives: A Call for Action*. Anchorage, AK: The Alaska Federation of Natives.

Alaska Native Review Commission Papers. General Correspondence Series 10, Box 43. Fairbanks, AK: Rasmuson Library, University of Alaska–Fairbanks.

Alinsky, Saul. 1969. *Reveille for Radicals*. New York: Vintage.

———. 1971. *Rules for Radicals*. New York: Random House.

———. 1972. "A Candid Conversation with the Fiesty Radical Organizer." *Playboy*, March.

Allen, Nancy H. 1981. "Homicide Prevention and Intervention." *Suicide and Life Threatening Behavior* 11:167–179.

Anderson, Charles W. 1978. "The Logic of Public Problems: Evaluation in Comparative Policy Research." In *Comparative Public Policy: A Cross National Bibliography*, eds. Douglas E. Ashford, Peter J. Katzenstein, and T. J. Pempel. Beverly Hills, CA: Sage Publications.

Applebome, Peter. 1988. "Along U.S. Border, a Third World is Reborn." *New York Times*, 27 March.

———. 1989. "At Texas Border, Hopes for Sewers and Water." *New York Times*, 28 December.

Arkes, Hadley. 1981. *The Philosopher in the City*. Princeton, NJ: Princeton University Press.

Arnold, Robert D. 1978. *Alaska Native Land Claims*. Anchorage, AK: Alaska Native Foundation.

Ashford, Douglas E. 1981. *Policy and Politics in Britain*. Philadelphia: Temple University Press.

Association of Village Council Presidents. 1985a. *Yulpit Kanlautciat*, July.

——. 1985b. "Policy Statement on ANCSA and Tribal Government." Adopted at the AVCP 1991 Convention, Aniak, AK.

Bachrach, Peter, and Morton Baratz. 1962. "Two Faces of Power." *American Political Science Review* 56:947–952.

——. 1963. "Decision and Non Decision: An Analytic Framework." *American Political Science Review* 57:632–642.

——. 1970. *Power and Poverty*. New York: Oxford University Press.

Bailey, Stephen Kemp. 1950. *Congress Makes a Law*. New York: Columbia University Press.

Ball, Wendy, and John Solomos, eds. 1990. *Race and Local Politics*. London: Macmillan.

Banton, Michael. 1985. *Promoting Racial Harmony*. Cambridge: Cambridge University Press.

Barker, Lucius J., and Jesse J. McCorry, Jr. 1976. *Black Americans and the Political Process*. Cambridge, MA: Winthrop Publishers.

Barnett, Marguerite R. 1976. "A Theoretical Perspective on American Racial Public Policy." In *Public Policy for the Black Community: Strategies and Perspectives*, eds. Marguerite R. Barnett and James A. Hefner. New York: Alfred Publishing Company.

Barnett, Marguerite R., and James A. Hefner. 1976. *Public Policy for the Black Community: Strategies and Perspectives*. New York: Alfred Publishing Company.

Barrera, Mario. 1979. *Race and Class in the Southwest*. Notre Dame, IN: University of Notre Dame Press.

——. 1985. "The Historic Evolution of Chicano Ethnic Goals." *Sage Race Relations Abstracts* 10:1–48.

Baumer, Donald C., and Carl E. Van Horn. 1985. *The Politics of Unemployment*. Washington, DC: Congressional Quarterly Press.

Baumgartner, Frank R., and Bryan D. Jones. 1991. "Agenda Dynamics and Policy Subsystems." *Journal of Politics* 53:1044–1074.

Bennett, Colin J. 1991a. "How States Utilize Foreign Evidence." *Journal of Public Policy* 11:31–54.

——. 1991b. "Review Article: What is Policy Convergence and What Causes It?" *British Journal of Political Science* 21:215–233.

Bennett, Colin J., and Michael Howlett. 1991. "When States Learn Do They Change? American Lessons and the Conceptualization of Policy Change." Presented at the annual meeting of the American Political Science Association, Washington, DC.

Bentley, Arthur F. 1949. *The Process of Government*. Evanston, IL: Principia Press of Illinois.

Ben-Tovim, Gideon. 1989. "Race, Politics, and Urban Regeneration: Lessons from Liverpool." In *Regenerating the Cities*, eds. Michael Parkinson, Bernard Foley, and Dennis R. Judd. Boston, MA: Scott, Foresman.

Benyon, John, ed. 1984. *Scarman and After*. New York: Pergamon Press.

Berger, Thomas R. 1985. *Village Journey*. New York: Hill & Wang.

Berry, Mary Clay. 1975. *The Alaska Pipeline: The Politics of Oil and Native Land Claims*. Bloomington, IN, and London: Indiana University Press.

Bezick, Denise. 1990. "It's Health vs Cheap Housing in Colonia Flap." *El Paso Times*, 1 July.

Birch, Doug. 1989. "Black Caucus Votes to Boycott Receptions at Annapolis Club." *Baltimore Sun*, 18 January, sec. H.

"Black Caucus Emerging Power in Legislature." 1987. *Durham Morning Herald*, 9 March, sec. B.

Black, Earl, and Merle Black. 1987. *Politics and Society in the South*. Cambridge, MA: Harvard University Press.

"Black Leaders Appeal to Carter For Meeting on Jobless 'Crisis.' " 1977. *New York Times*, 5 November.

Booth, Heather. 1988. "Identifying Ethnic Origin: The Past, Present, and Future of Official Data Production." In *Britain's Black Population: A New Perspective*, 2nd ed., eds. Ashok Bhat, Roy Carr-Hill, and Sushel Ohri. Brookfield, VT: Gower.

Boggs, Carl. 1983. "The New Populism and the Limits of Structural Reforms." *Theory and Society* 12:343–363.

Bosso, Christopher J. 1987. *Pesticides and Politics*. Pittsburgh: University of Pittsburgh Press.

Boyer, Edward J. 1985. "Group Strength." *Los Angeles Times*, 8 September.

Boyte, Harry C. 1980. *The Backyard Revolution*. Philadelphia: Temple University Press.

———. 1981. "Community Organizing in the 1970s: Seeds of Democratic Revolt." In *Community Organization for Urban Social Change*, eds. Robert Fisher and Peter Romanofsky. Westport, CT: Greenwood Press.

———. 1984. *Community is Possible*. New York: Harper and Row.

———. 1990. "The Growth of Citizen Politics." *Dissent* 37:513–518.

Boyte, Harry C., and Sara Evans. 1984. "Strategies in Search for America: Cultural Radicalism, Populism, and Democratic Culture." *Socialist Review* 14:73–101.

Bragg, Richard. 1979. "The Maryland Black Caucus as a Racial Group in the Maryland General Assembly." Ph.D. Diss., Howard University.

Briggs, Vernon M. 1984. *Immigration Policy and the American Labor Force*. Baltimore: Johns Hopkins University Press.

Browning, Rufus P., Dale Rogers Marshall, and David H. Tabb. 1984. *Protest is not Enough: The Struggle of Blacks and Hispanics for Equality in Urban Politics*. Berkeley, CA: University of California Press.

———. 1990. *Racial Politics in American Cities*. New York: Longman.

Buchannan, James M. 1975. *The Limits of Liberty: Between Anarchy and Leviathan*. Chicago: University of Chicago Press.

Buchannan, James M., and R. E. Wagner. 1977. *Democracy in Deficit: The Political Legacy of Lord Rynes*. New York: Academic Press.

Buckley, William F., Jr. 1984. "The Humphrey-Hawkins Bishops." *Washington Post*, 18 November.

Bullock, Charles S. III. 1987. "Redistricting and Changes in the Partisan and Racial Composition of Southern Legislatures." *State and Local Government Review* 19:62–67.

Bullock, Charles S. III, and Susan A. MacManus. 1981. "Policy Responsiveness to the Black Electorate: Programmatic Versus Symbolic Representation." *American Politics Quarterly* 9:357–368.

Bullock, Paul, ed. 1978. *Goals for Full Employment*. Los Angeles: Institute of Industrial Relations, University of California.

Bulpitt, Jim. 1986. "Continuity, Autonomy, and Peripheralisation: The Anatomy of the Centre's Race Statecraft in England." In *Race, Government, and Politics in Britain*, eds. Zig Layton-Henry and Paul B. Rich. London: Macmillan.

Button, James W., and Richard K. Scher. 1984. "The Election and Impact of Black Officials in the South." In *Public Policy and Social Institutions*, ed. Harrell Rodgers, Jr. Greenwich, CT: JAI Press.

Campbell, David, and Joe R. Feagin. 1975. "Black Politics in the South: A Descriptive Analysis." *Journal of Politics* 37:129–159.

Case, David. 1984. *Alaska Natives and American Laws*. Fairbanks, AK: University of Alaska Press.

Castells, Manuel. 1983. *The City and the Grassroots*. Berkeley, CA: University of California Press.

Ceasar, Paul, Sr. 1988. Interview with Benjamin Marquez. 18 July.

Chapados, Greg. 1991. Interview with Fae Korsmo. 28 August.

Cisneros, Henry. 1988. "Counter Power in San Antonio: Power, Politics and the Pastoral." *Commonweal* 115:75–79.

Clark, Kenneth B., and John Hope Franklin. 1983. *A Policy for Racial Justice*. Washington, DC: Joint Center for Political Studies.

Cobb, Roger W., and Charles D. Elder. 1972. *Participation in American Politics: The Dynamics of Agenda-Building*. Boston: Allyn and Bacon.

———. 1981. "Communications and Public Policy." In *Handbook of Political Communication*, eds. Dan D. Mimmo and Keith R. Sanders. Beverly Hills, CA: Sage Publications.

———. 1983. *Participation in American Politics: The Dynamics of Agenda-Building*. Baltimore: John Hopkins University Press.

Cobb, Roger W., Jennie Keith-Ross, and Marc Howard Ross. 1976. "Agenda Building as a Comparative Political Process." *American Political Science Review* 70:126–138.

Cohen, Felix S. 1982. *Handbook of Federal Indian Law*. Charlottesville, VA: Michie Bobbs-Merrill.

Cohen, Jean L. 1985. "Strategy or Identity: New Theoretical Paradigms and Contemporary Social Movements." *Social Research* 52:663–716.

Cohen, Michael D., March G. James, and Johan P. Olsen. 1972. "A Garbage Can Model of Organizational Choice." *Administrative Science Quarterly* 17:1–25.

Cohodas, Nadine. 1985. "Black House Members Striving for Influence: Growing Seniority Gives Them Clout." *Congressional Quarterly Weekly Report* 43:675–681.

Coker, Christopher. 1986. *The United States and South Africa, 1968–1985: Constructive Engagement and its Critics*. Durham, NC: Duke University Press.

Cole, Leonard A. 1977. "Blacks and Ethnic Political Tolerance." *Polity* 9:302–320.

Collier, David, and Richard E. Messick. 1975. "Prerequisites Versus Diffusion: Testing Alternative Explanations for Social Security Adoption." *American Political Science Review* 69:1299–1315.

Colston, Fred. 1972. "The Influence of Black Legislators in the Ohio House of Representatives." Ph.D. Diss., Ohio State University.

Congressional Record. 1986–1987.Washington, DC: U.S. Government Printing Office.

Conway, M. Margaret. 1991. *Political Participation in the United States.* Washington, DC: Congressional Quarterly.

Cook, Allison. 1988. "Just Add Water." *Texas Monthly* 16:70–74.

Copely News Service. 1978. "Buckley Easy to Forgive Despite His Archaic Views." 2 January.

Cortes, Ernesto, Jr. 1986. "Organizing the Community." *Texas Monthly,* 11 July.

———. 1988. Interview with Benjamin Marquez. 1 October.

Crenson, Matthew A. 1971. *The Un-Politics of Air Pollution.* Baltimore: Johns Hopkins University Press.

Dahl, Robert A. 1956. *A Preface to Democratic Theory.* Chicago: University of Chicago Press.

———. 1961. *Who Governs?* New Haven, CT: Yale University Press.

———. 1967. *Pluralist Democracy in the United States.* Chicago: University of Chicago Press.

Danaher, Kevin. 1985. *The Political Economy of U.S. Policy Toward South Africa.* Boulder, CO: Westview Press.

Daniels, Lee A. 1992. "Preliminary 1991 Figures Show Drop in Homicides." *New York Times,* 3 January.

Deakin, Nicholas. 1974. "On Some Perils of Imitation." In *Lessons From America,* ed. Richard Rose. New York: Halsted Press.

Delgado, Gary. 1986. *Organizing the Movement: The Roots and Growth of ACORN.* Philadelphia: Temple University Press.

del Olmo, Frank. 1983. "Two Latino Activists Travel Separate Paths." *Los Angeles Times,* 29 July.

Dobbins, Cheryl, and Dollie R. Walker. 1974. "The Role of Black Colleges in Public Affairs Education." *Public Administration Review* 34:552–556.

Domhoff, G. William. 1978. *Who Really Rules.* Santa Monica, CA: Goodyear Publishing.

Downs, Anthony. 1972. "Up and Down with Ecology: The Issue Attention Cycle." *The Public Interest* 28:38–52.

Drewry, Gavin. 1985. "The Home Affairs Committee." In *The New Select Committees,* ed. Gavin Drewry. Oxford: Clarendon Press.

Duchineaux, Frank. 1991. Interview with Fae Korsmo. 4 September.

Durant, Robert F., and Paul F. Diehl. 1989. "Agendas, Alternatives, and Public Policy: Lessons from the U.S. Policy Arena." *Journal of Public Policy* 9:179–205.

Dye, Thomas R. 1992. *Understanding Public Policy.* 7th ed. Englewood Cliffs, NJ: Prentice Hall.

Easton, David. 1965. *A Systems Analysis of Political Life.* New York: John Wiley and Sons.

———. 1971. *The Political System: An Inquiry into the State of Political Science.* New York: Alfred A. Knopf.

Easum, Donald B. 1975. "United States Policy Toward South Africa." *Issue: A Quarterly Journal of Africanist Opinion* 5:66–72.

Edsall, Thomas Byrne, and Mary D. Edsall. 1991. *Chain Reaction: The Impact of Race, Rights, and Taxes on American Politics.* New York: W. W. Norton.

Edwards, John, and Richard Batley. 1978. *The Politics of Positive Discrimination.* London: Tavistock.

Eisinger, Peter K. 1980. *The Politics of Displacement: Racial and Ethnic Transition in Three American Cities.* New York: Academic Press.

Ellana, Linda J. 1980. "Bering-Norton Petroleum Development Scenarios and Sociocultural Impacts Analysis." *Minerals Management Service Social and Economic Report TR-54.* 2 vols. Anchorage, AK: Minerals Management Service.

EPISO. 1987. *1987 4th Annual Friends of EPISO Ad Book.* Unpublished article in author's possession.

Ermer, Virginia B., and John H. Strange, eds. 1972. *Blacks and Bureaucracy: Readings in the Problems and Politics of Change.* New York: Thomas Y. Crowell Company.

Eyestone, Robert. 1978. *From Social Issues to Public Policy.* New York: Wiley.

Farmer, Francesca E. 1984. "The People's Platform." *Focus* 12.

Fears, D. D. 1985. "A Time of Testing for Black Caucus as its Members Rise to Power in House." *National Journal* 17:909–911.

Federal Bureau of Investigation. 1989. *Crime in the U.S.—1989.* Washington, DC: U.S. Government Printing Office.

———. 1991. *Uniform Crime Reports.* Washington, DC: U.S. Government Printing Office.

Ferman, Barbara. 1985. *Governing the Ungovernable City: Political Leadership and the Modern Mayor.* Philadelphia: Temple University Press.

Fiellin, Alan. 1962. "The Functions of Informal Groups in Legislative Institutions." *Journal of Politics* 24:72–91.

Finks, David. 1984. *The Radical Vision of Saul Alinsky.* New York: Paulist Press.

Fisher, Robert. 1984. *Let the People Decide.* Boston: Twayne Publishers.

Fitzgerald, Marian. 1986. "Immigration and Race Relations: Political Aspects—No. 15." *New Community* 13:265–271.

———. 1988. "Different Roads? The Development of Afro-Caribbean and Asian Political Organization in London." *New Community* 14:385–396.

Flanders, Nicholas E. 1989. "The ANCSA Amendments of 1987 and Land Management in Alaska." *Polar Record* 155:315–322.

Flickinger, Richard. 1983. "The Comparative Politics of Agenda Setting: The Emergence of Consumer Protection as a Public Policy Issue in Britain and the United States." *Policy Studies Review* 2:429–444.

Flores, Henry. 1989. "You Can't Win for Winning: Hispanic Mayoral Politics in San Antonio Texas." Presented at the annual meeting of the Western Political Science Association, Salt Lake City, UT.

Francis, Wayne L. 1985. "Leadership, Party Caucuses, and Committees in the U.S. State Legislatures." *Legislative Studies Quarterly* 10:243–255.

Freeman, Gary P. 1985. "National Styles and Policy Sectors: Explaining Structured Variation." *Journal of Public Policy* 5:467–496.

Frohock, Fred M. 1979. *Public Policy: Scope and Logic.* Englewood Cliffs, NJ: Prentice Hall.

Gamble, Don J. 1978. "The Berger Inquiry: An Impact Assessment Process." *Science* 199:946–952.

Gamson, J. 1989. "Silence, Death, and the Invisible Enemy: AIDS, Activism, and Social Movement 'Newness.' " *Social Problems* 36:351–367.

Gans, Herbert J. 1990. "Deconstructing the Underclass: The Term's Danger as a Planning Concept." *Journal of American Planning Association* 56:271–277.

Garcia, F. Chris, and Rudolfo de la Garza. 1977. *The Chicano Political Experience*. North Scituate, MA: Duxbury Press.

Garrow, David J. 1978. *Protest at Selma*. New Haven, CT: Yale University Press.

Ginsburg, Benjamin. 1982. *The Consequences of Consent*. Reading, MA: Addison-Wesley Publishing.

Gittell, Marylin. 1980. *Limits to Citizen Participation: The Decline of Community Organizations*. Beverly Hills, CA: Sage Publications.

Gomez-Quiñones, Juan. 1978. *Mexican Students Por La Raza*. Santa Barbara, CA: Editorial La Causa.

Goodin, Robert. 1982. "Banana Time in British Politics." *Political Studies* 30:42–58.

Goodin, Robert E. 1982. *Political Theory to Public Policy*. Chicago: University of Chicago Press.

Governor's Task Force. 1968. *Task Force Commentary on State Alaska Native Claims Act: Draft of January 24, 1968*. Juneau, AK: Alaska State Archives.

Gray, Virginia. 1973. "Innovation in the States: A Diffusion Study." *American Political Science Review* 67:1174–1185.

Greenberg, Edward S., Neal Milner, and David J. Olson. 1974. *Black Politics*. New York: Holt, Rinehart and Winston.

Greenhouse, Linda. 1989. "Court Bars a Plan to Provide Jobs to Minorities." *New York Times*, 24 January.

Gregory, Jeanne. 1987. *Sex, Race, and the Law*. London: Sage.

Gross, Bertram. 1974. "Statement." *Subcommittee on Equal Opportunities Hearing on H.R. 15476, House Committee on Education and Labor*. 93rd Congress, Second Session.

Gross, Bertram, and Kusum Singh. N.d. *Let Freedom Ring*. Forthcoming.

Grumm, John. 1965. "The Systematic Analysis of Blocs in the Study of Legislative Behavior." *Western Political Quarterly* 18:350–363.

Haas, J. E., and T. E. Drabek. 1973. *Complex Organizations: A Sociological Perspective*. New York: Macmillan.

Hagerty, Vaughn. 1987. "COPS Puts Stadium Vote on Hold; Says it Won't Back Tax Funds Use." *San Antonio Light*, 26 October.

Hamilton, Charles V. 1972. "Racial, Ethnic, and Social Class Politics." *Public Administration Review* 32:638–648.

———. 1981. "New Elites and Pluralism." *The Power to Govern: Proceedings of the Academy of Political Science* 34:167–173.

Harmel, Robert, Keith Hamm, and Robert Thompson. 1983. "Black Voting Cohesion and Distinctiveness in Three Southern Legislatures." *Social Science Quarterly* 64:181–192.

Hawkesworth, M. E. 1988. *Theoretical Issues in Policy Analysis*. Albany, NY: State University of New York Press.

Hawkins, Augustus F. 1975. "Planning for Personal Choice." *Annals of the American Academy of Political and Social Scientists* 418:13–16.

Heidenheimer, Arnold. 1985. "Comparative Public Policy at the Crossroads." *Journal of Public Policy* 5:441–465.

Heineman, Benjamin W., Jr. 1972. *The Politics of the Powerless: A Study of C.A.R.D.* London: Oxford University Press.

Henry, Charles P. 1977. "Legitimating Race in Congressional Politics." *American Politics Quarterly* 5:149–176.

Hensley, Willie. 1991. Interview with Fae Korsmo. 24 June.

Herbert, Adam. 1974. "The Minority Administrator: Problems, Prospects, and Challenges." *Public Administration Review* 34:556–563.

Hero, Rodney C. 1992. *Latinos and the American Political System: Two Tiered Pluralism?* Philadelphia: Temple University Press.

Hindell, Keith. 1965. "The Genesis of the Race Relations Bill." *Political Quarterly* 36:390–405.

Hogwood, Brian W. 1987. *From Crisis to Complacency? Shaping Public Policy in Britain.* New York: Oxford University Press.

Hogwood, Brian W., and Guy Peters. 1983. *Policy Dynamics.* New York: St. Martin's Press.

Holden, Matthew J. 1973. *The Politics of the Black Nation.* San Francisco: Chandler Publishing Company.

Holler, Tom. 1988. Interview with Benjamin Marquez. 12 July.

Holly, Dan. 1989. "Black Legislators Gather to Discuss Their Gains." *Tallahassee Democrat,* 29 November, sec. D.

Houser, George. 1976. "Meeting Africa's Challenge: The Story of the American Committee on Africa." *Issue: A Quarterly Journal of Africanist Opinion* 6:16–26.

Humphrey, Hubert. 1975. *Speech Delivered at the Congressional Black Caucus Weekend.* September.

Hunt, Deryl G. 1974. "The Black Perspective on Public Management." *Public Administration Review* 34:520–525.

Hunter, Floyd. 1980. *Community Power Succession.* Chapel Hill, NC: University of North Carolina Press.

Hyman, Mark. 1988. "Black Groups Agree in Minority Share." *Baltimore Sun,* 22 November, sec. D.

———. 1989. "Black Legislators Meet with Kirwan." *Baltimore Sun,* 6 June, sec. B.

Industrial Areas Foundation. 1978. *Organizing for Family and Congregation.* Franklin Square, NY: Industrial Areas Foundation.

———. 1988. "Sign-Up and Take Charge Campaign." Unpublished leaflet in possession of the author.

Jacobs, Brian. 1986. *Black Politics and Urban Crisis in Britain.* Cambridge: Cambridge University Press.

Joint Center for Political Studies. 1990. *National Roster of Black Elected Officials.* Washington, DC: JCPS.

Jones, Alex S. 1991. "Editors Report Gains in 1990 in Minority Journalists Hiring." *New York Times,* 12 April.

Jones, Charles O. 1977. *An Introduction to the Study of Public Policy.* 2nd ed. North Scituate, MA: Duxbury.

———. 1984. *An Introduction to the Study of Public Policy.* Monterey, CA: Brooks/Cole Publishing Company.

Jordan, Grant, and Jeremy Richardson. 1982. "The British Policy Style or the Logic of Negotiation?" In *Policy Styles in Western Europe,* ed. Jeremy Richardson. London: Allen and Unwin.

Jordan, Milton. 1989. "Black Legislators: From Political Novelty to Political Force." *North Carolina Insight* 12:40–58.

Jordan, Vernon. 1973. Testimony before the U.S. Congress.

Kairaiuak, Charlie. 1991. Interview with Fae Korsmo. 28 June.

Kann, Mark E. 1983. "The New Populism and the New Marxism." *Theory and Society* 12:365–373.

Karnig, Albert K., and Susan Welch. 1980. *Black Representation and Urban Policy*. Chicago: University of Chicago Press.

Katznelson, Ira. 1973. *Black Men, White Cities*. London: Oxford University Press.

———. 1981. *City Trenches: Urban Politics and the Patterning of Class in the United States*. New York: Pantheon Books.

Keech, William R. 1968. *The Impact of Negro Voting*. Chicago: Rand McNally.

Kenworthy, Tom. 1989. "CBC Facing New Circumstances after Twenty Years." *Washington Post*, 17 September, sec. A.

Kerr, Clark. 1983. *The Future of Industrial Societies*. Cambridge, MA: Harvard University Press.

Kesselman, Mark. 1982. "The Conflictual Evolution of American Political Science: From Apologetic Pluralism to Trilateralism and Marxism." In *Public Values and Private Power in American Politics*, ed. J. David Greenstone. Chicago: University of Chicago Press.

———. 1983. "From State Theory to Class Struggle and Compromise: Contemporary Marxist Political Studies." *Social Science Quarterly* 64:826–845.

King, Martin Luther, Jr. 1967. *Where Do We Go From Here*. Boston: Beacon.

Kingdon, John W. 1973. *Congressmen's Voting Decisions*. New York: Harper and Row.

———. 1984. *Agendas, Alternatives, and Public Policies*. Boston: Little, Brown, and Company.

Kirp, David. 1979. *Doing Good by Doing Little*. Berkeley, CA: University of California Press.

Kisken, Sybil R. 1989. "The Uncertain Legal Status of Alaska Natives." *Arizona Law Review* 31:405–422.

Kitka, Julie. 1991. Interview with Fae Korsmo. July 31.

Korcsmar, Reverend John S. 1988. Interview with Benjamin Marquez. 2 October.

Korsmo, Fae E. 1990. "Problem Definition and the Alaska Native: Ethnic Identity and Policy Formation." *Policy Studies Review* 9:294–306.

Langdon, Steve. 1986. "Contradictions in Alaskan Native Economy." In *Contemporary Alaskan Native Economies*, ed. Steve Langdon. Lanham, MD: University Press of America.

Last, John M. 1980. "Scope and Methods of Prevention." In *Public Health and Preventive Medicine*, 11th ed., ed. John M. Last. New York: Appleton-Century Crofts.

Lawson, Steven F. 1985. *In Pursuit of Power: Southern Blacks and Electoral Politics, 1965–1982*. New York: Columbia University Press.

———. 1991. *Running for Freedom*. New York: McGraw-Hill.

Layton-Henry, Zig. 1984. *The Politics of Race in Britain*. Boston: Allen and Unwin.

"Leading Negroes Agree on Goals." 1962. *New York Times*, 26 November.

Lee, Dalton S., and N. Joseph Cayer. 1987. "Recruitment of Minority Students for Public Administration Education." *Public Administration Review* 47:329–335.

Lenz, Mary. 1981. "Native Claims Settlement Act—Was it Meant to Fail?" *Tundra Times*, 24 September.

Lerma, Amalia. 1988. Interview with Benjamin Marquez. 30 September.

Lester, Anthony, and Geoffrey Bindman. 1972. *Race and Law*. London: Longman.

"Levantando La Voz." 1987. *The Texas Observer*, 17 July.

Levine, Charles F. 1973. "Understanding Alinsky: Conservative Wine in Radical Bottles." *American Behavioral Scientist* 17:279–284.

Levison, Andrew. 1980. *The Full Employment Alternative*. New York: Coward, McCann, and Georghegan.

Lind, Scott. 1984. "Reagan ACTION Chief Attacks Valley Interfaith and Public Works." *The Texas Observer*, 6 April.

Lindblom, Charles E. 1968. *The Policy-Making Process*. Englewood Cliffs, NJ: Prentice Hall.

Lineberry, Robert. 1977. *American Public Policy: What Government Does and What Difference it Makes*. New York: Harper and Row.

Lipsky, Michael. 1968. "Protest as a Political Resource." *American Political Science Review* 62: 144–158.

Little, Alan N. 1974. "Compensatory Education and Race Relations: What Lessons for Europe?" In *Lessons From America*, ed. Richard Rose. New York: Halstead Press.

Logan, John R., and Harvey M. Molotch. 1987. *Urban Fortunes: The Political Economy of Place*. Berkeley, CA: University of California Press.

Love, Janice. 1988. "The Potential of Economic Sanctions Against South Africa." *The Journal of Modern African Studies* 26:91–111.

Lowe, Stuart. 1986. *Urban Social Movement: The City After Castells*. New York: St. Martin's Press.

Lowi, Theodore J. 1964. "American Business Public Policy Case Studies and Political Theory." *World Politics* 16:677–715.

———. 1971. *The Politics of Disorder*. New York: W. W. Norton.

———. 1979. *The End of Liberalism*. 2nd ed. New York: W. W. Norton.

"Lugar Says He'd Lead Fight to Override Sanctions Veto." 1986. *New York Times*, 17 September.

McAdam, Doug. 1982. *Political Process and the Development of Black Insurgency*. Chicago: University of Chicago Press.

McClain, Paula D. 1990. "Agenda Setting, Public Policy, and Minority Group Influence: An Introduction." *Policy Studies Review* 9:263–272.

McClain, Paula D., and Albert J. Karnig. 1988. "Introduction: Minority Administrators—Another Frontier." In *Urban Minority Administrators: Politics, Policy, and Style*, eds. Albert J. Karnig and Paula D. McClain. Westport, CT: Greenwood Press.

McClain, Paula D., and David F. Pijawka. 1986. "Agenda Setting and Nondecisionmaking: Decommissioning Nuclear Generating Stations." *Policy Studies Review* 5:742–755.

McCrudden, Christopher. 1983. "Anti-Discrimination Goals and the Legal Process." In *Ethnic Pluralism and Public Policy*, eds. Nathan Glazer and Ken Young. London: Heineman.

McKnight, John, and John Kretzmann. 1984. "Community Organizing in the 80's: Toward a Post-Alinsky Agenda." *Social Policy* 14:15–17.

Manley, John. 1983. "Neo-Pluralism: A Class Analysis of Pluralism I and Pluralism II." *American Political Science Review* 77:368–383.

Maraniss, David. 1989. "El Paso's Perimeter of Policy." *Washington Post*, 17 August.

Marel, Robert Lee. 1989. *Poorest of Americans: The Mexican Americans of the Lower Rio Grande Valley of Texas*. Notre Dame, IN: University of Notre Dame Press.

Marquez, Benjamin. 1989. "The Politics of Race and Assimilation: The League of United Latin American Citizens, 1929–1940." *Western Political Quarterly* 42:355–373.

———. 1990. "Organizing the Mexican-American Community in Texas." *Policy Studies Review* 9:355–373.

Marris, Peter, and Martin Rein. 1972. *Dilemmas of Social Reform*. 2nd ed. London: Routledge and Kegan Paul.

Martinez, Gebe. 1987. "Cisneros Slams His Door on COPS for its 'Abuse.' " *San Antonio Light*, 28 November.

Martone, Frederick. 1977. "Letter: Comments on American Indian Review Commission's Final Report." *Lloyd Means Collection*. Seattle: University of Washington Manuscripts.

Meier, Kenneth J. 1979. "Affirmative Action: Constraints and Policy Impact." In *Race, Sex, and Policy Problems*, eds. Marian L. Polley and Michael B. Preston. Lexington, MA: Lexington Books.

Mercy, James A., and Patrick W. O'Carroll. 1988. "New Directions in Violence Prediction: The Public Health Arena." *Violence and Victims* 3:285–301.

Messina, Anthony M. 1989. *Race and Party Competition in Britain*. New York: Clarendon Press of Oxford University Press.

Metz, Steven. 1986. "The Anti-Apartheid Movement and the Populist Instincts in American Politics." *Political Science Quarterly* 101:379–395.

Meyer, John W., and Brian Rowan. 1977. "Institutionalized Organizations: Formal Structure as Myth and Ceremonial." *American Journal of Sociology* 83:340–363.

Miller, Cheryl. 1990. "Agenda Setting by State Legislative Black Caucuses: Policy Priorities and Factors of Success." *Policy Studies Review* 9:339–354.

Mills, C. Wright. 1959. *The Power Elite*. New York: Oxford University Press.

Mofford, Rose (Governor-AZ). 1989. *State of Arizona: Governor's Task Force on Aids Report*. State of Arizona.

Montejano, David. 1987. *Anglos and Mexicans in the Making of Texas, 1836–1986*. Austin: University of Texas Press.

Moore, Mark H. 1988. "What Sort of Ideas Become Public Ideas?" In *The Power of Public Ideas*, ed. Robert B. Reich. Cambridge, MA: Harvard University Press.

Morehouse, Thomas A. 1988. *The Alaska Native Claims Settlement Act, 1991, and Tribal Government*. Anchorage, AK: Institute of Social and Economic Research—University of Alaska.

"Morgan Bank Scored at Meeting On Share in South African Loan." 1967. *New York Times*, 16 March.

Morris, Aldon D. 1984. *The Origins of the Civil Rights Movement*. New York: Sage Publications.

Morris, Julie. 1989. "The Third World in Texas." *Gannett News Service*, 10 October.

Morris, Milton. 1975. *The Politics of Black America*. New York: Harper and Row.

Mosqueda, Lawrence J. 1986. *Chicanos, Catholicism, and Political Ideology*. New York: University Press of America.

Muñoz, Carlos, Jr. 1989. *Youth, Identity, Power: The Chicano Movement.* New York: Verso.

Murray, Charles. 1984. *Losing Ground.* New York: Basic Books.

Nakamura, R. T. 1987. "The Textbook Policy Process and Implementation Research." *Policy Studies Review* 7:142–154.

Native American Rights Fund. 1985. *Proposed Legislation—Discussion Draft.*

Navarro, Cecilia. 1986. "Understanding the Mexican American Voter: Legacy and Potential of the Mexican American Community." Master's Thesis, University of Texas at El Paso.

Navarro, Vincente. 1985. "The 1984 Election and the New Deal: An Alternate Interpretation." *Social Policy* 15:3–10.

Nelson, Barbara. 1984. *Making an Issue of Child Abuse.* Chicago: University of Chicago Press.

Nelson, Richard R. 1977. *The Moon and the Ghetto.* New York: Norton.

Nelson, William E. 1991. "Constraints on Black Political Emergence: Lessons from Liverpool." Presented at the annual meeting of the American Political Science Association, Washington, DC.

Neustadt, Richard. 1970. *Alliance Politics.* New York and London: Columbia University Press.

New York. 1987. State Laws, Chapter 30: 543–544.

New York State Department of Civil Service. 1987. *Report on the Distribution of Protected Classes in the New York State Agency Work Force: 1983–1984–1985.* Albany, NY: Department of Civil Service.

Nixon, Jaqi. 1982. "The Home Office and Race Relations Policy: Co-ordinator or Initiator?" *Journal of Public Policy* 2:365–378.

Nolan, Donald. 1987a. "Memorandum to New York State Agencies and Departments and the Legislative and Judicial Branch."

———. 1987b. "Memorandum to Chief Executive Officers of Four Year Institutions of Higher Education."

"Non-White Men Face Greatest Murder Risk." 1989. *Arizona Republic*, 3 January.

Oberschall, Anthony. 1973. *Social Conflicts and Social Movements.* Englewood Cliffs, NJ: Prentice Hall.

Obregon, Enedelia J. 1987. "Ministry Battling Poverty." *Austin American Statesman*, 7 September.

O'Carroll, Patrick W., and James A. Mercy. 1986. "Homicide Trends in the United States." In *Homicide Among Black Americans*, ed. Danell F. Hawkins. Lanham, MD: University Press of America.

Offe, Claus. 1985. "New Social Movements: Challenging the Boundaries of Institutional Politics." *Social Research* 52:815–868.

Ortiz, Isidro. 1984. "Chicano Urban Politics and the Politics of Reform in the Seventies." *Western Political Quarterly* 37:564–577.

Özgur, Özdemir A. 1982. *Apartheid: The United Nations & Peaceful Change in South Africa.* Dobbs Ferry, NY: Transactional Publishers.

Peters, Guy B. 1986. *American Public Policy: Promise and Performance.* Chatham, NJ: Chatham House Publishers.

Peters, Guy B., and Brian W. Hogwood. 1985. "In Search of the Issue-Attention Cycle." *Journal of Politics* 47:238–253.

Peterson, Paul E. 1981. *City Limits*. Chicago: University of Chicago Press.

Petracca, Mark P. 1986. *Agenda-Building and National Policy Formation: Effects on the Boundaries of Governmental Decision-making*. Ph.D. Diss., University of Chicago.

————. 1990. "Building the Institutional Agenda: From Political Issue to Public Policy." Presented at the annual meeting of the American Political Science Association, San Francisco.

Petry, Alcie. 1988. Interview with Benjamin Marquez. 18 July.

Pierce, Neal R. 1991. "Minorities Slowly Gain State Offices." *National Journal*, 5 January.

Pinderhughes, Dianne. 1987. *Race and Ethnicity in Chicago Politics*. Urbana, IL: University of Illinois Press.

Pitkin, Hanna F. 1967. *The Concept of Representation*. Berkeley, CA: University of California Press.

Piven, Francis Fox, and Richard A. Cloward. 1977. *Poor People's Movements: Why They Succeed, How They Fail*. New York: Vintage Books.

Plotkin, Jane. 1977. "Black Legislators Preserving their Independence." *Fayetteville Observer Times*, 6 March, sec. B.

Plotkin, Sidney. 1983. "Democratic Change in the Urban Political Economy: San Antonio's Edwards Aquifer Controversy." In *The Politics of San Antonio*, eds. David R. Johnson, John A. Booth, and Richard J. Harris. Lincoln, NE: University of Nebraska Press.

"Polaroid Under Attack, Plans to Aid Some South African Blacks." 1971. *New York Times*, 13 January.

Polsby, Nelson W. 1980. *Community Power and Political Theory*. New Haven, CT: Yale University Press.

————. 1984. *Political Innovation in America*. New Haven, CT: Yale University Press.

Prestage, Jewel. 1968. "Black Politics and the Kerner Report: Concerns and Directions." *Social Science Quarterly* 49:453–464.

Preston, Michael B., Lenneal J. Henderson, and Paul L. Puryear. 1987. *The New Black Politics: The Search for Political Power*. 2nd ed. New York: Longman.

"Protests Spreading in U.S. Against South Africa Policy." 1984. *New York Times*, 5 December.

Quimby, Ernest, and Samuel R. Friedman. 1989. "Dynamics of Black Mobilization Against AIDS in New York." *Social Problems* 36:403–415.

Raiffa, Howard. 1968. *Decision Analysis*. Reading, MA: Addison-Wesley. Quoted in William N. Dunn. 1981. *Public Policy Analysis*. Englewood Cliffs, NJ: Prentice Hall.

"Reagan, In Reversal, Orders Sanctions On South Africa: Move Causes Split in Senate." 1985. *New York Times*, 10 September.

Reed, Steve. 1989. "Austin Interfaith Quietly Taking Root in Politics." *Austin American Statesman*, 9 February.

Rein, Martin. 1976. *Social Science & Public Policy*. New York: Penguin.

Reitzes, Donald C., and Dietrich C. Reitzes. 1987. *The Alinsky Legacy: Alive and Kicking*. Greenwich, CT: JAI Press.

Richardson, Jeremy, ed. 1982. *Policy Styles in Western Europe*. London: Allen and Unwin.

Richardson, J. J., and A. G. Jordan. 1979. *Governing Under Pressure*. Oxford: Basil Blackwell.

Riley, Steve. "Confusion Reigns at the Assembly." *The Raleigh News and Observer*, 15 January, sec. A.

Ripley, Randall B. 1985. *Policy Analysis in Political Science*. Chicago: Nelson-Hall.

Ripley, Randall B., and Grace A. Franklin. 1991. *Congress, the Bureaucracy, and Public Policy*. 5th ed. Pacific Grove, CA: Brooks/Cole.

Robertson, David Brian. 1991. "Political Conflict and Lesson Drawing." *Journal of Public Policy* 11:55–78.

Robertson, David Brian, and Jerold L. Waltman. 1992. "The Politics of Policy Borrowing." In *U.S. and U.K.: Education and Training Policy in Comparative Perspective*, eds. David Finegold, Lewis McFarland, and William Richardson. London: Falmer.

Rocha, Elisa. 1989. "Fledgling Entity Faces Uphill Battle to Hook Up Lower Valley 'Colonias.' " *El Paso Herald Post*, 30 December.

Rodriguez, Elisa, Sr. 1988. Interview with Benjamin Marquez. 2 October.

Rose, E. J .B., et al. 1969. *Colour and Citizenship*. New York: Oxford University Press.

Rose, Harold M. 1981. "The Changing Spatial Dimension of Black Homicide in Selected American Cities." *Journal of Environmental Systems* 11:57–80.

Rose, Harold M., and Paula D. McClain. 1981. *Black Homicide and the Urban Environment*. Washington, DC: National Institutes of Mental Health.

———. 1990. *Race, Place, and Risk: Black Homicide in Urban America*. Albany, NY: State University of New York Press.

Rose, Richard. 1974. *Lessons from America*. New York: Halstead Press.

———. 1976. "On the Priorities of Citizenship in the Deep South and Northern Ireland." *Journal of Politics*. 38:247–291.

———. 1988. *Politics in England*. 5th ed. Boston: Little, Brown.

———. 1990. *Perspective Evaluation Through Comparative Analysis: Youth Training in a Time-Space Perspective*. Glasgow: University of Strathclyde Centre for the Study of Public Policy.

———. 1991. "What is Lesson-Drawing?" *Journal of Public Policy* 11:3–30.

———. 1992. *Lesson-Drawing Across Time and Space*. Tuscaloosa, AL: University of Alabama Press.

Roth, Dennis. 1981. "The Humphrey-Hawkins Act and the Nation's Current Economic Priorities." *Congressional Research Service Brief*. Number MB 80216.

Rothschild-Whitt, Joyce. 1979. "The Collectivist Organization: An Alternative to Rational-Bureaucratic Models." *American Sociological Review* 44:509–527.

Ruffins, Paul. 1990. "The Black Caucus: Twenty Years of Achievement." *Focus* 18:3–5.

Russell, Dave. 1990. "Equal Opportunities and the Politics of Race." *Talking Politics* 3:8–13.

Sack, Kevin. 1991. "Officials From Minorities Angered by Cuomo's Budget." *New York Times*, 25 February.

Saggar, Shamit. 1991. "The Changing Agenda of Race Issues in Local Government: The Case of a London Borough." *Political Studies* 39:100–121.

Salisbury, Robert H. 1969. "An Exchange Theory of Interest Groups." *Midwest Journal of Political Science* 8:1–32.

Sambo, Dalee. 1991. Interview with Fae Korsmo. 24 June.

Savage, Robert L. 1985. "Diffusion Research Traditions and the Spread of Policy Innovations in a Federal System." *Publius* 15:1–27.

Savas, E. S., and Sigmund G. Ginsburg. 1978. "The Civil Service: A Meritless System?" In *Current Issues in Public Administration*, ed. Frederick S. Lane. New York: St. Martin's Press.

Schattschneider, E. E. 1960. *The Semi-Sovereign People*. New York: Holt, Rinehart, and Winston.

———. 1975. *The Semi-Sovereign People*. Hinsdale, IL: Dryden Press.

Schon, Donald A. 1971. *Beyond the Stable State*. New York: W. W. Norton.

"Schultz Wary of Anti-Apartheid Move." 1989. *New York Times*, 17 April.

Sekul, Joseph D. 1983. "Communities Organized for Public Service: Citizen Power and Public Policy in San Antonio." In *The Politics of San Antonio*, eds. David R. Johnson, John A. Booth, and Richard J. Harris. Lincoln, NE: The University of Nebraska Press.

Selznick, Phillip. 1949. *TVA and the Grass Roots*. Berkeley, CA: University of California Press.

Shafritz, Jay M., Walter L. Balk, Albert C. Hyde, and David Rosenbloom. 1978. *Personnel Management in Government: Politics and Process*. New York: Marcel Dekker.

Sharp, Elaine B. 1990. "Agenda Setting and Policy Results: Lessons from Three Drug Policy Episodes." Presented at the annual meeting of the American Political Science Association, San Francisco, CA.

Shefter, Martin. 1985. *Political Crisis/Fiscal Crisis*. New York: Basic Books.

Shively, John. 1991. Interview with Fae Korsmo. 18 July.

Silberman, Charles. 1978. *Criminal Violence and Criminal Justice*. New York: Random House.

Skogan, Wesley G. 1990. *Disorder and Decline: Crime and the Spiral Decay in American Neighborhoods*. New York: Free Press.

Smith, C. Fraser. 1989. "Black Caucus Celebrates as Potential Clout Grows." *Baltimore Sun*, 22 May, sec. D.

Smith, Eric, and Mary Kancewick. 1991. "The Tribal Status of Alaska Natives." *University of Colorado Law Review* 61:455–516.

Smith, T. Alexander. 1975. *The Comparative Policy Process*. Santa Barbara, CA: ABC-Clio.

Sochart, Elsie A. 1988. "Agenda Setting, the Role of Groups, and the Legislative Process: The Prohibition of Female Circumcision in Britain." *Parliamentary Affairs* 41:508–526.

Solesbury, William. 1976a. "The Environmental Agenda." *Public Administration* 35:379–397.

———. 1976b. "Issues and Innovations in Environmental Policy in Britain, West Germany, and California." *Policy Analysis* 2:1–38.

Solop, Frederic I. 1990. "Protest and Public Policy: The Anti-Apartheid Movement and Political Innovation." *Policy Studies Review* 9:307–326.

Sooben, Philip N. 1990. *The Origins of the Race Relations Act*. Warwick, England: University of Warwick Centre for Research in Ethnic Relations.

"South Africa Is New Social Issue for College Activists." 1978. *New York Times*, 15 March.

"South Africa Protesters Take Part in Daily Drama." 1984. *New York Times*, 16 December.

"South Carolina Legislative Black Caucus." 1988. *Forum* 2:1–4.

Southern Regional Council. 1987. "Minority Summary of 1987 Legislative Sessions." *SLRC Legislative Bulletin* 3:3–4.

"Spaulding Named Black Caucus Head." 1982. *Durham Sun*, 11 November, sec. D.

Spivak, Howard, Alice J. Hausman, and Deborah Prothrow-Stith. 1989. "Practitioners' Forum: Public Health and the Primary Prevention of Adolescent Violence—The Violence Prevention Project." *Violence and Victims* 4:203–212.

Stanley, Harold W., and Richard G. Niemi. 1990. *Vital Statistics on American Politics*. Washington, DC: Congressional Quarterly.

Starling, Grover. 1979. *The Politics and Economics of Public Policy*. Homewood, IL: Dorsey.

Steinberger, Peter J. 1985. *Ideology and the Urban Crisis*. Albany, NY: State University of New York Press.

Stone, Clarence. 1980. "Systemic Power in Community Decision Making: A Restatement of Stratification Theory." *American Political Science Review* 74: 978–990.

Stringer, Joan K., and J. J. Richardson. 1980. "Managing the Political Agenda: Problem Definition and Policy Making in Britain." *Parliamentary Affairs* 33:23–39.

Studlar, Donley T. 1974. "Political Culture and Racial Policy in Britain." *Patterns of Prejudice* 8:7–12.

———. 1984. "Introduction: Dilemmas of Change in British Politics." In *Dilemmas of Change in British Politics*, eds. Donley T. Studlar and Jerold L. Waltman. Jackson, MS: University Press of Mississippi.

———. 1985. " 'Waiting for the Catastrophe' ": Race and the Political Agenda in Britain." *Patterns of Prejudice* 19:3–15.

———. 1986. "Non-White Policy Preferences, Political Participation, and the Political Agenda in Britain." In *Race, Government, and Politics in Britain*, eds. Zig Layton-Henry and Paul B. Rich. London: Macmillan.

Studlar, Donley T., and Zig Layton-Henry. 1990. "Nonwhite Minority Access to the Political Agenda in Britain." *Policy Studies Review* 9:273–292.

Swanstrom, Todd. 1985. *The Crisis of Growth Politics: Cleveland, Kucinich, and the Challenge of Urban Populism*. Philadelphia: Temple University Press.

Tarrow, Sidney. 1988. "National Politics and Collective Action: Recent Theory and Research in Western Europe and the United States." *American Review of Sociology* 14:421–440.

Tatalovich, Raymond, and Byron W. Daynes, eds. 1988. *Social Regulatory Policy*. Boulder, CO: Westview.

Thompson, Kenneth H. 1982. *The Voting Rights Act and Black Electoral Participation*. Washington, DC: Joint Center for Political Studies.

Tomlison, Sally. 1986. "Political Dilemmas in Multi-Racial Education." In *Race, Government, and Politics in Britain*, eds. Zig Layton-Henry and Paul B. Rich. London: Macmillan.

Tosi, Henry L. 1984. *Theories of Organization*. New York: John Wiley and Sons.

Touraine, Allain. 1985. "An Introduction to the Study of Social Movements." *Social Research* 52:749–787.

TransAfrica. 1986. "TransAfrica: The Black World's Bridge to US Foreign Policy Legislators." Unpublished article distributed by TransAfrica.

Trounstine, Philip, and Terry Christensen. 1984. *Movers and Shakers*. New York: St. Martin's Press.

Truman, David B. 1951. *The Governmental Process*. New York: Knopf.

United Nations General Assembly. 1962. *Resolution 1761*.

United States Conference of Catholic Bishops. 1984. "Catholic Social Teaching and the United States Economy." *Origins* 14:358.

United States. Congress. 1980. Public Law 96–487. Title XIV, Part A.

United States. Congress. Senate Committee on Energy and Natural Resources, Subcommittee on Public Lands. 1986. *Hearings on S. 2065, a Bill to Amend the Alaska Native Claims Settlement Act*. 99th Congress, 2nd Session.

———. 1987. *Hearings on S. 1145 and H.R. 278*. 100th Congress, 1st Session.

United States Department of the Interior. 1984. *ANCSA 1985 Study*. Falls Church, VA.

Valle, Isabel. 1987. "Minister: COPS Deals with Poor." *San Antonio Express News*, 28 December.

Villarreal, Roberto E. 1987. "EPISO and Political Participation: Public Policy in El Paso Politics." Presented at the annual meeting of the Western Political Science Association, Anaheim, CA.

Vroom, Victor H., and Arthur G. Jago. 1988. *The New Leadership: Managing Participation Organizations*. Englewood Cliffs, NJ: Prentice Hall.

Walker, Jack L. 1969. "The Diffusion of Innovations Among the American States." *American Political Science Review* 63:880–889.

———. 1977. "Setting the Agenda in the U.S. Senate: A Theory of Problem Selection." *British Journal of Political Science* 7:423–445.

———. 1983. "The Origins and Maintenance of Interest Groups in America." *American Political Science Review* 77:390–406.

———. 1991. *Mobilizing Interest Groups in America: Patrons, Professions, and Social Movements*. Ann Arbor, MI: University of Michigan Press.

Waltman, Jerold L. 1980. *Copying Other Nations' Policies: Two American Case Studies*. Cambridge, MA: Schenkman.

Waltman, Jerold L., and Donley T. Studlar, eds. 1987. *Political Economy: Public Policies in the United States and Britain*. Jackson, MS: University Press of Mississippi.

Walton, Hanes. 1972. *Black Politics: A Theoretical and Structural Analysis*. Philadelphia: J. B. Lippincott Company.

———. 1985. *Invisible Politics: Black Political Behavior*. Albany, NY: State University of New York Press.

Waste, Robert J. 1987. *Power and Pluralism in American Cities*. New York: Greenwood Press.

Weiss, Carol. 1987. "Where Politics and Evaluation Research Meet." In *The Politics of Program Evaluation*, ed. D. Palumbo. Beverly Hills, CA: Sage Publications.

Whalen, Charles, and Barbara Whalen. 1985. *The Longest Debate*. Cabin John, MD: Seven Locks Press.

White, Philip V. 1981. "The Black American Constituency for Southern Africa, 1940–1980." In *The American People and South Africa*, eds. Alfred O. Hero and John Barratt. Lexington, MA: Lexington Books.

Wilkinson, Charles F. 1987. *American Indians, Time, and the Law*. New Haven, CT: Yale University Press.

Williams, Andy. 1981. "Natives Get Cash But Little Land in First Decade." *Fairbanks Daily News Miner*, 16 November.

Williams, Eddie N. 1982. "Black Political Progress in the 1970's: The Electoral Arena." In *The New Black Politics: The Search for Political Power*, eds. Michael B. Preston, Lenneal J. Henderson, and Paul Puryear. New York: Longman.

Wilson, James Q. 1960. *Negro Politics: The Search for Leadership*. New York: Free Press.

———. 1983. *Thinking About Crime*. Rev. ed. New York: Basic Books.

Wilson, William J. 1987. *The Truly Disadvantaged*. Chicago: University of Chicago Press.

Wolfgang, Marvin E., and Ferracuti, Franco. 1967. *The Subculture of Violence*. London: Tavistock—Social Science Paperbacks.

Wolman, Hal. 1990. "Understanding Cross-National Policy Transfers: The Case of Britain and the U.S." Presented at the annual meeting of the American Political Science Association, San Francisco.

Wolman, Harold L., and Norman C. Thomas. 1970. "Black Interest, Black Groups, and Black Influence in the Federal Policy Process: The Case of Housing and Education." *Journal of Politics* 32:875–897.

Wright, Eric O. 1978. *Class, Crisis, and the State*. London: New Left Books.

———. 1985. *Classes*. London: Verso.

Wurf, Jerry. 1974. "Merit: A Union Way." *Public Administration Review* 34:431–434.

Wynia, Bob L. 1974. "Federal Bureaucrats' Attitudes Toward a Democratic Ideology." *Public Administration Review* 34:377–387.

Yates, Douglas. 1976. "Urban Government as a Policy-Making System." In *The New Urban Politics*, eds. Louis Masatti and Robert L. Lineberry. Cambridge, MA: Ballinger Publishing.

Young, Ken. 1983. "Ethnic Pluralism and the Policy Agenda in Britain." In *Ethnic Pluralism and Public Policy*, eds. Nathan Glazer and Ken Young. London: Heinemann.

Index

Contributors

CHARLES P. HENRY is an associate professor of African-American studies at the University of California, Berkeley. His two most recent publications are *Culture and African American Politics* (1990) and *Jesse Jackson: Search for a Common Ground* (1991).

FAE L. KORSMO is an assistant professor in the Department of Political Science at the University of Alaska at Fairbanks.

CHERYL M. MILLER is an assistant professor in the Department of Political Science and the Policy Sciences Graduate Program at the University of Maryland, Baltimore County. Dr. Miller is the author of numerous articles on institutional and bureaucratic participation in public policy formation. She is currently working on a manuscript on the policy entrepreneurship role and life cycle of state legislative black caucuses.

BENJAMIN MARQUEZ is an assistant professor of political science at the University of Wisconsin-Madison. His research interests include urban politics, minority politics, and political sociology, and he has written extensively in the area of Latino politics. His latest book, *LULAC: The Evolution of a Mexican American Political Organization*, is scheduled for release in 1993.

PAULA D. McCLAIN is professor of government and foreign affairs at the University of Virginia, whose primary research interests are in the areas of public policy, urban crime, and urban politics. She has published articles in numerous journals, including the *Journal of Politics*, *American Political*

Science Review, and *Urban Affairs Quarterly*. Her most recent book, co-authored with Harold M. Rose, is *Race, Place and Risk: Black Homicide in Urban America* (1990). She is a past president of the National Conference of Black Political Scientists, and she is the program co-chair for the 1993 annual meeting of the American Political Science Association.

CARL E. MEACHAM is an associate professor of political science at the State University of New York, College at Oneonta. He was formerly a program associate for the New York State Governor's Office (Rockefeller); a special assistant to the U.S. Commissioner of Education (Ernest Boyer); and a special assistant secretary in the New York State Senate. His publications have appeared in *Liberal Education, New Republic, The New York State Times, Journal of Church and State, Liberian Studies Journal*, and *Policy Studies Review*. Dr. Meacham is currently working on a book about political independence in South America.

FREDERIC I. SOLOP is an assistant professor of political science at Northern Arizona University. His research and teaching interests include U.S. politics, social movements, public opinion, and public policy. Dr. Solop also co-directs the NAU Northern Arizona Poll, a biannual public affairs survey of northern Arizona residents.

DONLEY T. STUDLAR is the Eberly Family Distinguished Professor of Political Science at West Virginia University. He has investigated public policy in the United Kingdom for twenty years, most recently as co-editor (with Jerold L. Waltman) of *Political Economy: Public Policies in the United States and Britain* (1987) and in a chapter (with Susan Welch), "Voting for Minority Candidates in Local British and American Elections," in *Ethnic and Racial Minorities in the Advanced Industrial Democracies* (Greenwood Press, 1992).

FRANCESCA SCHMID THOMAS concentrates on volunteer work with disadvantaged inner-city and minority children. Most recently, she is working at a school for homeless children.